"Stimulating, breezy, intellectual; this book has it all. Once I picked up this masterpiece, I found myself opening up a birthday present every time I turned the page. A must read for anyone serious about the most important problems facing humanity today."
—John A. List, Homer J. Livingstone Professor of Economics, University of Chicago

"This book wraps a world-changing idea in an immensely readable narrative. If we are going to overcome global poverty, we need more than good intentions, and Dean Karlan and Jacob Appel show us exactly what we need and how to get there."
—Peter Singer, Ira W. Decamp Professor of Bioethics in the University Center for Human Values, Princeton University

"An accessible account of 'the new development economics' based on field experiments and randomized control trials. . . . Valuable, insightful. . . . Anyone interested in a readable discussion of this truly new approach to poverty should pick up this book."
—Tyler Cowen, professor of economics, George Mason University; author of *The Age of the Infovore* and coauthor of the blog *marginalrevolution.com*

"The most urgent challenge in the world is economic development, and Karlan is right at its cutting edge. . . . An important book—and a captivating one."
—Tim Harford, author of *The Undercover Economist* and the Dear Economist column at *Financial Times*

"The types of research that Dean Karlan and his colleagues at Innovations for Poverty Action conduct are critical for helping foundations like the Ford Foundation."
—Frank DeGiovanni, director of economic development, Ford Foundation; former chair of the executive committee, Consultative Group to Assist the Poor

"Karlan is one of the world's leading experts on microfinance in developing countries, and he's done pioneering research around the globe. His work smashes old boundaries within economics to answer some of the most pressing issues facing poor countries today. Most of what we know today about how to make microfinance work for the poor flows from Dean's research."

—Edward Miguel, professor of economics,
University of California, Berkeley

"*More Than Good Intentions* offers a new way forward in the battle against poverty. It's a data-driven path, but one populated with real-life stories and full of the human spirit. Karlan and Appel call us to be rigorous in our decisions—and we need to listen to them, for the stakes couldn't be higher."

—Jacob Harold, program officer, philanthropy,
The William and Flora Hewlett Foundation

"This wonderful book, by one of the leading combatants, brings us directly to front lines of the battle for a more reasoned approach to fighting poverty."

—Abhijit Banerjee, the Ford Foundation
International Professor of Economics at MIT

"This book invites you to a conversation. The topic could not be more compelling: global poverty. Your partner could not be more fascinating: one of the leading scholars in the world working on it. The result is everything you would hope for."

—Sendhil Mullainathan, professor of economics, Harvard University

"Be prepared to have your preconceptions about international development sharply challenged, as Karlan and Appel break down what really works to alleviate poverty."

—Justin Oliver, executive director, Center for Microfinance,
Chennai, India

"Karlan offers that all-too-rare combination of academic research excellence and its application to international development practice. Karlan is creating a breakthrough."

—Chris Dunford, president of Freedom from Hunger

"Karlan and Appel write that their goal is 'to speak directly to readers, to lead them into some corners of the world they might not otherwise encounter, and bring them face-to-face with the people who populate those places.' They have succeeded admirably, as both advocates and analysts."

—*Kirkus*

"Engaging prose…vivid reportage…an enlightening and optimistic take on smartening up development aid."

—*Publishers Weekly*

MORE THAN GOOD INTENTIONS

HOW A NEW ECONOMICS IS HELPING TO SOLVE GLOBAL POVERTY

Dean Karlan
Jacob Appel

DUTTON

DUTTON

Published by Penguin Group (U.S.A.) Inc.
375 Hudson Street, New York, New York 10014, U.S.A.

Penguin Group (Canada), 90 Eglinton Avenue East, Suite 700, Toronto, Ontario M4P 2Y3, Canada (a division of Pearson Penguin Canada Inc.); Penguin Books Ltd, 80 Strand, London WC2R 0RL, England; Penguin Ireland, 25 St Stephen's Green, Dublin 2, Ireland (a division of Penguin Books Ltd); Penguin Group (Australia), 250 Camberwell Road, Camberwell, Victoria 3124, Australia (a division of Pearson Australia Group Pty Ltd); Penguin Books India Pvt Ltd, 11 Community Centre, Panchsheel Park, New Delhi–110 017, India; Penguin Group (NZ), 67 Apollo Drive, Rosedale, North Shore 0632, New Zealand (a division of Pearson New Zealand Ltd); Penguin Books (South Africa) (Pty) Ltd, 24 Sturdee Avenue, Rosebank, Johannesburg 2196, South Africa

Penguin Books Ltd, Registered Offices: 80 Strand, London WC2R 0RL, England

Published by Dutton, a member of Penguin Group (U.S.A.) Inc.

First printing, April 2011
1   3   5   7   9   10   8   6   4   2

Copyright © 2011 by Dean Karlan and Jacob Appel
All rights reserved

 REGISTERED TRADEMARK—MARCA REGISTRADA

LIBRARY OF CONGRESS CATALOGING-IN-PUBLICATION DATA
has been applied for

ISBN 978-0-525-95189-6

Printed in the United States of America
Set in Minion
Designed by Francesca Belanger

Dean: To Cindy, for all of your love and support.
And to Maya, Max, and Gabi, in random order.

Jake: To Poppop and Grandpa

CONTENTS

How Jake and I Met, and the Voice in This Book

How Jake and I Met

In late 2006, I got an automated e-mail alert from Google inform-
ing me that "Innovations for Poverty Action," the name of the
nonprofit organization I founded, had appeared on a Web page.
I clicked the link and found myself reading a blog entry by Jacob
Appel, then a recent hire who was working on one of our projects
in Ghana. The next thing I knew, an hour had passed and I had
read through the entire thing—which is extraordinary for someone with the attention span of a cornflake.

I knew Jake—I had interviewed him a few months before
and had been working with him on two different projects—but
I didn't know he was a writer. I'd hired him on the strength of
his math background, and in his interview he struck me as a fellow numbers geek. But through his blog I learned that Jake is a
sponge. He is the type of guy who doesn't just go to the market
and buy his groceries. He talks to the taxi driver on the way to
the market and learns about his life. At the market he asks about
business, how it is going, why the entrepreneur is doing what she
is doing. He soaks up the world around him, and squeezes it out

in gripping stories about daily life. And he writes wonderfully, in contrast to the boring, technical writing called for in academia. A team was born.

This book was a project I had had in mind for a long time. I really wanted to create a bridge between the wonky, specialized world of economic development and the wider world of people who care about and engage with the issues of poverty, but not necessarily as a full-time job. Much of the research my colleagues and I do ends up languishing in technical journals and is discussed mainly at conferences of academics, development professionals, and large foundations. To the extent that the public is aware of it at all, most have the impression that it's dense, dull, and dry stuff.

In truth, it's anything but. As anyone who has spent time doing research in the field will attest, it is engaging, thought-provoking, and inspiring work. Reading Jake's blog, I knew that he could communicate that, both through his accounts of interactions with everyday people and through writing about the research itself. So, as his project in Ghana was winding down, I approached him about working together on a book. It was a pretty attractive offer, all things considered. I was fairly jealous: travel the globe, visit projects, read current research, and write. Happily, he accepted. I did get to travel some with him too. Although the discovery of Scrabble on the iPod touch did not help our productivity when visiting sites or on our writing retreats together, it undoubtedly added to the fun. Eighteen months and many thousands of miles later, here we are.

The Voice in This Book

Above all, the goal was to make this book accessible and engaging, for it to speak directly to readers, to lead them into some corners of the world they might not otherwise encounter, and to bring them face-to-face with the people who populate those places. The last thing I wanted was for readers to get hung up on the authors, confused about whose voice they were hearing.

So, although this has been a thoroughly collaborative project, Jake and I have tried to keep things simple by writing in my voice throughout. The *I* in this book is me, Dean. But the writing is both of ours. And if there is a sentence on these pages that really pops, it is a good bet that Jake wrote it.

If I (or, rather, we) did a good job, then this is the only time you should have to think about who's who.

Thank you for reading.

Dean Karlan (I) and Jacob Appel (Jake)

1

INTRODUCTION

The Monks and the Fish

Morning in the harbor at Marina del Rey in Los Angeles is steely bright, and it smells of brine and of fish, and it is filled with the sound of pelicans. They congregate by the hundreds on the end of the jetty, strutting and chattering and throwing their heads back to slug down great bulging beakfuls of breakfast. Completely absorbed in the guzzling of their food, they seem not to notice the dinghies puttering by.

Jake was in one of those dinghies with his girlfriend Chelsea and her father, returning from a short ride out on the gentle rolling swell of the Pacific. They passed the gray-brown pelicans on the gray-brown rocks and continued into the marina. Coming down the causeway, they passed the gas pumps, the big prow of the Catalina ferry, and the Buddhist monks.

Yes, the Buddhist monks: those unassuming men and women, some dressed in saffron robes and others in street clothes, standing on the dock around a folding card table on which was erected a little altar with a statue of a sitting Buddha and an oil lamp. On the ground in front of the table was a plastic tub as big as a steamer trunk. From the boat, low in the water, Jake couldn't see what was inside. They were saying prayers over it.

Chelsea's father put the boat into idle and turned in a half-circle to stay even with the monks. They came to the end of their prayer and bowed deeply, and the two closest to the bin took it by the handles and dragged it forward to the edge of the dock. Then they tipped it.

Out came a great torrent of water and minnows, which landed in the causeway with a silvery clatter. The minnows disappeared instantly, darting away in every direction, and the ripples from the splash were drawn down the causeway to the ocean by the outgoing tide. The monks bowed again, deeply, and began to pack up their things.

What Jake had seen, Chelsea told him afterward, was a regular ritual. Those particular Buddhist monks set a tubful of fish free every couple of weeks. It was their small way of setting right something they believed was wrong. They didn't think those fish ought to be killed, so they bought their freedom. They would approach some fishermen, purchase their day's catch, say a prayer, and release the fish into the causeway to return to the ocean.

It was a moving gesture. Jake can attest to that. Whatever can be said against it—that it is merely symbolic, that those minnows might just be caught again later, that it does nothing to change the fact that fishing still goes on every day, that it is at best just a drop in a bucket (or a bucket in the sea)—it doesn't change the facts. The monks believed in something and they acted out of kindness and compassion.

When Jake and I talked about it together, though, there was one question we couldn't get around: The monks had clearly aimed to do a good thing—but could they have done better?

If their goal was to save a day's catch of fish from certain death, why not pay the fishermen ahead of time and just tell them to stay home? That would save the fish the trauma of being caught and dragged out of the water in the first place. It would save the fishermen the effort of waking up at dawn to complete the Sisyphean task of catching fish only to see them thrown back.

It would save the gas they used to run the boat. And it would save the bait they used too.

The monks clearly had good intentions, but they may not have found the best way to act on them. Granted, some might argue that this is a relatively minor tragedy, that freeing baitfish is not a dire global concern. But the lesson still stands: We need more than good intentions in order to solve problems. Nowhere is this more relevant than in the fight against world poverty—a truly dire and global concern, in the service of which good intentions are usually the first (and all too often the only) resource to be mustered.

A Two-Pronged Attack for Fighting Poverty (and Saving Fish)

It is the best part of us that endeavors to be like the monks, to act out of compassion and do something positive for others. The vast majority of the work being done around the world to fight poverty fits this description, and anything that springs from such a genuinely altruistic impulse should be encouraged.

But there is a lesson in the monks and their tubful of minnows. Sometimes, even when we have all the good intentions in the world, we don't find the most effective or most efficient way to act on them. This is true whether we want to save fish, make microloans, distribute antimalarial bed-nets, or deliver deworming pills. What we really need to know is: How can we act with more than good intentions? How can we find the best solutions?

The only real consensus view on the issue is about the gravity of the problem. Three billion people, about half the world, live on $2.50 per day. (To be clear, that's $2.50 *adjusted for the cost of living*—so think of it as living on the amount of *actual goods* that you could buy for $2.50 per day in the United States.) In the public dialogue about aid and development—that vast complex of people, organizations, and programs that seeks to alleviate poverty around the world—there are two main competing explanations for why poverty persists on such a massive scale. One camp maintains that we simply haven't spent enough on aid programs and need to massively ramp up our level of engagement. They point out that the world's wealthiest nations dedicate on average less than 1 percent of their money to poverty reduction. In their view, we haven't even given our existing programs a fair chance. The first thing we have to do is give more. A lot more.

The other camp tells a starkly different story: Aid as it exists today doesn't work, and simply throwing money at the problem is futile. They point out that $2.3 trillion *has* been spent by the world's wealthiest nations on poverty reduction over the past fifty years and ask: What have we accomplished with all that money? With poverty and privations still afflicting half the globe, can we really claim to be on the right track? No, they say; we need a fresh start. The aid and development community as it exists today is flabby, uncoordinated, and accountable to nobody in particular. It's bound to fail. They argue that we need to pull away resources from overgrown, cumbersome international organizations like the United Nations, wipe the slate clean, and focus instead on small, agile, homegrown programs.

Each camp claims prominent economists as adherents: Jeffrey Sachs of Columbia University, an adviser to the United Nations, and Bill Easterly of New York University, a former senior official at the World Bank. Sachs and his supporters regale us with picture-perfect transformational stories. Easterly and the other side counter with an equally steady supply of ghastly the-world-is-corrupt-and-everything-fails anecdotes. The result? Disagreement and uncertainty, which leads to stagnation and inertia—in short, a train wreck. And no way forward.

Jake and I propose that there actually *is* a way forward. My hunch is that, at the end of the day, even Sachs and Easterly could agree on the following: Sometimes aid works, and sometimes it does not. That can't be all that controversial a stand!

The critical question, then, is *which* aid works. The debate has been in the sky, but the answers are on the ground. Instead of getting hung up on the extremes, let's zero in on the details. Let's look at a specific challenge or problem that poor people face, try to understand what they're up against, propose a potential solution, and then test to find out whether it works. If that solution works—and if we can demonstrate that it works consistently— then let's scale it up so it can work for more people. If it doesn't work, let's make changes or try something new. We won't eradicate poverty in one fell swoop with this approach (of course, no approach yet has managed to do that), but we can make—and are making—real, measurable, and meaningful progress toward eradicating it. That's the way forward.

To get there, we need a two-pronged attack.

The first prong is to understand the problems in the first place. Some problems are systemic, in the way entire populations interact and exchange information, and in the way they buy, sell, and trade. Increasingly we are recognizing that the problems are also with *us as individuals,* with the way we make decisions. Here we turn to behavioral economics for insight.

In the past, economists would have thought about the monks in a pretty wooden, mechanical way. They would have talked about the cost of the fish, the value the monks imputed to their survival, the opportunity cost of the fishermen's time, and the social impact of running the boat on diesel fuel. They would have put you to sleep. More important, at the end of the discussion the monks probably would still be dumping tubs of fish into the Marina del Rey causeway.

This is a narrow view of what makes us tick. Traditional economics gives us economic humans, the archetypes for rational decision-making. Borrowing a term from Richard Thaler and Cass Sunstein (from their book *Nudge*), I call these folks *Econs*. When they need to choose between two alternatives, Econs weigh all the potential costs and benefits, compute an "expected value" for each, and choose the one whose expected value is higher. In addition to keeping a cool head, they are very methodical and reliable calculators. Given accurate information about their options, they always choose the alternative most likely to give them the greatest overall satisfaction.

Behavioral economics expands on narrow definitions of traditional economics in two important ways. The first is simple: Not everything that matters is dollars and cents. In a sense, this is nothing new. For instance, Gary Becker—by many accounts a "traditional" economist—has been using economic analysis to think about marriage, crime, and fertility for years. The second expansion is a bit more radical. Behavioral economics recognizes that, unlike Econs, we do not always arrive at decisions by calculating a cost-benefit analysis (or even act as if we had done so). Sometimes we have different priorities. Other times we are distracted or impulsive. We sometimes slip up on the math. And, more often than we'd like to admit, we are shockingly inconsistent. To mark all of the ways we are different from Econs, Thaler and Sunstein use the powerfully simple term *Humans*. I will do the same.

Behavioral economics incorporates more nuanced behavior,

and sometimes inconsistent behavior—like when we continue to sneak an occasional candy bar when we say we want to lose weight, or when we still eat dinners out while we try to pay down our credit card debt. It might suggest that the monks don't care what traditional economics has to say. Maybe they throw the fish back because paying for not-fishing wouldn't serve their purpose. Maybe it's important to them to hear that silvery splash, or to see the minnows dart away like a bursting firecracker. Maybe there is something psychological about the salience of seeing, with one's own eyes, fish jump free. And maybe the monks simply are willing to accept a less efficient solution in exchange for that moment of spiritual connection.

The breakthrough of behavioral economics has been to claim that if we want to understand the monks, then we must know how and why they make the decisions they do. Instead of deducing a way to think from a core set of principles, behavioral economics builds up a model of decision-making from observations of people's actions in the real world. As we will see throughout this book, this way of thinking can help us design better programs to attack poverty.

This does not imply that we should throw out the old models. Behavioral economics is a powerful tool, but the proverb still applies: Just because you have a hammer, doesn't mean everything is a nail. The inspiration for some of the antipoverty programs we'll see comes straight from nuts-and-bolts economics. Combining the old and new approaches gives us the best chance to understand exactly what problems we're up against, and to design and implement the best solutions.

This first prong of the attack—understanding the problems we face—is a start, but it's not enough. Imagine you are stranded on a desert island with a rusted-out rowboat. Understanding the problem, even deeply, is like understanding why boats full of holes don't float. That alone will not get you home. You need to find a way to build a better boat.

Hence, the second prong of the attack: rigorous evaluation. Evaluation lets us compare competing solutions—like different boat designs or plugs for the holes—and see which one is most effective. Creative and well-designed evaluations can go even further, and help us understand *why* one works better than another.

Here's how it might work with the monks. I could propose setting up a new market, a market for hiring fishermen to not-fish, which would enable the monks to save fish more efficiently. It might sound good in theory, but then we'd go to the field and test.

Sometimes things that sound good fail. Suppose the monks actually don't care about seeing the splash of the minnows and would be happy to pay fishermen to not-fish; maybe they are simply up against a problem that makes it unfeasible. It could be a trust problem, where the monks fear the fishermen would accept payment for not-fishing and go out fishing anyway. Or maybe it is a monitoring problem, where there just aren't enough monks to tail around all the fishermen on not-fishing days to ensure they keep their word. A rigorous evaluation could point us to the specific problem that keeps the not-fishing market from saving more fish.

In the context of development, rigorous evaluation can help resolve the debate about how best to attack global poverty, by going to the field and finding out whether specific projects work. (It turns out that some projects work better—sometimes much, much better—than others.) You might think this goes without saying. You might assume that aid organizations have always routinely conducted careful and rigorous evaluations to see if they're doing the best they can. If so, you would be surprised.

Until recently, we knew astonishingly little about what works and what doesn't in the fight against poverty. We are now beginning to get the hard evidence we've lacked for so long, by measuring the effectiveness of specific development programs, many of which you'll read about in these pages. The next chapter will go into a bit more detail about how we do this.

Microcredit, the provision of small loans to the poor, is a perfect example of an idea that generated tremendous enthusiasm and support long before there was evidence on its impact. The excitement is largely understandable, for the very design of microcredit is appealing. It strikes a lot of chords: Microcredit often targets women, and many believe that the economic empowerment of women redounds to the benefit of the entire family; microcredit often focuses on entrepreneurs, and many believe that such individuals, given access to a modicum of working capital, are capable of dramatically improving their lives through their ingenuity and enterprising spirit; microcredit often involves communities, and many believe that by involving the community rather than just individuals, we are more likely to succeed.

But in some sense the enthusiasm is surprising: It seems to be predicated on a double standard about the useful role of high-interest debt. At the same time that we see millions of dollars pouring into microcredit programs to lend to poor microentrepreneurs at rates ranging from 10 to 120 percent APR (all in the hope of alleviating poverty), we also see millions of people outraged at payday-loans outfits at home, which lend at similar rates to the poor in America.

Without some basic facts about whether these loans actually

make people better off, I would not know which side to believe, much less how to reconcile the two positions. But rigorous evaluation can—and does—help. Many were surprised by a study in South Africa, which we will see in chapter 4, that found that access to consumer credit, even at 200 percent APR, made people much better off on average. This does not imply that all credit is good for all people, but it should make us look critically at our strong opinions about what works and what doesn't, about what's good and what's bad. Do we have concrete facts to back them up?

The two-pronged attack we'll see throughout this book is a powerful economic tool. I use it (albeit in a slightly different form) whenever I teach development economics, both to undergraduates and doctoral students. Three questions organize our discussions. First: What is the root cause of the problem? Using both behavioral and traditional economics to answer this question is exactly the first prong of our attack in this book. Then two more questions: Does the "idea" at hand, whether a government policy, NGO intervention, or business, actually solve the problem? And how much better off is the world because of it? Using rigorous evaluations to answer these two questions together is the second prong of our attack.

Jump in Singer's Lake

Even in the absence of hard evidence about specific programs, people find compelling reasons to engage in and support the fight against poverty. One such reason comes from ethics, plain and simple: Suppose you are walking down a street by a lake on your way to a meeting, and if you miss the meeting you will lose two hundred dollars. You see a child drowning in the lake. Do you have an ethical obligation to stop and jump in and save the child, even though it will cost you two hundred dollars?

Most people say yes.

Don't you then also have an ethical obligation to send two hundred dollars right now to one of many organizations delivering aid to the poor, where it can save a child's life? Most people say no—or, at least, they don't cut that check.

The example comes from Peter Singer, a utilitarian philosopher at Princeton University and a hero of mine. I tend to think of it at some very specific moments, like when I am in a store and tempted to buy something that I don't really need. Couldn't that money go toward something better?

Singer's basic idea resonates, at least with me, but the logical conclusion of his argument is hard to swallow. The implication of his strict utilitarian reasoning is that we should all give away our money until we are so hard up that we honestly *couldn't* spare two hundred dollars to save a drowning child. Maybe an Econ would feel compelled by the cold force of logic to do so (assuming, of course, he'd had the heart to save the drowning child in the first place). But no Human I know of—not even Singer himself, a tireless advocate for doing more—goes that far.

Because the conclusion to the lake analogy makes us uncomfortable, we grope for holes in the logic. We raise objections. Often people's first response is to point out that when you dive in and pull the child to safety, there is no question that you've made a difference in the world. You can see with your own eyes that you've saved a life. But when you cut a check to an aid organization, the link is much less clear. How can you know your two hundred dollars is really doing good?

Most of this book is an attempt to respond to that objection. I hope that seeing some successes (and failures) up close convinces you that we *can* know we're doing good—if we commit to rigorously testing aid programs and supporting the ones that are proven to work.

The second objection people raise to Singer's lake analogy is about the "identifiable victim"—a vague sense that there's something morally significant about *seeing* the child flailing around in the lake, whereas we can't see the child our two-hundred-dollar check would be saving in, say, Madagascar. Logically, this objection is easy to refute. If someone runs to your house to tell you there is a boy drowning in the lake, you still have to go save him even though you haven't seen him with your own eyes. Wearing a blindfold does not solve ethical conundrums, and we cannot confine our responsibilities to a specific geographic area simply by narrowing our field of vision. A child is a child, wherever he is in the world, even if we cannot see him.

The trouble is that, while this refutation might be logically valid, it isn't viscerally compelling. We cannot simply reason our way into having a feeling of compassion, of responsibility for others. We need to be *moved* to act.

Behavioral Solutions Right Under Our Noses

Aid organizations, which depend for funding on our feelings of compassion, know from experience that appealing only to people's ethical obligations doesn't pay the bills. That's why tactics like the identifiable victim are longstanding staples of fund-raising. Think of Save the Children, which promises a photograph and a handwritten letter from *your* sponsored child in exchange for thirty dollars a month. Rather than approaching donors with facts, figures, and tables—which is what might sway an Econ—aid organizations take full advantage of the fact that we're Humans. They capitalize on our emotions.

This is exactly behavioral economics applied to the marketing of charities. Once you get inside the minds of those who give, you can come up with clever strategies to raise more money.

One such fund-raising strategy takes the financial sting out of giving by tacking donations onto other purchases. Recently I was in the checkout line at Whole Foods Market when the cashier asked me if I wanted to donate a dollar to the Whole Planet Foundation. She pointed to a small flyer on the counter. If I wanted to donate, she could scan a bar code on the flyer and add a dollar to my bill.

With a hundred dollars of groceries already rung up, an extra dollar is a tiny hit to take—so tiny you'd hardly notice it. And you get a lot of bang for that buck. Suddenly, you feel good walking out of Whole Foods Market with your bags of groceries. You've done something positive. It's not hard to see why the Whole Planet Foundation has been awash in donations.

Another behavioral approach to fund-raising involves separating the good parts of contributing (i.e., the satisfaction of doing a good deed) from the bad (i.e., the pain of parting with your money). Giving becomes much easier if you can enjoy the satisfaction up front, unencumbered by that irksome feeling that your wallet is thinner, and pay later.

That's exactly what happened in the phenomenally successful "Text to Haiti" campaign in January 2010. In the weeks following the devastating earthquake, people rose up in unprecedented numbers and acted to help those in need. Small individual contributions—the vast majority of them ten dollars or less— piled up at an unbelievable pace. Text donations from the first three days alone totaled more than ten million dollars.

Giving by text message takes a few seconds and is utterly gratifying. You type in "HAITI," press Send, and get an instant response thanking you for your generosity. You hardly have time to think of the phone bill coming at the end of the month. When it does arrive, your ten dollars is easier to part with because it's tacked onto the cost of phone service—a cost you're already prepared to bear.

Unless, that is, you are Cara. The following was pulled from a real Facebook page:

Cara's profile said: "I've texted Haiti to 90999 over 200 times . . . over $2000 dollars [sic] donated to Haiti relief efforts. Join me!"

COMMENTS

Noah: Your parents might not like your cell phone bill this month

Cara: It's not my money! Hah

Cara: Wait a second . . . this doesn't get added to the phone bill does it? I thought it was just a free thing . . .

Aaron: Cara shooot. No every text is $10!!!

Cara: Oh wow, are u sure? This could be very bad for me.

Aaron: Yeah I saw it on the football game they bill it to your cell phone bill.

Chloe: Yeah. Every text is 10 bucks. It said so when the Health and Human Services lady came on and told people about it on the Colbert Report. Uhh, Ask for people to help you pay your phone bill?

Cara: Thanks for letting me know! Haha Haiti must love me!

Kyle: A 2000 dollar phone bill? this is sitting in its own spe-
    cial zone of hilarious.
Aaron: Well . . . you may be screwed but, in this case there's
    a big upside at least
Cara: Just counted my texts . . . grand total is 188 texts.
    $1,880 phone bill . . . this is not hilarious Kyle!!!!!!

Never mind, Cara—there are worse ways to make a mistake
with $1,880. And this really doesn't happen very often—in the
vast majority of cases, people know exactly what they are giving
when they give it.

But behavioral marketing approaches can make it so donors
may not always know exactly what, or whom, they are giving *to*,
and this is more disquieting.

As an example let's look at Kiva.org, a tremendously popular
Web site that raises money for microlenders around the world.
Ask a user of the site how it works and this is what you're likely
to hear: You log on and read through the stories of people who
need loans. When you find one you like, you can fund her loan
by clicking and sending money through Kiva. When the client
repays her loan, you get your money back.

That's what most users would tell you, but most users would
be wrong.

Suppose you click to fund a Peruvian client's hundred-dollar
loan. Here's what happens behind the scenes: Some weeks before,
bank staff went out to the field to take pictures and write up profiles
of existing clients. Those profiles are what you see on the Web site.
When you click to fund the woman's loan, you make a hundred-
dollar no-interest loan to Kiva. Kiva then makes a hundred-dollar
no-interest loan to the client's Peruvian microlender. The hundred
dollars goes into the microlender's loan portfolio, and is lent out to

clients (but not the one you clicked on, who already has her loan) at around 40 to 70 percent APR. If the client you clicked on actually defaults on her loan, you could lose your hundred dollars, but that's rare. Most of the time, either another client repays the loan for her, or the lender pays back the loan itself (in order to keep its "record" on Kiva.org clean, so that it can attract more money). That's how it really works.

In innumerable casual conversations, people have told me that they use Kiva exactly because they love the idea that *their* money goes to *that* particular person whose story they read, whose story moved them. They feel a connection, and that inspires them to give.

I have mixed feelings about this. Raising more money is a good thing, of course. Kiva is out there raising millions (over a hundred million as of November 2009) for microcredit. The problem is that pitching a development program on something other than its impacts puts some distance between the means and the ends. Tactics that work brilliantly to mobilize donations—focusing on the identifiable victim, for instance—don't necessarily work best to design programs that truly help poor people improve their lives.

The very best organizations pursue effectiveness in their fund-raising *and* in their programs with equal tenacity—and they usually end up with very different approaches to each. The point is that they have to recognize and respect that difference. We have to trust them to know that anecdotes are a far cry from real, systematic impact. And then we have to trust that, even as they use anecdotes to court donors, they will demand rigorous evidence to shape their programs.

For an organization to be worthy of that trust is no small feat.

We Can Demand Better

Fortunately, we don't have to rely on development organizations to come around entirely on their own. If we want aid programs to do the most good, we have to recognize that as donors—the ones who pay the bills—we are the people who ultimately have the power to steer the ship. Yes, us. You and me.

Large donors—governments, major philanthropic foundations, the World Bank—clearly matter. But small donors matter even more. Individual donors in America contribute over $200 billion to charity every year, three times as much as the sum of all corporations, foundations, and bequests. As we've just seen, aid organizations have spared no effort in developing an acute understanding of what works to raise funds from you and me. You can be sure they'll respond to the incentives we give them.

Jake and I will conclude this book with some practical suggestions for what you, as an individual, can do to help steer the ship. I hope I won't spoil the suspense, though, if I give you one bottom line up-front. Cutting checks is good, but it's not enough—especially when, thanks to behavioral marketing, we can do it with such little effort or deliberation.

Instead, we ought to find out where our money will make the biggest impact, and send it there. Some large donors, like the Bill & Melinda Gates Foundation and the Hewlett Foundation, try to do this as a matter of policy—and, sure enough, organizations respond by showing evidence that their programs work. Naturally, a small donor acting alone can't drive that kind of change. But if enough small donors start to reward aid organizations for providing credible demonstrations of their impacts, you can bet that better programs will ultimately result. And perhaps, if a critical mass of donors does this together, we can slowly but surely contribute to a shift in how we as a society view the act of giving money. This isn't just about making better use of the money raised, but also about helping to convince skeptics, who think aid isn't worth giving, that development can work if done right.

Remember Cara's Facebook page? There's a serious point lurking there. Cara's initial post showed not only that texting to Haiti was easy, but that it was cool—cool enough for her to think it was worth sharing on Facebook. Whether we like it or not, for most of us there's an element of social display mixed up in our motivations for giving—and aid organizations know this, too, which is why visible signs of donation such as wristbands, stickers, and ribbons are also an effective fund-raising tool.

Anyone acting on good intentions deserves praise, no matter how far from optimal their actions may be. But how much more good could we do in the world if impact-informed giving came to be seen as the coolest kind of all?

Where This Book Is Going

So much for the theory. How do we actually tell which programs are doing the most good? We'll get to the nitty-gritty in the next chapter. And in the rest of the book, Jake and I will share some of what we've learned about specific programs that really do work. The inspiration for many of these programs is surprisingly simple, and close to home: It's taking innovative insights and solutions that have given us new ways to succeed in so many of the things we all do—rich and poor alike—and adapting them to the fight against poverty. For that reason, the chapters are organized and named according to those basic, universal activities, from Buying to Mating (and a quite a bit in between).

Chapter 3 examines an often-overlooked aspect of development programs: selling them to the poor. We often assume that designing a good program is all that matters. This is odd because nobody in the developed world thinks it's sufficient to design a good product without also getting the sales pitch right.

Chapters 4 through 7 explore different aspects of microfinance, from the various flavors of microcredit to saving. The topic deserves this depth for two reasons. First, it touches practically all of us. In the United States, formal finance is universally available. If you have a credit card, a mortgage, or a bank account, you're part of that vast network of borrowers and savers. The simple fact that financial solutions work for so many—and such a wide variety of—people in the developed world is a compelling argument that they can be tailored to help the poor. This has not gone unnoticed: Microcredit has generated more enthusiasm and support than perhaps any other development tool in history, and that's the second reason for taking such a close look at it. It is so much a poster child of the aid industry that you might think it was a universal cure-all, and first we want to show that, for all its virtues, it is not a panacea—but it can generate some real benefits. Second, when it is designed well, it isn't just about credit, but about savings too. Some of the most exciting work in microfinance has shifted away from borrowing and toward saving, with big donors like the Bill & Melinda Gates Foundation leading the charge.

Chapters 8 through 11 expand the search for poverty solutions beyond the realm of dollars and cents and into some places where you might not expect to find economists at work. From the public sphere—farmers tending their fields in the open, parents sending their children to school—to the more intimate spaces of doctors' offices and finally people's bedrooms, we'll look at some innovative approaches to the problems surrounding agriculture, education, health, and sex. We will see that many of the tools we now use to do better in those areas of our own lives can serve the poor as well.

Finally, the book concludes with some ways forward—specific ideas that have the power to make a big difference in the lives of the poor, and things that each of us can do to help them succeed.

Most of the research I'll talk about in this book is evaluation. It gives us concrete evidence, and concrete evidence truly should be the driving force in deciding which development approaches to support. But I don't believe it should be the only consideration. There is room for creativity, for trying new things, and for failure. We need new ideas to push us forward, and as donors we should reward those too.

Jake and I don't claim to have all the answers in this book. As we shall see repeatedly, behavioral economics reveals that, just like everyone else, poor people make mistakes that end up making them poorer, sicker, and less happy. (If they didn't, they could quickly escape poverty by selling self-help classes to the rest of us.) Identifying and correcting these mistakes is a prerequisite for solving global poverty, and we don't have a foolproof way of achieving that any more than we have a foolproof way to make every person in the developed world win all of his or her personal battles.

That said, we in the developed world are beginning to chip away at these insidious and persistent problems for ourselves, one by one. We *have* found specific ways to improve our decisions and make our lives profoundly better. We can and do use new tools—like the Save More Tomorrow program and stickK.com, which we'll see later—to spend smarter, save more, eat better, and lead lives more like the ones we imagine. The leap is in understanding that solutions like these, that have so enriched our own lives, can do the same for the people who need them most.

This book is about finding out which of them really work for the poor, and finding new solutions for the problems that remain.

2

TO WORK AGAINST
POVERTY

How We Do What We Do

In 1992, my best friend and I were looking into ways to travel in
Latin America for a year before going to graduate school. We had
vague ideas about development projects, and an interest in human
rights. He found a brochure for FINCA International in his college career services office. (FINCA stands for Foundation for
International Community Assistance, but mostly goes by FINCA,
and is now one of the better-funded microcredit organizations in
the United States.) Neither of us had ever heard of FINCA, but the
pamphlet caught our attention. It talked about "microcredit." Neither of us had heard of that either. I remember being exhilarated
by the description of FINCA's program—making small loans to
entrepreneurs in developing countries, which would allow them
to expand their businesses and escape poverty.

At the time, I was two years into an investment banking job;
I was constantly thinking about finance. Giving loans to the poor
was a captivating idea, and we sent in a letter and our résumés.

We first proposed to visit FINCA's offices in Latin America one
by one and help them share information and ideas across countries
(we wanted to travel throughout Latin America!), but the folks at
FINCA International spotted some computer background on our
résumés, and came back with a better idea: to go to El Salvador,
learn the specialized banking software they used there, and adapt
it for use in their other offices in Latin America. Off we went.

It wasn't quite what we expected. What was supposed to be six weeks became thirty months, and the single biggest failure of my professional career.

My friend and I built a brand-new software system from scratch, tailored it to meet the byzantine accounting standards of four different countries, and customized it to accomodate the wide variety of lending practices that prevailed around the region. I later learned that it languished unused (except for a few years' stint in El Salvador and Peru), and eventually was completely discarded. I was crushed. I felt that I had come up short.

But there was a silver lining to my experience with FINCA. I learned what I wanted to do.

Over the course of those thirty months, the most exciting moments took place not in the office or at the computer, but at the hundreds of meals I shared with FINCA employees and fellow aid workers. We talked about microcredit, what it was doing, why we thought it was working, and how we thought it could be done better. Our conversations were interesting, but that's as far as they went. We didn't have any solid ground on which to build. My first instinct was to look at the data, and to be a bit analytical about gauging the effectiveness of FINCA's lending program. But there was no data to look at! The simple and sad fact was that neither we nor FINCA knew how—or even whether—microcredit was really helping the poor.

What we needed was some hard evidence of the impacts microcredit had on the lives of FINCA's clients.

The first "impact evaluation" I ever saw of microcredit made my stomach ache. It was clearly intended to generate pretty numbers for a brochure to donors—not to determine whether something was really working. It asked clients something like, "You are eating better now, compared to before you joined FINCA, yes?" I was not yet trained in economics or surveying techniques, but I knew enough to know that this was not proving anything. (For the record, this was twenty years ago, so I can't swear to the exact wording of the question posed to the clients. But I do know with certainty that the survey was given only to existing clients, which, as we will discuss later, is a deep flaw if you really want to know the impact of a program.) What I have since learned is that FINCA was doing just as much to measure its impact as anyone else. Which is to say, very little.

I thought about continuing to work with a microcredit organization, like FINCA—but what could I do to really make a difference? What did I know? Not much. And as far as I could tell, getting informed wasn't just a matter of finding the right reading material. The information really wasn't out there. So I decided to pursue a Ph.D. in economics, hoping that it would give me the skills I needed to return to microcredit and help figure out what really works and what does not.

When I got to graduate school it became clear that there were two types of people in the development universe: thinkers and doers. The doers were out in the real world, doing the best that they could—but they were essentially blind. Meanwhile, in the halls of academia, the thinkers were doing interesting analytical research—but they were often mute when it came to talking to the doers. Much of the research never made it out into the world.

Thinkers would argue that their research was "deeper than that, helping to understand the fundamentals of the way society works." Fair enough. But this left me unsatisfied. I knew that at some point we had to get beyond the "deep" and move into results that tell us what to do. There were some notable exceptions to this separation between thinkers and doers. I vividly remember having coffee with Michael Kremer, then a professor at MIT, about potential topics for my dissertation. A few years before, Michael had begun running experiments (which we will see later in this book) measuring the impact of providing inputs like uniforms and textbooks to schools in Busia, Kenya. His work in Busia set the stage for me and many others. But I feared that it all seemed too simple compared to dissertations my peers were doing. The topic I wanted to research—which, albeit grounded in fancy theoretical questions about credit markets, basically boiled down to "flip a coin to determine whether or not a person gets a loan"—just didn't feel hard or complicated or "smart" enough to count toward a Ph.D. in economics. I asked Michael whether he thought it would even be allowed as a dissertation topic, or if I would have to pursue it as a side project. To this day, I can remember his simple, poignant response: "What matters is the question, and the credibility with which you can answer it. That is what the world needs. You are asking an important question that has not been answered well, and this method is a better way to get at it. So go and do it!"

When I finished my graduate course work and started off as a professor, I wanted to make sure that my research, and the research of other like-minded professors, did not simply get published and sit on dusty bookshelves in academic halls. I saw a void, a need for a new kind of organization with a head for academia, but with its feet squarely in the real world. It would serve as a loudspeaker and an advocate for policy-relevant research, and be full of people ready and eager to help generate research results, and, most important, it would work to scale-up the ideas that are proven to work.

I pitched the idea to my graduate school advisers, Abhijit Banerjee, Esther Duflo, and Sendhil Mullainathan. They agreed that such an organization was sorely needed and, even better, they agreed to join the board (along with Ray Fisman, a professor from Columbia who knew us all well but was not doing this type of field research himself). Development Innovations was born, though its name would soon change. A year later, in 2003, Abhijit, Esther, and Sendhil started MIT's Poverty Action Lab (now the Abdul Latif Jameel Poverty Action Lab, or J-PAL), a center at MIT and network of like-minded researchers from around the world. J-PAL has an equally strong fervor for finding rigorous solutions to the problems of poverty.

Esther is a true *force de la nature,* having just in the past two years collected numerous accolades—including a MacArthur Foundation "genius" fellowship and the John Bates Clark medal, often considered a precursor to the Nobel Prize in Economics— that make us all proud to be part of her circle (and I'm particularly proud to have been her first student!).

From the beginning, Abhijit, Esther, Sendhil, and I knew how closely the two organizations would work together, so we changed the name of Development Innovations to Innovations for Poverty Action (IPA), and continue working together to this day.

Each year IPA has managed to at least double in size, starting with $150 total revenue in 2002 (the filing fee in the state of New Jersey), to $18 million in grants and contracts income in 2009. We now have some four hundred employees and projects in thirty-two countries. While in some countries we do run antipoverty programs ourselves, the vast majority of our work around the world is collaborative: We partner with other implementing organizations— mostly local and international nonprofits—to design and manage program evaluations to find out what works and what doesn't, and then we let the world know what we've learned.

No Way Forward?

As we saw in chapter 1, economists Jeffrey Sachs and Bill Easterly have butted heads for years over a very simple but elusive question: Does aid really work? At the root of their differences is a disagreement over what constitutes "evidence," and that's the rub. Until recently, the debate about aid effectiveness has been tied up in complicated econometrics and a mire of controversial country-level data. The cutting-edge research that IPA has done in evaluating the effectiveness of specific development programs is finally giving us a new way to think about this question.

The next step in resolving the aid debate isn't more arguments from podiums and isn't back-office analysis of huge country-level data sets. It's far simpler, and more direct: Find individual programs that work, and support them. Find programs that don't work, and stop doing them. And observe the patterns of both to learn which conditions are conducive to success, so that our first attempts at designing solutions get better and better.

To do this, we need to get on the ground and work directly with development practitioners on evaluations. As early as the 1970s, economists were doing rigorous evaluations of specific social programs like job training and work-incentive taxation with the Department of Labor here in the United States. But for some reason—perhaps because we tend to be less demanding as donors than we are as taxpayers—the practice never took off in development. Until very recently, with virtually no hard evidence to guide us in choosing which tools to use in the fight against poverty, we were flying blind.

Consider this analogy: For thousands of years, there was a general consensus in the medical community that the best way to treat hundreds of ailments, from acne to cancer to insanity, was by bloodletting. Sure, there were variations across doctors— some favored lances, others leeches—but they agreed on the basic principles: People were ill because of toxins in their blood, and the way to fix the problem was to bleed them out. Only in the mid-nineteenth century, with the advent of scientific medicine, did the practice begin to fall into disfavor. The reason? Somebody finally proved rigorously that it didn't work.

The sad fact is that much of the work being done around the world to fight poverty is in a sense like bloodletting. There is a wealth of conviction and some agreement about the driving principles—people are in need, and we should provide them with *something* to help—but that's about the extent of it. The process of systematic testing, and the corresponding refinement of methods and treatments, is just beginning.

The coming chapters will let you know what we've learned so far about what works, and what does not—and give you the basics of how we tell them apart. I'll try not to bore you with technical details. (For the geeks out there—like me—who want such things, the endnotes have citations and comments on relevant research.) I can't claim to answer all the will-this-work questions you might have (or even a majority of them), but I do hope to give you a jumping-off point, a way of thinking critically about impact that you can use wherever you engage with the issues of poverty—in the news, in conversation, or as a donor.

Randomized Control Trials: Asking the Right Question

So how exactly do we find out what works? The tool we use, called a Randomized Control Trial (RCT), is hardly cutting-edge. It's actually about a thousand years old—much older than economics itself—and it has long been the gold standard throughout the sciences for determining effectiveness. To take one example, the Food and Drug Administration requires data from an RCT to warrant approval for new medicines. In general, if you need rigorous and systematic evidence of effectiveness on a large scale, you use an RCT to get it when you can.

The power of an RCT lies in its ability to give an objective, unbiased picture of the impact a program has on its participants. What do we mean by *impact*? Simply put, measuring impact means answering (at least) one simple question: How did people's lives change with the program, compared to how they would have changed without it?

Often, evaluations of development programs only answer the first half of the question: How did people's lives change with the program? That is, they measure how people were before (the "before") and compare it to how they were afterward (the "after"). These are aptly called "before-after" evaluations.

Before-after analyses usually aren't very good. In fact, they can be so bad that in many cases I suggest that, rather than do a before-after, an organization should pass on evaluation altogether and just provide more services. I consider it unethical to measure impact so badly that it really does not tell you anything. That just wastes money that could have gone to better uses.

Here's why the before-after approach is flawed. Suppose you are conducting a study in eastern Washington in the spring of 1980 to evaluate a new treatment for respiratory infections. On the morning of Sunday, May 18, BOOM! Mount St. Helens erupts. Soon, many of the subjects of the study (who also live in eastern Washington) develop severe respiratory infections, and your before-after comparison reveals that, indeed, many more subjects had infections at the end than at the beginning. What can you conclude about the treatment you tested? Did it really cause the subjects to develop more infections, or was that a consequence of something else—like the ash from the eruption?

The before-after approach fails when something external (like a volcanic eruption) causes a change in the outcomes we care about (like respiratory infections). In the case of Mount

St. Helens, it is quite easy to identify the outside influence. But with many development programs it is difficult, if not downright impossible, to observe them all. We need something extra that lets us account for those external factors—especially when they are hard to identify.

That something extra is a set of people who don't get the treatment being tested, but whom we monitor anyway (called a "control group"). Any external factors that come into play should affect both the treatment and control groups equally. If they do, then we can still compare the two at the end to see the impact of treatment. In the Mount St. Helens example, suppose the number of respiratory infections tripled in the control group, but only doubled in the treatment group—then we'd know that the new treatment really did help, despite the fact that there were more respiratory infections at the end than at the outset.

Flip a Coin for Science

But is any control group enough? Can we simply take a set of people who were not treated and compare their outcomes to those of the treated folks? Not quite. The two groups have to be similar enough that we can make a meaningful comparison between them.

What exactly do we mean by *similar*? It is easy to find people who were not part of a program. Many evaluations of development programs do just that; and that's where they go wrong. The very fact that certain people were excluded from the program often means they are not right to use for comparison! We have to ask *why* they were excluded. Did they choose not to join? Did they not qualify to participate? The answers to these questions can have big implications.

Let's say a microfinance bank wants to evaluate a new

entrepreneurial loan by giving it to some clients as a pilot. At a large group meeting, the bank's managers describe the loan and ask for twenty volunteers to form the pilot group. Then they choose twenty of the remaining clients (who didn't volunteer) to monitor for control. Sure enough, the pilot is a success: Those receiving the new loans make more of their payments on time and in full. Based on these results, the bank's management concludes that the features of the new loan cause better repayment behavior. It launches the product and offers it to all clients. Many take up the new loans, but they don't fare so well—they actually default more than before. Did the test lead them astray?

Not necessarily. The pilot showed the difference between twenty clients who volunteered to receive—and actually did receive—the new loan, and twenty clients who did neither. Maybe those who stood up to volunteer were excited by the offer because they had good business ideas and well-developed plans to execute them. And maybe those who didn't volunteer (some of whom ended up in the control group) had fewer good business ideas or were less motivated. That would help to explain why the volunteers outperformed the comparison group, even if the new entrepreneurial loan had nothing to do with it.

Because so many development programs—especially microcredit, but others as well—seek to leverage the intangible qualities of participants, this is a common problem. When you design an evaluation, how can you be sure you don't put all the go-getters (or all the creative ones, or all the ambitious ones, or the ones with the strongest work ethic) in one group? If traits like these were easy to identify and measure, you could just deal them out evenly between treatment and control. But they aren't easy to identify or measure—they are hidden.

So how do you divide people evenly based on characteristics you can't see?

You flip a coin for each person to decide whether she is offered a program or not. If it comes up heads, assign to treatment. If it comes up tails, assign to control.

That's it. That's the big secret. The coin does the work for us. Of course, it doesn't have any idea who the go-getters are, but on average it will send half of them to each group. And as long as the total number of individuals is large enough, the treatment and control groups will have similar people on average across all characteristics. This is true for the things we observe, like gender, age, education, as well as the things we cannot observe and verify, like entrepreneurial spirit and ambition.

The "on average" part is important. If you flip a coin a hundred times, it should come up heads close to 50 percent of the time. Flip that same coin a thousand times and the proportion should be even closer to 50 percent (though you still probably won't get exactly five hundred heads). The point is, flipping a coin does not guarantee a perfect split, but it gets you close—and the more coin flips, the closer you get. So it is with randomization. On average, treatment and control groups constructed by random assignment will be comparable across all characteristics, and the larger the groups, the more confident we can be about the balance.

So now you know: An RCT is not a complicated thing. This machine, powerful enough to find out the truth about what works in the fight against poverty, does not run on Ph.D.-level mathematics. It works by using randomization to split a set of people into two groups, taking a "before" snapshot of each, giving one of the groups the program in question, and comparing "after" snapshots of both groups.

A Hard Question for Ernest

Now, treatment and control groups and flipping of coins may not sound as sexy as some behavioral research, but that doesn't mean doing an RCT of a development project is boring. Far from it. The structure of an RCT requires you to get your hands dirty, to encounter poverty firsthand. You want to collect solid and consistent data for the treatment and control group snapshots? Go out and get it. RCTs take place in the field—in slums, in teeming markets, in mud huts, in rice paddies—and they work by looking at real people as they make real decisions in the real world.

Jake and I can both say from experience that doing field research is by turns inspiring, maddening, hilarious, tragic, joyous, and mysterious; but it is always enlightening. With almost equal frequency, seemingly intractable problems are resolved in an instant, and tasks that appeared straightforward are found to be impossibly complex. There simply is no such thing as a ho-hum day in the field.

Here is an example from a project of mine on microcredit interest rates. Jake, who was a research assistant on the project at the time, conducted an interview with a phone card salesman in Ghana while pilot-testing a survey.

Ernest was sitting in the shadow of a yellow umbrella. The dusty sidewalk shone, bleached by the bright white sunlight, and the frontier of the shadow cut a sharp edge against it. The umbrella was anchored by a small wooden cabinet painted bright yellow. On its top were a foolscap notebook, a ballpoint pen, and two mobile phones.

Jake ducked his head under the rim of the umbrella and greeted him. "Good afternoon, sir."

"Yes, sir, good afternoon to you too."

"Sir, my name is Jake. Today I am doing a survey to learn about the businesses in this area and about their owners. Do you mind if I ask you a few questions about your phone card business?"

"Oh, that will be fine, Jake. My name is Ernest."

Jake began with the first survey question, and soon came to the fifth question. "Ernest, how many people belong to your household? By that I mean: How many are you that share a single living space and take meals together?"

Ernest didn't waste any time. "Oh, that is just me, sir."

"I see. So you live alone?"

"Oh, no, sir. I have a wife and three children. But myself, I wouldn't eat with them. My wife brings my food to me alone."

"Ah. But normally your wife cooks for the whole family."

"Yes. She will prepare the stew and the *fufu* for all."

"So for how many people does your wife prepare food each evening?"

"That is"—and Ernest counted silently on his fingers—"eight."

"Eight. So it is yourself, your wife, your three children, and three others. Who are the other three?"

"Hm. They are my grandmother and my wife's sister." He cocked his head and waited.

"Well, that sounds like two."

"Yes."

"So that makes seven altogether: you, your wife, your three children, your grandmother, and your wife's sister."

"Yes, we are seven. And also the sister's children. They are two."

"Oh, so seven and the two children—nine in all?"

"Yes."

"And your wife's sister, is she married?"

"Yes, she has husband."

"And does he join you for meals most days?"

"No, he stays with his family at the Central Region."

"I see. But what about his wife and two children you mentioned? Do they live at your house?"

"No. They are with him."

"Oh. I thought you said they normally share meals with your family."

"Yes, we have been eating together."

"I'm afraid I don't understand. Your wife's sister and her two children—how can they live in the Central Region and also normally share meals with you?"

"Oh, Jake! They have come to stay with us." Ernest was smiling. Maybe he was thinking of his full house.

"Are they just visiting, or do they live in the house with you?"

"Oh, no, they don't live there. They have only been staying for a very short time."

"Okay. So how long have they been with you?"

"They came around the Christmas season."

It was July.

What We Talk About When We Talk About Poverty

Spend some time doing this kind of fieldwork—in sprawling, chaotic urban centers, in impossibly dense favelas climbing up steep hillsides, in tiny villages perched on the edge of a cliff, places that are accessible only by ancient rusty buses, or by gutted vans with bench seats made of bare wood planks, or by foot—and you pretty quickly stop talking about "fighting poverty" in lazy metaphors. Poverty is not a shackle that can be broken, not a tumor that can be excised, not a millstone that can be shattered, not a choking vine that can be clipped. Or at least seeing it in those ways accomplishes nothing.

Here's what the UN says about it: "Fundamentally, poverty is a denial of choices and opportunities, a violation of human dignity. It means lack of basic capacity to participate effectively in society." This may be entirely true and accurate. But is it useful?

When we articulate the problems of poverty in these terms, we're bound to find solutions that traffic in the same currency. Witness the recent emphasis on "sustainable" programs—ones that, after an initial period of oversight and external funding, become self-sufficient and even self-propagating.

The case for sustainability is often explained with a flourish of Chinese proverb: "Give a man a fish and you feed him for a day. Teach a man to fish and you feed him for life."

This gets donors and socially minded investors excited. People prefer to give a hand up rather than a handout. That makes sense: Instead of giving fish to the poor, let's give them rods and reels and lessons about casting. Then we won't have to provide fish in perpetuity. Outfitted with equipment and training, they will be able to eat long after we leave. What could possibly go wrong?

The teach-a-man-to-fish approach has been around for decades. The results have not been as universally great as one might hope. For natural-born fishermen, it can work. But the problem is that some people are bad at baiting the hooks; some can't cast worth a damn; some have arthritis and can't grip the reel to haul in a catch; and some don't live near a river with enough fish in it. Some people think fishing is just plain boring. Come dinner, all these folks are out of luck. They can't eat rods and reels and lessons about casting. So what can this kind of development do for them?

Up in the realm of high-minded concepts and metaphor—choices, opportunities, dignity, fishing—the air is thin and there are no actual poor people to be found. This isn't where development needs to be. It needs to be on the ground. If we want to solve poverty, we need to know what it is in real—not abstract—terms. We need to know how it smells, tastes, and feels to the touch.

And maybe this is why it's such a hard thing to grasp: Poverty doesn't have many positive sensory attributes, because to be poor means *not* to have things, in the most immediate sense. It means not having enough food, not having shelter, not having access to clean water or to essential medicines when you're sick. The day-to-day experience of being poor is about lacking day-to-day necessities. It's about not being able to get the things you need.

Let's talk about basics. People need to eat. And that means sometimes we have to give them food. People need medicine. That means sometimes we have to hand out pills and give immunizations. People need to go to school. That means sometimes we need to get students and teachers into classrooms.

Addressing world poverty is a dynamic, complex problem. But we won't solve it if we see it only as that.

We need to see individuals. Individuals with different capabilities and different needs. Individuals like Vijaya, whom we'll meet in chapter 7. What she really needs is a way to stop her husband from drinking away the money she earns. Individuals like Elizabeth, whom we'll meet in chapter 10. What she really needs is better customer service from her local hospital.

When we think about poverty this way, in concrete terms, we begin to see a path forward. Actually, many paths forward. The possible solutions are as numerous and as varied as the people they serve and the needs they address. To find them we need to think creatively, cast a wide net, and recognize that we are unlikely to find a single answer for everybody. At the same time, we must be methodical and tenacious. If a development program is supposed to help solve a specific, concrete problem, let's put it to a specific, concrete test. If it passes, great. If not, fix it or try something else. In this way, step by step, we can refine the tools we use and the ways we use them; we can make real progress against poverty.

3

TO BUY

Doubling the Number of Families with a Safety Net

According to archaeologists, the use of blankets began during the reign of Neanderthal man. Which means that, in some sense, the Snuggie was thirty thousand years in the making.

Down through the ages, all the great thinkers and creative geniuses of human history muddled through with the same old flat-as-a-pancake bedcovers, leaving the landscape of blanketry more or less as they had found it. Then, in 1998, there was a breakthrough.

Gary Clegg, a freshman at the University of Maine, was set upon by the harsh New England winter. Even in his own dorm room, he couldn't do his homework. He was cold just sitting at his desk. Regular blankets helped, but they were cumbersome and restrictive. So he asked his mom to make him a blanket with sleeves. The first version wasn't perfect, but successive prototypes got better and better. By the spring thaw, the Slanket was born.

Oblivious, most of the world did not take notice; the sleeved blanket languished in obscurity for a decade. Few realized what they were missing until 2008, when a campy commercial for the Snuggie, a copy of the Slanket, began to air on late-night television. In the space of two minutes, it articulated a thorny and pervasive problem and presented an elegant solution. "You want to keep warm when you're feeling chilled, but you don't want to raise your heating bill. Blankets are okay, but they can slip and slide. And when you need to reach for something, your hands are trapped inside. . . . The Snuggie keeps you totally warm and gives you the freedom to move your hands. So now you can work the remote or read a book in total warmth and comfort." Spoof ads on YouTube also helped spread the word.

Finally the masses knew. Mankind had been brought to the threshold of a new era. Now it had only to leap.

And leap it did. Four million Snuggies were sold in the first year. Snuggie fan clubs sprang up by the hundreds. There were Snuggie pub crawls. The cast of *Good Morning America* did a show wearing Snuggies. As of February 2010, the number of sleeved blanket users worldwide is estimated at twenty million and rising every day. It is nothing short of a revolution.

Of course, you could be a cynic and go around taking the wind out of everybody's sails. You could say that the Snuggie isn't a revolution, but a cheap, thin blanket with two holes cut in it and stovepipe sleeves attached. And you might be right. But who cares? The people have spoken. (The earlier Slanket continues to sell well, but not as well as the Snuggie.)

You Can Sell Anything

Advertisers have a saying: There's no such thing as a bad product, only a bad salesman. We saw in the introduction that, in our donating as much as in our consumption, we respond to the suggestive power of marketing—often to the exclusion of the facts about the thing being sold. When that happens, quality and popularity can diverge. Just because something is good for you doesn't mean people will buy it (think lima beans); and just because people buy something doesn't mean it's good for you (think cigarettes and salty french fries).

Sophisticated businesses understand this and act accordingly: In the United States alone, companies spent about $412 billion on advertising in 2008.

But there is a strange disconnect between the way we sell everyday products at home and the way we sell development solutions abroad. Namely, we often don't think we need to *sell* development solutions at all, but rather expect them to be adopted on their merits alone. (Note that this approach has not worked very well for lima beans.)

This is shortsighted. It ignores the fact that development is a two-way street. If we want to help the poor by offering programs and services, two things have to happen: First, we need to make programs and services that work; second, the poor have to *choose* to sign up for them. Or, in the case of rainfall insurance policies, microloans, and prepaid fertilizer coupons (all of which are among the examples we'll see later on in the book), they have to buy them.

In recent years we have begun to make some headway on the first part by coordinating the efforts of researchers and practitioners to rigorously evaluate development programs. But we're really lagging behind on the second. In some sense, the more we learn about what works, the more we need to get the marketing right—because letting a proven-effective program fail due to lack of interest is a wicked waste.

A significant portion of advertising money is spent on making good first impressions. This is something development organizations need to think about when they launch brand-new products. If they get the marketing right, they have the potential to generate Snuggie-like levels of excitement.

The Last-Mile Problem

The Snuggie is a textbook case of an unknown bursting onto the scene and making a splash. But many of the programs you'll see in this book are not quite analogous to the Snuggie. They've been around, and people know they exist. This is both an advantage and a disadvantage. Familiarity breeds awareness, but it also breeds numbness. To borrow an advertising term, the products don't pop.

A prime example is oral rehydration therapy, a dirt-cheap and highly effective treatment for diarrhea. It is a small plastic envelope of salts that, when eaten, allow the body to absorb and retain water. Combined with fluid intake, it effectively neutralizes the threat of mortality from the disease. The salts cost a couple of pennies at most, and in many diarrhea-prone areas of the developing world they are fully subsidized—available for free.

A cheap and proven cure (with no side effects, by the way) for a deadly disease would seem to sell itself, but the sad fact is that it doesn't. Nearly two million people, mostly children, die every year from diarrhea. Either they don't know about the salts, or they don't want them. Either way, it means we are failing.

Fortunately, we don't have to look very hard to find ways to improve on the marketing front. We are constantly bombarded by examples—on the Web, in billboards, in magazines, on television, and on the radio. And in the grocery store, where lima beans still languish more or less unloved, but where there's a lesson to be learned from the equally humble raisin.

In biological terms, 1986 was an unremarkable year for the California raisin. It was a dried grape all the way through, from the first day to the last. There were really no developments to speak of. Nor were there any big changes in the availability of California raisins to the American public. They were sold in most grocery stores around the country, as they always had been. There was no scientific discovery that showed raisins to be a miracle food with previously unknown health benefits—they continued to be a reasonably healthy snack option—nor is there any evidence that the nation's collective palate changed during that short span.

Nonetheless, 1986 was a turning point. In the words of the raisins' primary advocacy group, the California Raisin Advisory Board, they were "at best dull and boring" at the beginning of the year; by the end, people were "no longer ashamed to eat [them]." Now, industry groups may be prone to hyperbole, but in this case the proof was in the pudding. And the pudding was full of raisins. For the rest of the decade, sales increased by 10 percent.

As the Advisory Board's words implied, the surge in sales had little to do with California raisins themselves, and everything to do with the way the public *thought about* California raisins. Which, in turn, had everything to do with *the* California Raisins, a quartet of singing Claymation raisins that burst onto American television screens in 1986, brandishing electric guitars and sporting cool sunglasses, and singing "I Heard It through the Grapevine." If you remember the California Raisins—and I know many of you do—then you're living proof: It was a stroke of marketing genius.

Almost overnight there was a profusion of fan clubs, T-shirts, lunch boxes, and, most important, raisins.

Sendhil Mullainathan, one of my Ph.D. dissertation advisers at MIT, coauthor of some of the work discussed in this book, and certified MacArthur Foundation "genius," has thought and written a lot about this issue (though not typically in terms of Motown and dried fruit). He calls it the Last-Mile Problem. It goes as follows: Faced with a stubborn challenge, we employ brilliant minds and vast resources to design a solution. We combine science, engineering, creativity, and careful testing, and often we succeed in solving the technical problem—thus completing 999 miles of a thousand-mile journey. Then, inexplicably, we pack it in. Instead of taking the same rigorous approach to adoption, we just put the solution out there and expect it to speak for itself. All too often—as in the case of oral rehydration salts, an example Sendhil uses in many of his talks on the subject—it doesn't.

So let's put it bluntly: We need to learn from the Snuggie and the California Raisins.

How Much Is a Photo of a Pretty Woman Worth?

Part of the problem is that economists aren't trained to think about the last mile. Take the example of credit: How does a person decide whether to borrow money? In undergraduate and graduate economics courses, students learn models of borrowing that consider the interest rate, the person's investment opportunities, and the rate at which he values current versus future consumption.

It all makes analytic sense, but it's extremely limited. Models are just equations; they can't see or say anything beyond the variables they comprise. So when a model with these three inputs is used to design a loan product, it spits out a recommendation about those three parameters and nothing more.

In South Africa, I set out with Jonathan Zinman, a friend and classmate from MIT, to work on a nuts-and-bolts question—exactly the kind of thing our standard economic models are designed to talk about—and ended up learning even more interesting things about the last mile. We wanted to understand how borrowers reacted to different interest rates, so we partnered with a local consumer lender called Credit Indemnity (which has since been bought out by a larger bank) and designed an RCT.

We were excited to sink our teeth into an important policy issue that has been hotly debated in microcredit circles over the years. (In fact, the dearth of evidence on exactly this issue was one of the main things that had set me on the path toward development economics a decade earlier.) One of the key questions we wanted to answer was whether higher interest rates led to higher default. To find out, we needed a big study in which we offered people different interest rates on loans, and we needed a lot of people to borrow in order to have enough data to answer the question.

So we had to court a boatload of potential borrowers. We settled on a direct-mail campaign to some fifty-three thousand of Credit Indemnity's current and former clients. When we sat down with their management to talk about designing the campaign, we asked them what they knew about how to generate the highest response rate to a direct-mail solicitation. As it turns out, they had not done prior tests—so they were full of questions, just as we were. All of a sudden, the study on interest rate sensitivity was a marketing study too.

Marianne Bertrand, Sendhil Mullainathan, and Eldar Shafir think a lot about exactly these issues of psychology and economics. After the discussion with Credit Indemnity, I was visiting Marianne and Sendhil in Chicago, and we sat down to brainstorm about how we could boost the response rate to direct-mail marketing. As is typically the case with them, five minutes of talking led to ten ideas for potential improvements to the direct-mail solicitations. The ideas were interesting, but we were all struck by the fact that we were just spinning our wheels. There simply was no good data from the "real world" to guide or justify our thinking. (Which is not to say marketing firms don't do RCTs themselves; they do. In fact, they do tons of them—but they don't typically share the results with dorky academics like us, nor do they design them in ways that test specific theories of human behavior.)

This ignorance became the killer insight: What *does* actually work? And how important are subtle marketing features, relative to the most important factor in our traditional model—the interest rate?

To pit the marketing tweaks against the interest rate, we had to vary both. So we got the most current flyer from Credit Indemnity and started tinkering.

In addition to substantive product features, like the interest rate and the application deadline, we varied purely presentational features of the mailer. Should the flyer show a picture of a pretty woman, and if so, what *kind* of pretty woman? South Africa has a long history of racial issues; would people respond better to a photo of someone of their own race? Would proposing uses for the loans or presenting more example loans (suggestions of how much one could borrow and how long one could borrow for) entice customers? How about displaying the interest rate in different ways, or showing competitors' rates?

Putting the variations together, we produced dozens of different flyers and assigned them randomly to the fifty-three thousand names on the mailing list. Months later, when all the application deadlines had passed, we could see which flyers had brought in the most customers.

The first thing the data showed was that, across the board,

customers clearly cared about interest rates. As a standard model would predict, they were significantly more likely to apply for low-rate loans. What was surprising was how much they appeared to care about things besides the price.

Two marketing features—photographs of pretty women and the number of example loans—proved influential although they had nothing to do with the actual terms of borrowing. From the perspective of classical economic theory, this is strange: Surely no customer would say that his decision to borrow boiled down to the picture in the corner of his pamphlet, but there it was in the data, clear as day. In terms of generating applications, adding a picture of an attractive woman to the flyer had the same effect on men as lowering the loan's interest rate by 40 percent!

The response to example loans, a simple table breaking down the monthly payments for a few different loan amounts, was surprising for two reasons. First, flyers with four example loans in the table attracted far fewer applicants than flyers with just one, suggesting that presenting more options actually *drove away* customers. This directly opposes standard economic theory, which maintains that having more choices is always better for the chooser.

The second surprising result from the example loans table was just how strong this choice aversion appeared to be. Showing one example loan instead of four attracted as many additional applicants as dropping the interest rate by about a third.

If I had doubts that marketing could make a difference in the developing world, the South Africa study put them to rest. When simple changes to a promotional mailer (like cutting out three rows on the table of sample loans) generate as much new business as drastic price cuts, you can't afford to ignore it.

Now, knowing *that* marketing matters is one thing; knowing exactly *which* changes to make to a promotional mailer is far from straightforward. The hardest part about this study was predicting what would work and what would not. (In fact, before the study began, we guessed at the impact of each marketing tweak—and many of our guesses were wrong.) Race, for instance, has always been a hot-button issue in South Africa; but customers didn't respond any differently when we varied the race of the person photographed in the flyer. Similarly, many businesses in South Africa ran "cell-phone giveaway" raffles. Assuming that the marketing experts were onto something, we tested it on some flyers. But it didn't do any good in our test. It actually dampened the response.

The results that *did* stand out in South Africa—especially the aversion to more example loans—pointed clearly toward behavioral economics.

Too Many Choices

Recent behavioral research has shown traditional economics' more-choices-are-always-better rule to be far from universal. Sometimes options can paralyze. When they are too numerous or too hard to compare, we often just procrastinate: "This is a lot to think about right now; I'll get to it tomorrow."

People have recognized this tendency in their daily lives for a long time—maybe for as long as they have been making decisions—but nobody put a fine point on it until recently. Behavioral psychologists and economists dubbed it, appropriately, "choice overload," and set out to measure it.

In 2002 Sheena Iyengar, a social psychologist at Columbia University (and author of the recent book *The Art of Choosing*), and Mark Lepper, a psychologist at Stanford University, did a choice experiment at a fancy grocery store in California. They set up a table where shoppers could taste exotic jams. Each person who stopped at the table was allowed to try any number of jam flavors and was given a coupon for a dollar off a jar of their choice. Iyengar and Lepper wanted to see whether choice overload afflicted even casual shoppers, so hour by hour they changed the number of flavors available to sample, from six to twenty-four.

Sure enough, it did. More shoppers were drawn to the unmistakable bounty of the twenty-four-flavor table, at least initially—60 percent of passersby stopped to have a sample, compared with 40 percent at the six-flavor table—but ultimately it proved to be more than they could swallow. Customers were *ten times* more likely to buy jam (30 percent versus 3 percent) after visiting the six-flavor table.

The simple explanation was that people were overwhelmed by the two-dozen options and, rather than navigate the complicated choice, decided to write off exotic jams altogether. Goodbye, gooseberry. Hello, strawberry. Whatever was already in the refrigerator at home would be just fine after all.

Now, you could object that in the South Africa example-loans table we weren't bombarding people with a ton of options—at most, four! But if choice overload features in such trivial decisions as what to put on our toast, then surely it could afflict people— perhaps even more strongly—when they take on big choices, like whether to take out loans.

Doubling the Number of Families with a Safety Net

If you are feeling a twinge of unease about using insights from jam sales and pictures of pretty women to entice poor people into taking on consumer debt, that's a good sign. We have not seen yet whether Credit Indemnity's loans are actually a good thing! In the next chapter we'll address that question, and the issue of microloans in general, in much greater depth. First, though, let's see whether the lessons from South Africa hold up in a much different context, marketing a product that is much more transparently beneficial—rainfall insurance policies for poor farmers in India.

These policies work. They pay off in the event of lower-than-average rainfall, so policyholders can be assured of having at least some income in dry years, even with a diminished (or completely failed) crop. In effect, they offer financial protection against unpredictable changes in the weather—protection that, based on farmers' own descriptions of struggling through bad growing seasons, is much needed.

But they have not been adopted as widely or consistently as you might expect. Why not? In 2006, Shawn Cole, Xavier Giné, Jeremy Tobacman, Petia Topalova, Robert Townsend, and James Vickery (an eclectic group of economists drawn from academia, the World Bank, the International Monetary Fund, and the Federal Reserve Bank of New York) designed an RCT to find out: How do you get farmers in rural India to buy insurance? Partnering with local microfinance organizations in the states of Gujarat and Andhra Pradesh, they developed and tested a slew of strategies for marketing a basic rainfall insurance policy.

As Zinman and I had done in South Africa, the research team in India aimed to find the secret to selling by randomly assigning various marketing approaches to different potential customers and tracking sign-ups. But there were big differences between the two studies—not just the fact that the insurance product was more of a no-brainer.

First, there were the people. Most of the people we worked with in South Africa, despite being fairly poor on the whole, had formal jobs and earned steady salaries. The majority of men and women being offered insurance in India were small-scale rural farmers living off the land, with all the uncertainty that implies. They had known fat years and they definitely had known lean years.

Then there was the setting. In South Africa we worked in urban and semiurban areas and sent promotional flyers through the mail. In India, marketing had to be done in person, either at the village level or door-to-door. People didn't have street addresses, let alone mailboxes. (Even if they had, there was no postal delivery in the rural areas of Andhra Pradesh where the study took place.) It was the kind of project where you got your feet muddy walking along the raised dirt paths between fields of sorghum, where farmers invited you to sit down on little wooden stools in the shade in front of their houses.

Now, we need not belabor the point that the South African and Indian contexts are different. You get it. But I do want to show that the differences are stark enough that we should not expect to find the same set of advertising features driving consumers' choices in both places. That said, the India research team's findings agreed with what Zinman and I saw in South Africa on the central point: Marketing matters. A lot.

Again, knowing *that* marketing matters is one thing; knowing *which* pieces of a marketing campaign matter is another. As we had done in South Africa with race, the India research team tested a sensitive issue by randomizing the religious content of photographs on the insurance flyers. Some featured a Hindu man standing in front of a temple, others featured a Muslim in front of a mosque, and the rest showed a neutral-looking man in front of a nondescript building. They found, as we had, no difference in sign-ups. Nor did it make a difference whether the flyer emphasized the benefits of insurance for the purchaser alone or for her family.

If subtle advertising variations weren't having a big effect, maybe a bigger information problem was to blame. Many potential customers did not understand exactly what the rainfall insurance policy was or how it worked. The researchers figured people might warm up to the product if they learned more about it. So some marketing treatments were randomly chosen to include a few minutes' presentation about measuring rainfall and the connection between rain, soil moisture, and optimal planting practices. But that was a wash too—people didn't buy any more (or less) insurance after hearing the educational material.

What did generate a significant response was a personal touch. In communities where marketing was done face-to-face by agents from the insurance company, getting a sales visit at home increased the likelihood of signing up by two-thirds, though most everyone (including those not visited at home) knew that policies were available. But that isn't all. Those in-person marketing visits became a third more effective when the insurance salesman was introduced by a known and trusted agent from a local microfinance bank.

Taken together, those two tweaks—making in-home sales visits and getting a foot in the door with an introduction from a trusted organization—fully *doubled* the chances that a person would sign up. Apply them across the board and you get twice as many insured people. In the overall poverty picture, that's twice as many families who have a safety net; twice as many who don't need to worry about going hungry when the rains are bad.

The Importance of Selling

Often when I talk about these projects to noneconomists, to nonacademics, I am struck by how out of touch they think I am. And, frankly, how stupid I feel. News flash: We've got to *sell* this stuff!

Maybe the reason we don't think much about the marketing of aid and development is that we don't want to feel like we are peddling something. It clashes with our idea of what aid should be. Most people who have a hand in development programs around the world—practitioners, policymakers, and donors great and small—are in it for the right reasons. They want to help people in need. And (at the risk of oversimplifying) many of the people in need really do want help. Since both parties' basic intentions are aligned, why should we have to resort to the dark arts of advertising to get people on board?

Whether we should have to or not, the fact is that we *can* dramatically increase participation by presenting programs in the right way. And the more we find out about what works, the more we—and the poor—stand to succeed by doing it.

Most of the research in this book—in fact, most of the recent push in rigorous development research—focuses on developing effective programs. And that's great. Finding the things that work to fight poverty is the first step.

Making those things enticing is the second.

There is nothing to be ashamed of here. Actively marketing development programs does not mean misleading recipients or presuming that they cannot make good decisions on their own. It just means acknowledging that they're like anyone else: susceptible both to reason and to suggestion, subtle and otherwise.

Why not see that as an opportunity? If we've managed to convince millions upon millions of people—most of whom, by the way, already have blankets—that they need Snuggies, then surely we can find a way to sell proven solutions to the problems of poverty.

4

TO BORROW

Why the Taxi Driver Didn't Take a Loan

When a European compact sedan dies, I do not know where its soul goes. Often its body goes to Ghana, where it may be reborn as a taxi. In heaven, some believe, we are made whole again; but in Ghana cars are not. Neither their window cranks nor their turn signals have been restored. Instead of being made whole, they are made orange. The government mandates that every licensed taxi have four bright orange panels on its body: one above each wheel well. This makes them especially easy to spot, but more often than not you can identify a taxi without the aid of vision. You know them by the squealing, jostling sound they make as they trundle down the road, and by the acrid smell of exhaust and burning transmission fluid that follows them like an angry ghost.

One such taxi swerved across two lanes of traffic toward the curb where Jake stood. It sailed in with the grace of a misshapen bowling ball. The driver leaned over toward the open window on the passenger side and said, "Good afternoon, sir. Where going?"

Jake told him where and named his price. Then ensued the usual lively joust of lamentations, appeals, and umbrage taking, and soon they had an agreement. They set out toward the Labadi Bypass, which runs along the beach that marks the southern boundary of Accra, the capital city.

As they drove Jake began to ask the driver his usual suite of questions: whether he owns his taxi; who pays for upkeep and repairs; whether he's married; how many children he has; whether he keeps any formal savings. He also asked Jake about his work. When Jake said he was working with the savings and loans company where he had flagged down the cab, the driver wanted to know more.

The driver's goal was to own his own car, and he felt he would need a loan to buy one. He asked good questions about the process of accessing credit through the bank. Would he have to hold a savings account to be eligible for a loan? (Yes.) What kind of interest rate do they charge? (3.17 percent per month, flat, calculated on the initial balance of the loan.) How often would he have to make repayments? (Monthly.) Could he repay over a year? (No, the maximum tenor of a client's first loan is six months.) Would he need to offer land as collateral for the loan? (No, he would have to provide a guarantor for security—not collateral.)

By the time he eased the car around the traffic circle at Independence Square, he was enthusiastic. "Tomorrow morning I will come straight to the banking hall before I start work," he said. He knew which documents would be needed to open an account, and whom to ask about starting a loan application. The path forward had been illuminated. Here was a man with the will and aptitude to succeed; he had just been unaware of the resources already available to him.

He and Jake shared a few minutes of pleasant silence as they traced an arc around the football stadium and the edge of Osu Cemetery. Jake could tell he was satisfied. As they came closer to the destination the driver asked one more question: "Do you know another *obruni* [foreigner] at that very bank? He is called James." Jake did know James, a member of the bank's executive management team, and told the driver so.

The driver said he remembered picking James up from the

same office and driving him home. This had been some time ago, "at least one year. I think even more than that." The ride had stuck in his memory because it was, like his ride with Jake, relatively eventful. On that evening James had answered "so many questions" about the process of accessing credit at the bank.

Jake asked, "Well, what did you say to James once he told you all of that?"

He said, without so much as a whiff of irony, "I told him I would come tomorrow."

But he didn't come tomorrow. Not a year before, and not this time either. He did say he wanted a loan, athough that alone is a fairly weak signal of intent. An unscientific review of conversations with Ghanaians over two years suggests that the number of people who say they want loans is much, much larger than the number of people who actually do something about it. What makes this case especially puzzling is that the driver's enthusiasm only increased as he learned all the gory details—about account opening, loan features, security requirements, and the like— and that he actually made a plan (albeit a simple one) to follow through. He knew what he had to do and seemed eager to do it. What went wrong?

Getting poor people to borrow money has become one of the best hopes for alleviating global poverty. So should the taxi driver's failure to show up be a cause for puzzlement and regret? The next few chapters are devoted to finding out.

The Miracle of Microcredit

Maybe the taxi driver hadn't read enough of the promotional literature published by microfinance organizations and their advocates. If he had, he would have known that this is life-changing stuff—not the kind of thing to be casually passed up. Client testimonials practically jump off the pages and grab you by the lapels: "Look! We used to suffer, but now we're prospering thanks to a loan from . . ." Beside the uplifting story is a photograph of a woman dressed in bright clothes, smiling widely. She is standing in front of the stocked shelves of her recently expanded convenience store or opening the door of her new bread oven, her smile full of dignity and satisfaction and her gaze fixed on a point beyond the camera, fixed on a bright future. Have you seen this woman?

If not, check out the Web sites or annual reports of a few microlenders. You won't have to look too hard. Here is an example from FINCA, the organization that introduced me to microcredit:

> María Lucía Potosí Ramírez . . . has spent her lifetime knitting beautiful wool sweaters and selling them in the local market. But the income she earned from selling her handiwork went toward providing daily necessities for her family, which never allowed her to save so she could buy wool in bulk at a lower cost. And, because she had no collateral, she couldn't access a loan from a traditional lending institution. When Mrs. Potosí learned about FINCA in 2001, she took out a loan for two hundred dollars. This allowed her . . . to purchase more wool at a lower price. Now her family eats better and her loans have tripled, allowing her to purchase and save more. Mrs. Potosí says she is grateful to FINCA for things that go beyond the tangible.

To readers in wealthy countries, stories like these are powerful for two reasons. First, they show loans improving borrowers' material standard of living. Where a family used to have to choose between, say, eating nutritious meals and buying necessary medicines, now it can do both. Second, they suggest profound changes taking place—changes that extend, as Mrs. Potosí says, "beyond the tangible," and into the lofty realms of empowerment and transformation. This is about more than dollars and cents, and donors value that.

Opportunity International, a global microfinance network serving over a million clients, features a testimonial in its quarterly newsletter from an American donor who visited with some Ghanaian borrowers:

> We heard from Marta, who buys and sells palm oil. She uses her Opportunity loans to pay for her products, giving her the funds to set up a kiosk in town. Her children are in secondary school and have a brighter future. She looked at us and said, "Now I am free!" This statement said it all. Without question, the women we met have experienced transformation. We witnessed it directly and felt their incredible spirit. Our trip to Ghana . . . reaffirmed our reasons for supporting Opportunity International and helped us understand the power of microfinance to change lives.

Before we are swept away in the tide of good feeling, let's get our bearings. While the shiny veneer of microcredit is new, debt is old. People in every corner of the world, rich and poor alike, have borrowed money for millennia. We usually think of debt as a burden and an obligation, not as a miracle cure for poverty. There must be something truly alchemical about microcredit to have turned the act of borrowing money into the kind of transformative, life-affirming experience described by Marta.

The heartwarming success stories we hear about microcredit date from 1976, when Muhammad Yunus, then the head of the Economics Department at Chittagong University in Bangladesh, embarked on a research project about the feasibility of delivering formal credit and banking services to the poor.

Yunus made his first loan, of twenty-seven dollars, to a group of forty-two bamboo craftswomen who, up to that point, had financed the purchase of raw bamboo by borrowing from moneylenders at high interest rates. He was interested in poverty alleviation, not profiteering, so he gave the women a better interest rate—low enough so that they could keep a greater share of their profits than before, but high enough to recoup his investment.

The new loan enabled the women to escape from the cycle of moneylender borrowing, and Yunus saw that his lending idea could work. But he had bigger ideas. Unlike the moneylenders he replaced, Yunus had an explicit social agenda—namely, pulling borrowers out of poverty—and he saw the loans themselves as just one arrow in a big quiver. The other arrows were behaviors and habits, like sending children to school, having smaller families, digging sanitary latrines in homes, and growing vegetables to supplement purchased food. These arrows, unfortunately, were not Yunus's to shoot; they were choices that clients would have to make on their own.

What he could do was to encourage them, using the loans as an incentive. Yunus founded the Grameen Bank to make group loans like the one he had made to the bamboo craftswomen. He wove in the behavioral goals directly. Women who wanted to borrow had to commit not just to paying off their debts, but also to a set of Sixteen Decisions (from which the above four are taken), which would contribute to prosperity and progress for themselves and their families. Suddenly, and for the first time, borrowing money had become a socially redeeming activity.

The rest is history. Since receiving a banking license from the government of Bangladesh in 1983, the Grameen Bank has grown steadily. Today it serves over six million clients with a total loan portfolio approaching $650 million. Along the way, Yunus and the Grameen Bank jointly picked up the 2006 Nobel Peace Prize for their efforts and, more important, inspired millions around the globe to follow their lead. Today, over a thousand microcredit institutions operate on six continents, serving some 155 million borrowers.

As the numbers and accolades attest, people are excited about microcredit. Everyone is singing its praises, from UN secretaries general to rock-star economists to bona fide rock stars. Some see it as the storied "golden bullet"—the singular big idea that will solve poverty once and for all. Jeffrey Sachs, the noted economist and special adviser to the UN on its ambitious Millennium Development Goals antipoverty initiative, whom we mentioned in the introduction, is one of its most influential advocates. He writes, "The key to ending extreme poverty is to enable the poorest of the poor to get their foot on the ladder of development. . . . They lack the amount of capital necessary to get a foothold, and therefore need a boost up to the first rung."

Celebrities from other quarters are on board too. For instance, the actress Natalie Portman serves as Ambassador of Hope for FINCA, the same charity that finances Mrs. Potosí's sweater venture. And antipoverty crusader Bono, lead singer of the rock band U2 and an outspoken ally both of Sachs and of the poor all over the world, adapts a proverb we met earlier: "Give a man a fish, he'll eat for a day. Give a woman microcredit, she, her husband, her children, and her extended family will eat for a lifetime."

With so much hype about microcredit, what we need to do is drop our preconceptions and take a clear-eyed, unbiased look at the evidence. In this chapter we'll do just that. We'll see that there are real success stories, but that, as with "teach a man to fish," it's not as simple or as universal as we'd all like. In the following two chapters we'll look at evidence for ways that microcredit programs might be improved, and we'll conclude our foray into the world of microfinance by arguing that we should likely be paying a whole lot more attention to micro*savings* instead.

Erlyn Drops Out

Sari sari translates literally from Tagalog, the most widely spoken indigenous language of the Philippines, as "this and that." It's a phrase you will learn quickly if you visit the country, because you'll find it emblazoned on signboards in every city and every village. The signboards will be red and rectangular, with Coca-Cola logos on either side, and in their centers will be white lettering in all caps declaring: SARI SARI STORE.

True to their name, these are stores that contain a grab-bag of goods. Depending on the neighborhood, you might walk down to your local sari sari store to buy a plate of hot stewed pork and rice, some new pencils, a cup of hot coffee, an individual serving of laundry detergent, packs of dried spaghetti, prepaid mobile phone credit, or fresh-picked coriander.

There is a method to the miscellany, though. The principle behind a successful store is simple: What do people want? The answer, of course, is always changing; but on any given day a fair approximation is written in the products on the narrow shelves and in the display cases.

Jake and I met one particular sari sari store owner, Erlyn, in the summer of 2009. Evidently, the people who shopped in Erlyn's neighborhood wanted pork rinds. Assorted pork rinds, in all different sizes and flavors and levels of crispiness.

Erlyn was happy to oblige. Above the counter in her sari sari store a great waterfall of pork rinds was frozen in midcascade, suspended in plastic bags and in bandoliers of foil pouches, hung from the lintel with binder clips and fishing line. The other popular item was Tang, and it was also well-represented, a kaleidoscope of colored sachets strewn among the shelves.

Erlyn did more than cater to her patrons' tastes. She also found ways to accommodate their budgets so they could buy the things they wanted without breaking the bank. She sold individual cigarettes and half-servings of Coke, which were really just little plastic bags, each filled with a few ounces of soda and tied shut. (I first experienced soda-in-a-bag in Central America. Shopkeepers like the concept because they get to keep the glass bottle for the bottle refund, but an unintended consequence is that the buyer has to drink it almost immediately, as it is hard to put down a bag of liquid! Each bag was about fifty cents. I remember offering a store owner in Honduras a dollar to have the bottle, too, but evidently there simply was no price for such a luxury.)

Through this myriad of goods, sold bit by bit, Erlyn built a successful business.

Just as she had assembled a motley assortment of products to meet her customers' needs, she had cobbled together a financial solution to meet her own. Well, to a point.

At first glance Erlyn might seem like an ideal microcredit client, and for a while she was one, borrowing from one of the largest nonprofit lenders in the Philippines. She had been very successful with her first few microloans, and so her coborrowers and loan officer encouraged her to borrow more. She did. But when she came home with twenty thousand pesos (about four hundred dollars), her largest loan yet, she found she couldn't put it all into the business at once. There simply was not enough room in the store for that many pork rinds. They would have been spilling out into the street. So she invested what she could in inventory, and the rest commenced to burn a hole in her pocket. There were opportunities everywhere: "When it is twenty thousand, then I would spend some in the house, on clothes or a TV. Then I know it is too much. It is so easy to spend!"

The store had reached capacity. Erlyn could have simply capped her borrowing at the amount she could spend on inventory, but that wouldn't have served her needs, either. The bank only made loans over six months, and the store needed restocking every two. It would not serve to borrow three times the restocking amount, since money lying around had a habit of disappearing. She was stuck.

But not completely stuck. Formal microcredit is not the only source of credit for the poor. In fact, even in places where microcredit is widespread, we see individuals using credit from neighbors, family members, store owners, and yes, the reviled (but reliable!) moneylender. In their recent book *Portfolios of the Poor*, Daryl Collins, Jonathan Morduch, Stuart Rutherford, and Orlanda Ruthven use detailed analyses of households in South Africa and Bangladesh to learn about the plethora of options and mechanisms the poor use to save and borrow. The story clearly is not as simple as "microcredit provides the poor with loans that they otherwise could not get."

In this vein, Erlyn had a specific solution, and the solution made house calls. The local moneylender offered forty-five-day and sixty-day loans, and he came by the shop each day to collect payments. His interest rate was higher than the nonprofit lenders, but he could lend Erlyn just the amount she needed, and for just as long as she needed it. To her, it was worth the additional cost. She left the bank and has been borrowing steadily, and quite happily, from a moneylender for the past two years.

This is not the way it's supposed to work. According to the promotional pamphlets, microcredit is supposed to help you wrest yourself away from the usurious clutches of the local moneylender, not convince you that, on balance, he offers a service better suited to your needs. What can explain this mystery?

Stripping Down to Bare-bones Loans

Actually, it's not such a mystery; there is less of a clear dividing line between microcredit and moneylending than you might imagine. People are often surprised to learn that the terms of many microloans around the world would violate the usury laws of most U.S. states. Consider a few examples from Mexico: The local affiliate of FINCA, a nonprofit microlender, lends at an 82 percent APR yield when all fees are included; Pro Mujer, another major nonprofit, lends at 56 percent. The for-profits aren't charging any more (but they get more of the heat—why is that?): Compartamos, for example, a publicly traded for-profit company, charges 73 percent. That's far worse than any American credit card. Even the low end of the microcredit interest rate spectrum, with annual rates in the neighborhood of 20 percent, is high by our standards.

This begs the question touched on earlier: What *is* microcredit, if it's not just another way of saying "small loans"? Despite the buzz surrounding the concept, that's not an easy question to answer. Some modern incarnations of microfinance bear little resemblance to the system pioneered by Yunus with the bamboo craftswomen. Perhaps the best one can do is invoke former U.S. Supreme Court Justice Potter Stewart's famous description of pornography: "I know it when I see it." Still, there are some persistent features of microcredit—an explicit social mission, an emphasis on entrepreneurship, a requirement to spend loans on microbusinesses, group lending, frequent group meetings to make loan payments, a focus on women's empowerment through borrowing—that are commonly thought to distinguish it from plain-vanilla moneylending.

We can ease our way into the big questions about whether, how, and why microcredit works by stripping back all of these distinguishing features till we're left with the bare essentials: a dollar amount, a maturity date, and an interest rate. If even barebones loans like these can be beneficial to borrowers, then there is good reason to be optimistic about microloans in general.

In 2004, Jonathan Zinman and I were wrapping up a marketing and interest-rate study (which we saw in the last chapter) with Credit Indemnity in South Africa. The people there were friendly, smart, and fun to work with, but Credit Indemnity was *not* a warm, fuzzy microcredit operation. It was a for-profit consumer credit business with no social agenda—a closer cousin to payday-loans outfits in the United States, or Erlyn's friendly door-to-door moneylender, than to Muhammad Yunus's Grameen Bank. It didn't target women or entrepreneurs, didn't care what borrowers did with the money (so long as they paid it back!), and lent only to working people. And it charged about 200 percent APR. In short, it was in no danger of winning a Nobel Peace Prize.

What we need to know is: Do these loans actually make people better off?

Jonathan and I spotted a chance to find out. Over the course of our interest-rate and marketing study, we had been struck that Credit Indemnity spent a surprising amount of time turning away potential clients. In fact it was rejecting fully *half* of its applicants on account that they were too risky to lend to. But our analysis of the data suggested that clients who barely met the lending requirements were extremely profitable customers for the lender. So we had to wonder: Could it be that the barely rejected applicants would have been profitable too?

After a bit of prodding and a lot of brainstorming with their credit team, we came up with a simple idea for an RCT that would serve everybody. It would help Credit Indemnity to improve its operations (and potentially its bottom line), and would also allow us to answer our question about whether borrowers benefited from credit. Where researchers usually face a struggle between answering meaningful questions and limiting interruptions to partners' operations, this project struck a perfect balance.

It worked by piggybacking on the existing lending process. When a new customer came in to apply for a loan, a staff member fed some basic information, like age, income, and number of years in their job, into a computer program, which instantly returned a basic recommendation about creditworthiness—either a thumbs-up, a thumbs-down, or a "maybe." We modified the software so that some "maybes" would randomly be assigned a thumbs-up and others thumbs-down. While credit officers were allowed to ignore the computer's recommendation, the net effect was that some marginally creditworthy applicants were randomly granted loans. By tracking all the applicants on the cusp—both those who were randomly assigned to be accepted and those who were randomly assigned to be rejected—and comparing their experiences, we could see whether receiving a loan made people better off.

A year later, a coherent picture had emerged. Applicants who received a random thumbs-up were significantly more likely to have kept their jobs, and had significantly higher incomes to show for it. Clients' families—not just the borrowers themselves— enjoyed greater prosperity too. The randomly approved applicants' households earned more money overall and were less likely to be below the poverty line. Survey responses showed that they were also less likely to go to bed hungry.

Most important, the strength of the results on income and job retention allowed us to effectively rule out the possibility that these loans were, on the whole, pernicious.

This was great news for advocates of microcredit. Actually, it was great news for advocates of payday loans too. Lenders around the world were being attacked left and right for pushing their evil debt on borrowers, but much of the ammunition was invective and innuendo—not facts. Given the paucity of reliable information on the impacts of credit, any evidence showing it to be *good*— even at high rates—was a welcome addition to the conversation.

Providing some hard evidence in favor of lending was a start, but the study with Credit Indemnity did more than that. It also showed us something interesting about the specific ways that loans can lead to prosperity. In many cases, we learned, the loans were used to deal with unexpected shocks.

Two common stories emerged. First, many borrowers used the loan to pay for transport-related costs. They repaired broken-down cars and motorbikes and bought bus fares, all of which allowed them to get to work on time and avoid getting into hot water with their employers. Second, borrowers sent money home to needy relatives in rural areas. Had they been unable to send assistance, many would have been obliged to pull up stakes and go in person to help their loved ones, a move that would have spelled disaster for their steady jobs at home. But with the aid of credit—even the high-priced consumer variety—both stories had comparatively happy endings. The paychecks kept rolling in.

Golden Eggs and the Case for Microcredit

So far, so good. We have learned that bare-bones small loans can work for Credit Indemnity's eligible borrowers, people in formal employment. Now what about the usual target market of microcredit, small-scale entrepreneurs?

The basic idea behind microcredit is that the poor actually have great economic opportunities, but that they lack the resources to take advantage of them. Here's a typical example: Lucia, a seamstress, makes her living sewing and mending clothes by hand. The $5 profit she makes each day is just enough to feed her family and pay their rent. With a $100 electric sewing machine she could double her output (and her profits), but that's money she doesn't have—until she pays a visit to a microlender.

Lucia takes a six-month loan for $100, buys the sewing machine, and starts earning $10 per day. Even if the lender charges 100 percent APR—which, again, would be an unthinkably (and probably unlawfully) high interest rate in the United States, but is entirely realistic for a microloan—Lucia still comes out ahead, and by a wide margin. She has to set aside just under a dollar each day to make her monthly payment of $21.85, leaving her with $9 a day for her family instead of the $5 she earned previously. Once the loan is paid off, she keeps that last dollar for herself and goes home each day with the full $10. And so, without much fanfare, Lucia nearly doubles her income thanks to a 100 percent–APR loan.

Simple, right?

If such lucrative business opportunities do exist for the poor, then high interest rates on microloans are not such a problem; borrowers and banks can both win. But that's a big "if." A one-time hundred-dollar investment that doubles long-term profits, like Lucia's sewing machine in our example, is a goose that lays golden eggs. Are there really, as microcredit advocates claim, so many of those golden geese waddling around the stalls of Dakar's or Dhaka's outdoor markets, or making themselves at home in the flooded rice paddies of Thai smallholders' farms?

We have to answer this fundamental question to know whether and when microcredit can be beneficial at all. Because one thing is certain: It can only work if clients pay back their loans. No matter what the interest rate, if clients rely on an increase in profits from borrowing to make their payments, then the viability of the whole system depends on how much that increase will be. In economic jargon, the question to ask here is "What is the marginal return to capital for the enterprise?" In other words, if a microentrepreneur puts an extra dollar into her business, how much more profit will she earn?

In 2005, three economists, Suresh de Mel from the University of Peradeniya in Sri Lanka, David McKenzie from the World Bank and IPA, and Chris Woodruff from the University of California at San Diego, set out for southern Sri Lanka to answer that question and find out what kind of business prospects the poor really had. How powerful were the economic engines of microenterprise, after all? Their strategy was simple and direct: They would inject money into some businesses and see how much additional profit was generated.

Going door-to-door, the researchers found 408 microentrepreneurs. They were tailors, lace tatters, bamboo craftspeople,

owners of small grocery stores, bicycle repairmen—the pro-
totypical microentrepeneurs that we hear about every time we
hear about microcredit. Half of them were randomly selected to
receive a grant of either one hundred or two hundred dollars (the
amount was also randomly chosen). This was a sizable amount,
roughly equivalent to three or six months' profits from the typical business.

The researchers tracked the profits of all 408 businesses
with quarterly surveys over the following fifteen months, and
compared those of grant recipients with those of nonrecipients.
Recipients' monthly profits increased by about 6 percent of the
grant amount on average. That is, investing an additional hundred dollars in the business generated six dollars more in profits
per month, or seventy-two dollars more in profits per year. And
potentially even more if the additional profits were reinvested
back into the business. As a reference, if you put all your money
into an investment with 70 percent annual returns (and kept
reinvesting the profits), your wealth would almost double every
year. That's a golden-egg-laying goose if ever there was one.

Why Isn't Microcredit More Popular?

If microentrepreneurs around the world can earn high returns
like their counterparts in Sri Lanka, then it's looking even better for microcredit. But hold on a moment. This apparent profusion of golden-egg-laying geese is actually a profound puzzle. If
returns really were so high, traditional economics would expect
people to funnel every available dollar toward their outrageously
profitable businesses. Microentrepreneurs should be knocking
down lenders' doors.

Trouble is, they aren't.

In the part of southern Sri Lanka where de Mel, McKenzie, and Woodruff conducted their study, microloans were widely available and reasonably cheap—interest rates were in the neighborhood of 20 percent APR, far lower than the returns the microentrepreneurs they had studied stood to make on average—so there seemed to be potential for profitable borrowing by these folks. But in fact there had been very little. Only one in nine had ever taken any kind of formal loan.

It's not just the southern Sri Lankans who are strangely reticent. For, despite widespread enthusiasm in the developed world, it would appear that one very important group is not entirely sold on microcredit: the poor. At first blush the figure of 155 million clients worldwide is an impressive one, but let's look a little closer. Compare that with the number of poor people. About half the world's population—well over three billion people, or twenty times the number of microcredit clients—live on less than $2.50 per day. So even if every microcredit client was poor (and not all of them are), still less than 5 percent of the poor would be borrowers.

Realistically, 5 percent is a conservative estimate. Not every poor person is eligible for microcredit, or has access to it in the first place. But that number actually doesn't seem too far off. A landmark study in Hyderabad, India, found a similar figure to the one from Sri Lanka—that somewhere between 10 and 20 percent of eligible borrowers choose to take loans. If people vote with their feet, microloans aren't winning any elections. And that means the Ghanaian taxi driver we met at the start of this chapter is far from alone. What can explain this puzzle?

Maybe the eight in nine microentrepreneurs in the Sri Lanka study who failed to take out loans were simply ignoring the knock of opportunity. But let's suppose they weren't. There are still two plausible explanations for the low level of borrowing.

The first explanation is a mathematical quirk. Maybe the big average annual returns observed in Sri Lanka only tell half the story. After all, an *average* of 70 percent doesn't mean that *everybody* saw a return of 70 percent on the nose. Let's say that half had 140 percent returns and the other half had zero: Then the average return would still be 70 percent, but we wouldn't be surprised to see the zero-percenters passing up microloans.

In fact, there was evidence to support this kind of story. Returns weren't the same across the board; they were different for different types of people. Some of the differences were just what you'd expect. For instance, more-educated and smarter microentrepreneurs seemed to do better (although, statistically speaking, these weren't robust results; the study wasn't designed to get at such granular analysis with only 408 participants). An additional year of schooling increased returns by a quarter, and success on a simple test of cognitive ability was a strong predictor for high business returns.

But other differences in returns were surprising and troubling, most notably the disparity between the sexes. There was strong evidence that men had high returns from their businesses, and much weaker evidence that women did. Men in the study had average annual returns of about 80 percent, while women's average returns were actually negative. Could it be that only men can run successful microenterprises?

Now, the general claim that women can't succeed as microentrepreneurs seems patently false. Take a walk through a crowded market in just about any developing country: The voices you will hear calling out the prices of vegetables are women's voices; the hawkers making their way down the aisles are announced by the rustling of their long skirts. Indeed, women are the lifeblood of microenterprise in much of the developing world. Moreover, much of the microfinance movement, from Yunus's Grameen Bank on down, has emphasized lending to women—largely because they are believed to be more responsible as borrowers than men. But if their businesses are destined to be unprofitable, then clearly they are not the right people to take on entrepreneurial loans.

Is all the emphasis on women really misplaced? I hope not; but the findings from Sri Lanka force us to confront that uncomfortable question.

Fortunately, there is a second possible explanation for the low level of formal borrowing. Maybe people were driven away from microlenders by excessive restrictions on the use of borrowed money. In Sri Lanka as in the rest of the world, many microlenders require that loans be used exclusively to finance business activities. That means, for instance, that a tailor could take a loan to buy a sewing machine, but not to buy ready-made clothes for her children.

The problem was that the entrepreneurs in Sri Lanka didn't want to finance just their business activities. They had other ideas.

De Mel, McKenzie, and Woodruff had designed their study to see just how far these other ideas went. The grants they made to entrepreneurs came in two flavors. Half were "in-kind": Recipients could choose any business-related items up to the grant amount, and the researchers went with them to buy it. The other half were made in cash with no strings attached. Recipients were told they could spend the money on anything they liked.

The researchers found that recipients of no-strings-attached cash grants spent just over half (58 percent) on business purchases. The rest went toward savings, paying off debts, and everyday consumption items like food, clothes, medicine, and bus fare. If this is really how they wanted to spend their money, is it any surprise that they weren't taking more entrepreneurial microloans?

Maybe we should think of this question another way: Why were microlenders making so many rules about how loan money could be spent? (The answer, ultimately, is that we as donors tell them to. Look at Kiva.org. We like the idea that our loans go to microentrepreneurial types. Would people give as much to Kiva if the appeals read: "Help fund this person's loan so she can buy a new television or pave her floor"?) We will see more about the wisdom—and the futility—of these rules in the next chapter.

A Little Meat on the Bare Bones

Two years after we had worked with Credit Indemnity to measure the impact of credit on borrowers in South Africa, Jonathan Zinman and I had a chance to replicate our Credit Indemnity study with a Filipino lender that made entrepreneurial loans. It was a great opportunity to see whether a more traditional version of microcredit (i.e., one that targeted entrepreneurs) could produce the same positive impacts as its consumer-oriented cousin. Maybe we would even find evidence to support those uplifting success stories we read in the brochures: the bread baker whose business takes off when she buys a new oven, FINCA's Mrs. Potosí and her thriving sweater concern.

As is the case with much of IPA's microfinance work in the Philippines, we have microfinance guru John Owens to thank for introducing us to our partner. He led us to Reggie Ocampo, president of First Macro Bank, a lender in and around the capital city of Manila with some seven thousand clients.

Much more so than Credit Indemnity, First Macro sits squarely in the microcredit universe. It lends exclusively to entrepreneurs, and loans are supposed to be spent solely on borrowers' businesses. Most of its clients have no formal employment, no credit history, and no collateral to secure their loans. And while First Macro is a for-profit business, it does have an explicit social agenda. Its mission statement talks about "community development," "customer-driven products," and "sustainable growth." First Macro's loans are also about two-thirds cheaper, at 63 percent APR, than the ones we studied in South Africa.

But operationally there were a lot of similarities between the two lenders. Like Credit Indemnity, First Macro made loans to individual borrowers, typically with maturities of a few months, and they fed information about each applicant into a computer program that instantly produced a basic creditworthiness recommendation. So it was fairly straightforward to adapt our earlier experiment.

The replication with First Macro worked almost exactly like the Credit Indemnity study. Zinman and I modified the creditworthiness software so that some first-time applicants whose scores were just on the edge (i.e., the "maybes," who actually made up about three-quarters of the applicants) were randomly approved. Over the following two years, we surveyed everyone, including those who were rejected, to see how their lives had changed. Had the ones who got loans prospered?

Yes and no. Looking at all the applicants together, the results were unremarkable. Business profits were 10 percent higher for those who got loans, but statistically the increase was not significant, so we can't say with any confidence that the change in profits had anything to do with getting loans.

Looking at specific groups of applicants, it turned out there were some striking things to say, after all—but they were not the things microcredit evangelists wanted to hear. Not everybody succeeded. First, as in Sri Lanka, men did much better than women. They saw three times the increase in business profits as their female counterparts. Second, better-off borrowers proved much more adept at putting their loans to work: for the (relatively) wealthier half of applicants, getting a loan led to a 25 percent jump in business profits, whereas for those less well-off, we could not say with confidence that the loans had any effect on profits at all. So poor women, the stock heroes of microcredit lore the world over, did not steal the show in Manila.

For that matter, there was something else about the story emerging from First Macro that didn't square with conventional wisdom. The endpoints of the narrative arc matched—in general, businesses that received loans went from less to more profitable—but the middle part of the plot was a surprise. We had thought we might find an excuse to dust off those durable bromides about microcredit allowing enterprises to grow, spreading outward like great hydrangea blossoms, bursting with the life and vivid color of a magnolia in early spring, et cetera. No such luck. We found that where businesses actually improved, most did so not through a process of unfettered growth, but through pruning.

That's right: Increases in profits were driven mostly by *shrinking* firms, not expanding ones. Applicants who (randomly) received loans consolidated and pared down their operations. They had fewer businesses overall, and the businesses they did have employed fewer paid workers. Costs fell and profits rose. It was that simple.

Simple, but also unexpected. After all, nobody pitches

microcredit with stories about closing down businesses and lay-
ing off workers. But maybe they should try; if nothing else, they
would have evidence to back them up.

Can Microcredit Transform Communities?

What we've seen so far suggests that at least *some* people can and
do prosper from access to microcredit. But the stories one hears
from staunch advocates—think again of the adapted proverb
"Give a man a fish, he'll eat for a day. Give a woman microcredit,
she, her husband, her children, and her extended family will eat
for a lifetime"—imply something much stronger: not only that a
huge breadth of individuals around the world can benefit directly
from these loans, but that the rising tide lifts all boats. The great
promise of microcredit is that it can be plunked down almost
anywhere and be expected to pull entire communities up out of
poverty.

One way to find out whether this is true is to go ahead and
try: See what happens when microfinance arrives in a community
for the first time. In 2005, Abhijit Banerjee, Esther Duflo, Rachel
Glennerster, and Cynthia Kinnan, four economists from J-PAL
and IPA, converged on Hyderabad, India, to conduct an RCT. They
partnered with Spandana, an Indian microlender serving some
1.2 million clients with group loans. At the time, Spandana was
planning to expand by opening branches in new neighborhoods.
Working with the researchers, they identified about a hundred
neighborhoods where microloans were not yet available, and randomly selected half to receive a branch during the following year.

In late 2007, about a year after the branch openings, the
researchers surveyed widely in all hundred neighborhoods.
Where branches had been built, they spoke not only with those

who had borrowed, but also with those who hadn't. They were interested in the experience of the community as a whole—not just of the go-getters who were first in line at the new branches.

The first thing they noticed was that there actually weren't all that many go-getters. Just as we saw earlier in the Sri Lanka study, fewer than one in five people who met Spandana's eligibility criteria were sufficiently enticed to come in and take loans. Fewer still invested those loans in a microenterprise. In fact, the most common reason for borrowing was to pay off other debt—usually of the high-interest, moneylender variety.

In light of those facts, maybe it is not so surprising that, despite the shiny new Spandana branches on their streets, communities were not transformed overnight. The surveys found no marked changes in women's empowerment, children's school enrollment rates, or spending on health, hygiene, and food. Another way to see this was by tracking the total amount households spent each month—on everything from dinners to diapers, school fees to cigarettes. A year after the branch openings, total expenditures hadn't increased. It looked like people were, on the whole, no wealthier than before.

So for poor communities in Hyderabad, the introduction of microcredit didn't mean instant prosperity for all; but this was not the whole story. As with First Macro in Manila, the interesting dynamics here were below the surface. They had to do with different *kinds* of people and the different ways they responded to increased access to credit.

The researchers broke down the residents of the hundred Hyderabad neighborhoods. First they separated out everyone who already owned a business. Then they used a model to predict whether a person was likely to start a new business based on some demographic information about his or her entire household—how much land it owned, how many working-age women it included, and whether the wife of the household head was literate and had a paying job. They used the model to split the remaining people into two groups according to the strength of their entrepreneurial bent. Once each person had been labeled as an actual entrepreneur, a likely entrepreneur, or an unlikely entrepreneur, the researchers could compare the groups to see how credit impacted each of those groups.

This three-way division gets at the heart of our question. Do the poor share a common and equal capacity to exploit microloans for their own—and their families', and their communities'—benefit? Or does that ability belong to some more than others?

Comparing the three groups side by side, the differences were striking. And they told a coherent story.

Business-minded folks did well. Actual entrepreneurs tended to funnel money into their existing enterprises. Likely entrepreneurs cut back on consumption—especially consumption of so-called "temptation goods" like alcohol, cigarettes, lottery tickets, and roadside cups of tea (the Indian equivalent of Starbucks)—and ramped up spending on durable goods. They bought exactly the kinds of things you'd need to start a business: sewing machines if they were tailors, ovens if they were bakers, refrigerators if they were grocers.

All this business-related spending meant people were building and fueling economic engines. Despite the researchers' finding that people were not wealthier on the whole, they appeared to be heading in that direction. And the cutback in spending on temptation goods suggested that, with their entrepreneurial dreams now in reach, people were making smart sacrifices to achieve their goals. So far, the classic story about microcredit was safe.

But the unlikely entrepreneurs threw a major wrench into the works. They didn't buy durable goods or invest in businesses; they just consumed more. More of everything, from clothes to food to cigarettes and cups of tea. And at the end of the day, they weren't any wealthier than when they started. All they had left was their obligation to Spandana. So they wound up looking more like characters from a cautionary tale about, say, credit card debt than like the inspiring figures of microcredit literature.

The Means, Not the End

Now, we really need to be clear about the evidence we've reviewed in this chapter. It does *not* mean that microcredit is a failure, or that the enormous amount of enthusiasm it has generated is necessarily misplaced. All it means is that the jury is still out. Since the initial trials haven't come up all roses, the burden shifts slightly on to microcredit's advocates to make a strong case for it, and on to researchers to dig deeper and learn in what contexts it works best—or works at all. No single study, conducted in one place and at one point in time, can generate sufficient evidence to make worldwide prescriptions. One of the biggest challenges in development is to replicate evaluations in enough places and contexts that we finally arrive at universal lessons. This challenge is part of what motivated me to found IPA, an organization dedicated to the hard, slogging work that will ultimately bridge the gap between single studies and comprehensive, consistent evidence that we can take to the bank, so to speak.

The punch line is that what we've learned in this chapter about the limitations of microcredit is *not* a tragedy! It just means that not everybody is a born entrepreneur—or a born

microcredit client—any more than everybody is a born fisher-
man. In the next chapter, we'll have more to say about why.

So the problem with microcredit is not microcredit. The
success of microlenders, as viable businesses serving the poor,
is genuinely impressive. And, more important, thanks to the
explosion of the industry in the past three decades, millions of
people around have more choices than they did before. These are
truly great things.

The problem with microcredit is the way it has been pitched:
as a one-size-fits-all solution to poverty that can be adopted
effectively even without careful impact evaluations, and as
something that every poor person should want. For all its merits,
it is not that.

I am reminded of something I heard at a gathering on microcredit hosted by the Center for Global Development in early 2010.
A group of academics, policymakers, and practitioners had been
brought together to discuss the negative spin the media gave to
the microcredit evaluations I've talked about in this chapter.
Someone at the gathering summarized the palpable sense of concern and foreboding among the attendees: "The future of microcredit is at stake."

What really is at stake here? Microcredit is the means to
the end, not the end itself. What's at stake is an opportunity to
improve the lives of the poor. Millions of dollars pour into development aid, but it's not nearly enough to solve the problems of
poverty. My inner economist, the part of me that sees the world in
terms of trade-offs, gets frustrated that when we direct so much
of our money, efforts, and good intentions toward microcredit,
we don't direct them toward other things—like savings, insurance, education, and health. Some of those other things, many

of which you'll read about in this book, work, and are cheaper and more inclusive ways to get to our ultimate goal of reducing poverty.

So how can we do the best with the resources we have? And can we inspire more people to get involved, by giving them the confidence that there are programs that really work? That's what is at stake.

The tool is not what matters; reducing poverty is.

TO PURSUE HAPPINESS

Having Better Things to Do

Oti pulled up just after six thirty. The equatorial sun had already set and Jake was standing in the cacophony of the dark street. If the car ride had taken a toll on Oti, it didn't show; he looked fresh and nonchalant and he greeted Jake warmly. But Jake had been standing there for two hours. He was ready to have a serious talk about customer service.

The two had first been introduced by Daniel, the night guard at the compound where Jake was living, in the Labadi Beach neighborhood of Accra. Daniel had suggested that, instead of taking taxis to and from work every day, Jake could hire his friend Oti by the month to chauffeur. They agreed on a price and a timetable. Oti would come at eight o'clock each morning at the house and at four thirty each afternoon at the office. Oti was very friendly and personable, and he had a comfortable and light car that was reasonably functional. When it acted up, at least it was easy to push.

And so began a fine working relationship. But soon it became clear that it was not only Oti's vehicle that suffered from reliability issues. After a few nights waiting in the hot, sticky dark, it was undeniable: The bloom was off the rose. Rather than fire Oti, though, it seemed a better idea to see whether a little elbow grease on the relationship would suffice, as it often did with his car.

Jake thought the situation might be salvageable because the task in question seemed very simple. There was an element of mystery in the erratic timing; after all, it was barely four miles from Oti's house to the office. So what did it mean when he missed the appointed time by two hours?

Well, it's hard to say exactly what it meant. If nothing else, Oti proved that what is true of cat-skinning is also true of arriving late: There's more than one way to do it. Some ways are ordinary, like waiting until an hour after the pickup time to leave the house because you were watching a movie with your girlfriend, or getting stuck in a horrific traffic jam near the office of the National Lottery Board. Other ways are more involved, like setting out for the office with the tank on empty, then running out of gas on the way and realizing you forgot your jerry can at home, then walking over a mile back home to get the can, then walking to the gas station to fill it, then walking back to find that your car has been pushed out of the shoulder and onto the sidewalk by angry rush-hour motorists (much to the dismay of the many pedestrians who are now gathered around it, waiting to give you a talking-to), and finally filling the tank and making the pickup. Yes, there are myriad ways to be two hours late, and Oti knew a lot of them.

Even more remarkable than the breadth and variety of contingencies, though, was the utter equanimity with which Oti endured—or actively authored—them. On the night in question, as on many other nights, he arrived with a smile and a cheery "Oh, Jake! How is it?" and Jake was left to wonder about the rest. If the mistake was his, he was unrepentant; and if the fates had conspired against him, stranding him for hours in an intractable knot of traffic, he was quiescent and no worse for the wear.

It was one thing if Oti didn't mind wasting his customer's time. Most of us have met somebody like that. The bizarre thing was that Oti didn't seem to mind wasting his own time. And so that was the topic of his and Jake's serious conversation on the ride home, weaving through the lumbering vans and rattling taxis on the pitted roads of the Ghanaian capital.

The Right Place at the Right Time

You've heard it a thousand times, that fundamental equivalency between business and real life, stated with appropriate brevity: Time is money. At some point during the dot-com boom this maxim was applied to Bill Gates, with an eye-popping result. Calculating his average hourly earnings over the course of a year, it was determined that should he pass by a hundred-dollar bill sitting on the sidewalk, he should not bend down and pick it up. The reasoning went that it wasn't worth his time, because he could have made more than a hundred dollars by spending those two seconds at work.

The example is not exactly right, of course (for starters, Bill Gates doesn't actually get paid by the hour), but the principle behind it is solid. Whenever we spend time doing a particular thing, we can compare it to the other things we could be doing instead. And when we think about the total cost of doing that particular thing, we should factor in the value of the alternatives we pass up in the process. Economists call that factor "opportunity cost."

Opportunity cost isn't just for Bill Gates; it's for everyone. It's the reason why going to graduate school is more expensive than the mere cost of tuition—because those years could be spent working and earning money. It's also why you might choose not to work on a Saturday so you can go to the park with your family—presumably you're passing up a few extra dollars of economic gain, because the fun you would miss out on by spending the day at work is too great. You could make the same argument about the whole question of career choice: People move to lower-paying jobs because they enjoy the work more, or they quit to become stay-at-home parents.

The fact that these choices might leave us with less in our bank accounts at the end of the day doesn't mean they are uneconomic; they are just a reflection of our priorities, of the things that matter to us. Money is hardly the sole measure of that. Ultimately, opportunity costs are all about satisfaction—about making the choices that make you happiest, and also recognizing what you are not doing and how happy (or unhappy) that would make you.

So even though Oti could have earned money by picking up Jake ontime, there might have been mitigating factors that made it a bad choice overall. Suppose the traffic was so horrendous that it would take Oti three hours to make the eight-mile round trip. In this case the frustration and extra time associated with driving could be more costly than the money he would earn, making it a reasonable decision to cancel.

Still, there are plenty of times when, even if we have the big-picture choices right, we can make little errors that cost us. Suppose Oti wanted to watch a movie at some point during the afternoon. He could watch it from noon to two o'clock, when he didn't have anybody to pick up. In this case the opportunity cost is close to nil (he could, of course, go try to drum up more business, so there is some cost). Or he could watch it from four to six o'clock, and call Jake to cancel the day's pickup. In this case the opportunity cost of watching the movie is the money he would have earned by driving Jake home.

As far as Jake could see, Oti was hardly calculating opportunity cost with the cool acumen of an Econ. He did not cancel when traffic was horrible, nor did he make it on time when it clearly would have been easy to do. He said, regarding the movies, "Hey, if I am watching some movies with my girlfriend, what can I do? Should I off it to leave the house? I know I will come to pick you later, or else tomorrow morning at least." And he said, regarding the traffic, "Oh! If the traffic is too slow, what can I do? I am already sitting inside the car and I have said I would come, so I have to reach and pick you, even if it should take long. I don't mind if it takes up to two or even three hours."

Well, there it was, Zen-like in its simplicity, round and smooth as an eggshell. It was complete and, for the moment, irreproachable. It meant that on some days Jake would see Oti, and on other days he would take taxis.

Perhaps you are asking the obvious question: Why didn't Jake fire Oti and find someone else? Well, sometimes we all let sentiment sway us—Jake isn't an Econ either. He liked the guy. Maybe the problem was just that Oti knew that all too well.

The Pursuit of Happiness

For the sake of argument, let's assume that Oti had not struck the ideal balance between work (driving) and leisure (watching movies with his girlfriend). Let's assume that—if he thought through it clearly—on days without traffic, Oti really would prefer to pause his movie and earn money by picking up Jake. Well, if it's any consolation, he is not the only one making these mistakes. His counterparts in New York City don't appear to be doing much better.

A team of behavioral economists, Linda Babcock, Colin Camerer, George Loewenstein, and Richard Thaler, analyzed the records of thousands of New York City cabdrivers to figure out how they chose the number of hours they'd work on a given day. Specifically, they wanted to know: Were they allocating their working hours efficiently?

The basic idea is that, for taxi drivers, there are busy days and slow days. If the weather is bad, or if there is a convention in town, for instance, there are likely to be more fares, and in particular more short fares (which are more profitable per every mile driven). On the other hand, if it's a beautiful spring day, people are less likely to hail a cab. On busy days, a driver's average hourly earnings are significantly higher than on slow days. And though they can't control which days are busy and which are slow, drivers can choose their working hours. Each time a driver takes a car out, he gets to choose how long to work (usually up to a twelve-hour limit on shifts). Meanwhile, we assume that taxi drivers like their leisure time too.

According to standard economics, the solution to the time-allocation problem is simple: Drivers should choose to work longer on busy days—getting in while the getting's good—and knock off early on slow days—getting out when it is bad. This way they can work the same number of hours per week, but allocate those hours so that they earn the most money possible. The opportunity-cost interpretation is no different: Leisure time is cheaper on slow days than busy days, since drivers are passing up less income with every hour they spend on the couch.

The theory has its place, but perhaps that place is not in New York City's cabs. (Or Singapore's, for that matter—a study conducted there by Yuan Chou of the University of Melbourne yielded similar findings.) The economists concluded that drivers were not acting according to standard theory. In fact, they were doing quite the opposite.

On busy days drivers worked less, and on slow days they stayed out longer. This is doubly counterintuitive if one assumes that taxi drivers value their leisure time more on beautiful spring (slow) days than on dreary, rainy (busy) ones. The researchers proposed an alternate explanation: Rather than trying to maximize their average hourly wage, maybe drivers were working toward a specific income goal each day. If this was actually the case, then the data make perfect sense. On busy days drivers reach their targets quickly and close up shop, while on slow days they stay out longer, trolling for those last few fares in an effort to hit their marks.

If we accept the daily targeting theory, we might still ask: What's the difference? Do a few hours here or there really have a big impact on earnings? Using the drivers' daily records, the Babcock team estimated how much each driver would have made had he allocated his work hours differently. They found that, on average, drivers could earn about 5 percent more over time by simply working the same number of hours every day; and that they could earn about 10 percent more over time by working more on good days and less on bad days, while keeping the same number of total hours per week. Imagine increasing your salary by 10 percent without clocking any extra hours!

Now, hearing that you're effectively passing up a 10 percent raise because of your choice of shifts should be enough to prick anyone's ears. But particularly for the poor, who have the skimpiest of cushions to fall back on, oversights like these can mean significant changes in the conditions of daily life. They are the ones who stand to benefit most from small, piecemeal improvements in their economic decision-making, precisely because they live on the margins.

Oti and Microcredit

Of course, making a mistake to the tune of 10 percent of your income hurts; but it hurts even more when you're carrying a debt whose interest piles up at six or seven times that rate. That's where the rubber meets the road with microcredit.

The majority of the world's poor—and practically all of the world's microcredit clients—are either self-employed or casual workers, which means they make substantive and complex economic choices on a daily basis. For microentrepreneurs especially, it's not only about how many hours they will work on a given day, but also about which products to stock and sell; where to operate their businesses; whether to hire other employees and at what wages.

In the United States, sorting through these issues would likely be the work of an executive or strategic consultant. But MBAs are few and far between in the developing world, and in any event you're not likely to find one selling vegetables or plastic toys off a floor rug on the sidewalk.

The fact is that most microfinance clients are entrepreneurs not by design, but by necessity. Most developing countries lack social safety nets like unemployment checks or food stamps; if you want to eat, you have to work. And since there simply are not enough salaried jobs to accommodate everyone who needs to make a living, people go into business for themselves.

This is a far cry from the American notion of entrepreneurship, which evokes images of people who break out from the crowd because of their energy, independence, creativity, and drive. I do not mean to say that entrepreneurs in developing countries lack these characteristics. Quite the opposite: Were it not for an abundance of determination and ingenuity, a great many of them wouldn't survive at all. But if you ask them, most would concede that building and running small businesses wasn't their top career choice. Conversely, entrepreneurs anywhere, who exhibit that extraordinary dynamism and drive we so often imagine, would surely attest that their line of work is not for everyone.

So why does the microcredit movement act like it is? Muhammad Yunus, Nobel Prize–winning founder of the Grameen Bank, articulates it as follows:

> I firmly believe that all human beings have an innate skill. I call it the survival skill. The fact that the poor are alive is clear proof of their ability. They do not need us to teach them how to survive; they already know. So rather than waste our time teaching them new skills, we try to make maximum use of their existing skills. Giving the poor access to credit allows them to immediately put into practice the skills they already know. . . .

Yunus is a brilliant man, but this romantic point of view is wrong. Survival is one thing; building an enterprise from scratch—especially one profitable enough to sustain borrowing at typical microcredit interest rates—is quite another. In the last chapter we saw evidence from a project in Sri Lanka that showed there were good business opportunities out there, but that not everyone was equally able to take advantage of them.

That really shouldn't come as much of a shock. Would anyone propose that every random man on the street in the United States or Europe, for instance, has the capacity to conceive and manage a thriving small business? More to the point, would anyone propose we start lending money to random men on the street with that in mind? The recent financial crisis has shown that even highly educated individuals in the world's wealthiest nations sometimes behave irrationally and to everyone's disadvantage, including their own, when it comes to borrowing. Debt can be the shackles just as much as it can be the key.

But let's even concede that microcredit can be a valuable tool, at least for some. Still, might it work better if we provided some instructions along with it? If not every poor person is a born entrepreneur, maybe a little guidance would help. That's the idea behind business training programs, which some microlenders offer to—or, in a few cases, require of—their borrowers.

Now, if Muhammad Yunus were right, and the poor already had all the survival skills they needed, then presumably they would already be operating efficiently, maximizing their profits. And, as he declares in no uncertain terms, providing any kind of skills training (business skills included) would simply be a waste of time. On the other hand, what if business training did prove useful? That would seem to suggest that at least some people are not inherently knockout entrepreneurs. Maybe they're not inherently microcredit clients either.

After my two years with FINCA in El Salvador, this was one of the persistent questions rattling around my head. It stayed that way well into my last year of graduate school, when I met Martín Valdivia at a conference in Peru. Martín is a researcher at GRADE, a Peruvian think tank full of social scientists engaged in research on poverty. (He is also a great host at all the amazing restaurants in Lima, no doubt an essential ingredient in our collaboration and friendship). Martín and I found that we both had the same quandary, so we teamed up with Iris Lanao, the executive director of the Peruvian microlender FINCA Peru, and sought funding for an RCT on business training.

Soon after, I was invited to give an informal talk to the newly formed Henry E. Niles Foundation on the topic of what we knew about microcredit. Instead, I told them how little we knew, how even the basic workings of microcredit were still not fully understood. They were intrigued by the same puzzle I had been grappling with: How were microentrepreneurs borrowing (successfully!) at these interest rates with no business training at all? Their interest also helped to get the FINCA Peru project started.

FINCA Peru's borrowers were required to make weekly or monthly deposits corresponding to the size of their loans, and were also encouraged to hold voluntary savings in interest-bearing accounts. So there was some training, at least in the sense of behavioral conditioning: Clients learned about timely repayment and savings because they were required to do it. But there was nothing in the way of skills development, money management, or business or financial literacy education.

Would expanding the training program help borrowers do better? To answer this question, Martín and I identified over two hundred existing FINCA Peru village banks in Lima and Ayacucho (a university town in the Andes) and randomly assigned half to receive thirty-minute business training sessions during their weekly meetings. This lasted for one to two years for each group. They learned basic business lessons, including orderly record keeping, understanding their markets, diversifying their inventories, and keeping business funds separate from personal funds. The other half of the groups continued to have meetings focused strictly on the loans, as usual. They were monitored for control.

The results were not thrilling, but there were some bright spots. Clients in the treatment groups did adopt some of the strategies they had learned in the trainings. And their business revenues increased, particularly in bad months, though not by a lot. Microentrepreneurs everywhere face seasonal fluctuations in their business revenues, from changes in both supply and demand. Sometimes the stars align for a good month, when inventory is cheap and there always seems to be a line of customers around the block. But things can go badly too. There is the month when nobody is buying anything, when school fees or annual rent payments are owed, when the wholesaler raises his prices, when the flu gets passed around. As a result, this month the kids have to skip school to help out at the shop. Or this month they miss meals because income is down.

But if you received the training and changed some business practices, maybe you manage to avoid these bad outcomes. Clients who received training implemented strategies to guard against seasonal swings. Of the few differences between treatment and control, this was the largest, suggesting that the training's impact, while mediocre across the board, was concentrated where it was needed most.

FINCA Peru was glad to see its clients doing better, and it might have continued offering business training for that reason alone. Happily, looking at its own bottom line only made the decision easier. Even after accounting for the price of running the training sessions, the program amounted to a net gain for the bank, because clients receiving training were more likely to repay their loans on time, and less likely to drop out of the lending program. FINCA Peru took this good news and ran with it. Soon after the study ended they mandated training for all their clients.

But could it have been better? IPA works constantly to refine and replicate, testing ideas in different settings and with different people. This is essential if we hope to break through from particular findings to general lessons about what works. In a second study, led by Antoinette Schoar of MIT Sloan School of Management (and now the managing director of IPA's Small and Medium Enterprise Initiative), Greg Fischer of London School of Economics (and a board member of IPA), and Alejandro Drexler of the University of Texas-Austin, a microfinance program in the Dominican Republic tried to put a finer point on the impacts of business training for its clients.

Rather than just testing one training module, they tested two, and compared each to a control group. They found that standard accounting training did not work so well. But specific "rule of thumb" training, which gave microentrepreneurs simple heuristics for keeping track of money, did. In fact, the effect of the "rule of thumb" training was identical to what we had seen in Peru: Individuals found ways to smooth out their income so that bad months weren't so bad anymore. They didn't suffer so much when times were lean.

But neither of these studies found training recipients making the leap from microbusiness into small and medium enterprises. No transformations. No picture-perfect stories that jibe with the publicity we hear about microcredit. So Miriam Bruhn of the World Bank, Antoinette Schoar, and I joined forces on a project in Mexico that focused on individually tailored training, more like business consulting, for small and medium enterprises in this study. Here, individual mentors were assigned to small and medium enterprises not to teach basic skills, but to get to know the businesses and entrepreneurs closely and advise them on how to improve. The program, funded by the state government, primarily sought to increase employment. It did not achieve that goal. But profits more than doubled for the firms in the program, rising by 110 percent!

What is the lesson? Between the Peruvian, Dominican, and Mexican examples, it appeared that training featuring immediately practicable, concrete lessons, and more intensive, personalized consulting-style mentoring worked better than generalized skills training. Naturally, more intense training is also more expensive, but in the Mexican study the increase in profits outweighed the higher price. Overall it was even more cost-effective than FINCA Peru's training program.

These studies show that microentrepreneurs can improve

their businesses through training, but the bigger takeaway was the evidence that they had something to learn in the first place. As I said before, the fact that the poor are not all innately top-flight entrepreneurs should not come as a big surprise—but, judging from Muhammad Yunus's words, it's something many microcredit advocates need to hear.

Not everyone (in developing countries, or anywhere else, for that matter) is cut out to run a business—or to take on entrepreneurial debt. For some it's because they lack expertise or aptitude, but for most the answer is probably simpler. They are not great entrepreneurs because being great entrepreneurs isn't their main goal in life. People pursue happiness in other ways: doing work they enjoy more, spending time with their families, watching movies with their girlfriends in the afternoon.

What happens when the commonsense fact of people's varying abilities and priorities collides with the worldwide enthusiasm for entrepreneurial microcredit? You end up trying to fit some square pegs into some round holes, lending to people who aren't going to succeed. You make loans and watch hopefully, waiting for the businesses to sprout up like so many blades of new grass; but what ends up growing is not a uniformly lush, verdant carpet of green. There are some bare spots.

The Pursuit of Rice Cookers

When you get down and poke around in that bare dirt, you notice that some of the seed you thought you had scattered there never made it into the ground. Some microcredit clients don't even appear to have tried to build enterprises with their loans. Lenders—and donors—often get irritated when they hand out money for one reason, only to see it used for something else entirely.

Jake can personally attest to this. While he was living in Ghana, he befriended a man named Philip, who had a way of getting himself into tight spots.

One day as they were walking to lunch, Philip said he needed help. He had rented a room he couldn't afford, with the intention of staying just a couple weeks while he found cheaper lodging. But during that time he had run up a rent bill that already exceeded his savings, and the owner of the room would not let him check out for fear that he would disappear. That meant Philip was digging himself further and further into debt with each passing night.

"Jake," he said, "the way it has come down, I have to ask you for support. If you can help me, then by all means I will settle the balance on my bill at the guesthouse, and I will pay you back at the earliest when I take my salary." Jake was doubtful. He'd lent Philip money in the past and not been repaid, and he wasn't keen on getting burned again.

The tension grew in the afternoon, when two uniformed police officers appeared in the office where both Jake and Philip worked. They stood in front of Philip's desk and asked him to step outside. Philip went quietly and returned about twenty minutes later. He came straight to Jake's desk. "See, Jake?" he said. "It's serious." Jake gave him the money the next morning.

About two weeks later, around the time when paychecks went out, Jake asked how things were going. Philip seemed upbeat. "I am out of that guesthouse. I wouldn't let them catch me again," he said, shaking his head and pantomiming grabbing an animal by the scruff of its neck.

"And did you settle the whole bill? You don't owe anything more to them?"

"Well, there is some small balance left, but for that they wouldn't chase me."

"A balance?" Jake had lent Philip enough to repay his whole debt. Where had it gone, if not to the owner of the guesthouse?

"Well," Philip said, looking away, "I also bought a rice cooker. Now I can cook on my own."

This kind of scenario infuriates donors. We dig deep into our own pockets to help a guy like Philip with his rent and he turns around and buys a kitchen appliance. Jake dressed Philip down.

A picture of composure, Philip held his ground. He smiled and heaved a tired sigh: "I knew you would be upset with me. But you don't understand how it is with this guesthouse man. Once I gave him something, I knew he would not make trouble again for some few weeks. I can pay him the rest from my salary check."

Philip had gone back on his word. He really had said he would use the money to pay his rent.

But then his way of dealing with the world did work in its way. Neither the police nor the guesthouse proprietor was seen or heard from again, and Philip enjoyed many heaping bowls of perfectly cooked white rice in his new room.

Slippery Money

Money is fungible, as economists say. It is slippery. It moves like mercury on a tabletop, sliding effortlessly from place to place and leaving no residue. If Jake had cut a check directly to the guest-house proprietor, things might have been different. But cash—unlike, say, a coupon—is not tied to any particular person, product, or store. As Philip so ably demonstrated, it can be spent on anything. Short of tracking the serial numbers on bills—or physically tailing somebody around to watch him spend the money, like the researchers in the Sri Lanka study we saw last chapter—it is virtually impossible to follow any particular wad of it as it passes from hand to hand. (Besides, as we'll see later in this chapter, tracking the particular wads of cash we lend out doesn't necessarily tell us what we need to know.) So when we make rules or restrictions about the use of a cash loan or donation, we typically have no more than the recipient's word that they will be followed.

The question of right and wrong here is complicated. Organizations who act like Jake did, stipulating that aid money be spent in a particular way, often do so with good intentions. I have seen some microlenders require, for example, that clients bring in receipts for investments that match their businesses. Still, recipients often know more about their immediate and changing needs than anyone else. Philip did. So did the borrowers we saw last chapter in the Credit Indemnity study, who made themselves better off with unrestricted loans.

There's a larger point here than who's right and wrong. In fact, there are two larger points—we'll come to the second one later. The first is this: When we insist that microloans be spent on microenterprises, and then we ask people how they spent their last loan and how they plan to spend the next one, we shouldn't be surprised to find a lot of lying. If people were always straightforward about their intentions, many would never qualify for assistance. Many potential donors (Jake included) would hesitate to lend money to Philip if we knew how he actually planned to use it, or even if we believed he could decide later how he would spend it. In cases like these, where a person's eligibility depends on their willingness to commit to behaviors we cannot (or will not) monitor or enforce, it's hard to see the merit in forcing the issue. Aren't we just angling for false promises?

If we are, then we're ultimately hurting ourselves. When people cannot—or choose not to—be honest about how they put resources to use, we get the wrong ideas about how these programs actually function. That was exactly the upshot of the evaluations we saw last chapter, which began to tease out the true impacts of microcredit. They suggested that our picture is incomplete. If we really want to make microcredit work for the poor, we cannot delude ourselves into thinking that all microloans go toward enterprise investments. For how can we hope to fix a machine when its inner workings look nothing like our schematic?

Getting the Truth

This is a critical point in our approach to addressing the problem of world poverty. If we want to act with more than good intentions, we must have an accurate picture of the process of development, and of the specific ways it improves—or fails to improve!—lives. Thanks to the combined tools of behavioral economics and rigorous evaluation, this is actually within reach.

Regarding the use of borrowed money, there is a clever way to find out how people are really spending their loans without forcing them to fess up directly. The trick is realizing that people are willing to reveal sensitive truths as long as they can hide them in a cloud of mundane ones. So rather than asking a touchy question point-blank, we can imbed it in an innocuous list.

It works as follows: Imagine you wanted to find out whether people had been stealing Milky Way bars from the corner store. You could just ask—but you probably wouldn't be surprised if everyone said no. And you would be right to doubt their answers. Instead, make two lists of statements, hand one (randomly chosen) to each customer, and ask: "How many—not which ones, but just how many—of the following statements are true?":

List 1

1. I visit the corner store at least once a week.
2. Milky Way is my favorite candy bar.
3. I eat at least one candy bar per week.

List 2

1. I visit the corner store at least once a week.
2. Milky Way is my favorite candy bar.
3. I eat at least one candy bar per week.
4. I have stolen a candy bar from the store.

List 2 gives Milky Way thieves the cover they need to admit their actions without fear of being found out. Suppose a customer (who knows himself to be a thief) is presented with the second list. He says he agrees with two of the four statements. You can't peg him for stealing because he might lie and say he was only agreeing, for instance, with statements (2) and (3). But the information is in there; we just need to extract it.

Randomization is precisely the tool for the job. Because the customers were randomly assigned to lists, there should be no systematic differences between those who got List 1 and those who got List 2. In particular, they should not differ (on average) in their agreement with statements (1) through (3), which are common to both lists. That means the average agreement with all of List 1 is the same as the average agreement with just statements (1) through (3) of List 2. Subtracting that from the average agreement with all of List 2 gives us what we want. The quantity we care about—average agreement with statement (4), or the portion of customers who are Milky Way thieves—is exactly what's left over when we take away agreement with (1) through (3).

This technique reveals very clearly what the group is doing without exposing the behavior of any individuals. And it can do more than help solve the case of the missing Milky Ways. Pia Raffler, former Uganda country director for IPA and now a Yale political science Ph.D. student, Julian Jamison, an economist at the Federal Reserve Bank of Boston (and someone who considers a marathon a "training run"), and I used it in Uganda, where we were evaluating a Grameen Foundation and Google program that provided answers to health questions by text message. We wanted to know about people's sexual behavior—specifically on the sensitive topic of infidelity—but of course we knew folks might not tell the truth when asked directly. When we did ask directly, 13.3 percent of respondents admitted to having been unfaithful in the past three months. But when the infidelity question was embedded in a list, we found that 17.4 percent of respondents—about a third more—had been sneaking around.

Jonathan Zinman and I used the same technique in a project with the Peruvian microfinance organization Arariwa to learn what clients were actually doing with their loans.

According to Arariwa's rules, loan funds could only be used to invest in a business. If a borrower admitted to spending her loan on food, medicine, school fees, or any other kind of consumption (as opposed to investment), she would likely be barred from borrowing in the future. Still, the bank wanted to know where all the loan money was going. So it asked.

To hear the borrowers tell it, almost everything was—predictably—aboveboard. When questioned directly about what needs their loans had covered, 8 percent said they had spent some of their loan on household goods. Another 7 percent admitted to spending on their children's education. And a measly 2 percent claimed to have spent on health care. Everybody else, apparently, had followed the bank's instructions to the letter and eschewed consumption entirely.

Which would have been great, except that it was not true.

Using the list randomization approach yielded drastically

different answers. Once the sensitive questions (like "Did you spend part of your microloan money on household goods?") were surrounded by easy ones (like "Did you spend part of your microloan money on business supplies?"), we started to see the real picture. Now it looked like 32 percent of borrowers had used some loan monies for household goods, 33 percent for children's education, and 23 percent for health care.

These were huge differences we had uncovered. They suggested a radically different story about the way Arariwa's loans actually helped poor Peruvians improve their lives. Not everyone, it turned out, was building a microenterprise from the ground up. A big portion of clients simply paid lip service to Arariwa's vision of dignified success through entrepreneurship, then turned around and did what they pleased with the money. This is not uncommon. In Indonesia, Don Johnston and Jonathan Morduch of New York University found that over 50 percent of clients reported using loan proceeds for consumption.

Programs that distribute money or other valuable resources should question the wisdom of imposing rules that are unlikely to be followed. Making policies you can't enforce shows impotence. Besides, all those scofflaws—think of Philip enjoying his rice—might actually be onto something.

But there's another problem too.

The Bigger Problem with Slippery Money

I said there were two larger points here. Here is the second, and more compelling, reason why we need to see beyond restrictions that aim to limit the ways people can use programs and program resources to improve their lives: Even when they follow all the rules to the letter, the true impact of participation often pops up in an unexpected place. (This is why, even if it were feasible for lenders to do so, it wouldn't suffice to track the borrowed funds themselves.) Like water, money finds its own level. When it falls on uneven terrain it tends to fill the deepest holes first, no matter what you say to it—or to the person holding it. That's its nature.

Sometimes people help the leveling process along deliberately, like when Philip bought his rice cooker. Once he'd paid off enough of the guesthouse bill to get the proprietor off his back, his debt had ceased to be the deepest hole; now the money could go elsewhere.

But the same process often takes place without any conscious effort. Imagine water cascading down the tiers of an Italianate fountain. Gurgling out of the spout at the top, it enters the top bowl, which overflows and spills into the second bowl, which overflows and spills into the third, and so on. The water was added to the first bowl, but ultimately it's filling the last. So it is with the swag from development programs: Something of value—maybe a milk-producing goat or a school uniform for a child or money to start a microenterprise—is given to meet a specific need, but its effects might ultimately be felt in some distant quarter of the recipient's life.

Here is an example. Imagine a woman who sells tomatoes in a busy street market. Each morning she buys $50 worth of tomatoes from a wholesaler and, over the course of the day, sells them for $55. At the end of the day she takes $5 for herself and puts the remaining $50 in her back pocket to buy tomatoes the next morning. One day she gets approved to take out a $100 microloan to grow her tomato business. She goes to the bank first thing in the morning, picks up an envelope containing $100 in cash, and heads straight for the wholesaler's shop where, using the $100 from the envelope, she buys twice as many tomatoes as usual. Over the course of the day she sells them for $110. Voilà—a growing business!

As she closes up her stall in the evening, she remembers the $50 that she had set aside the previous afternoon. It's right where she left it, in her back pocket. Riding high on the excitement of the day, she decides to celebrate. So she stops on the way home and buys a DVD player for her family.

Did you see the money spill from one tier to the next? When the bank asks her how she used her loan, she answers (honestly!) that she spent it all on inventory for her tomato business. But from our bird's-eye view we can see that the true impact of the microloan was to allow her to buy $50 more of tomatoes and a $50 DVD player. Even when the slipperiness of the people is not a problem, the slipperiness of the money itself remains.

We can prescribe specific solutions to the problems we see, but our prescriptions are usually nonbinding. Sometimes people (like Philip) intentionally flout the rules; other times people (like the tomato seller) genuinely try to keep their promises, but wind up doing the same thing.

In the last chapter we saw evidence from the field suggesting that strictly entrepreneurial loans probably are not the answer for everybody. And now we see that, even if they were, the differences in people's priorities and the slipperiness of money itself mean even the most concerted efforts to restrict borrowers' choices are likely to be in vain.

But that doesn't keep lenders from trying. The most widely used tactic for keeping clients in line is creating incentives for borrowers to monitor one another. The reasoning goes: If they won't adhere to rules imposed from outside, maybe an insider— or, better yet, a whole slew of insiders—could do the trick.

In the next chapter we'll look at the main vehicle lenders use to apply peer pressure—the group liability loan—and see how well it works after all.

TO COOPERATE IN GROUPS

What About the Weakness of the Crowd?

If you looked at just the Art Deco marquee of the Roxy Theater, jutting triangularly up against the sky, you might think of a tropical city in its colonial heyday. Linen suits; close, steamy night air stirred by a gentle breeze; lazy clatter of palm fronds; the sweet smell of plantains frying in roadside stalls; music issuing from the door of a nightclub called the Copacabana, a nightclub with little round tables and a bandstand and good imported gin.

But you can't look at just the marquee of the Roxy Theater. Your eye also takes in its crumbling facade, the elegant curved glass window of its ticket booth webbed with dust and traversed by a long diagonal crack, the dead bugs laid upside-down in its empty poster displays. You cannot ignore the fine chalky silt of the parking lot inhaled against the back of your throat like lime, caustic as cement dust. You cannot tune out the drone of idling semi trucks on the road behind you or the buzz-saw snorts of the motorbikes that tear past them up the narrow shoulder. And it isn't a steamy night, but the blinding, white-hot morning of Tuesday, February 5, 2008.

Accra, Ghana, is a city whose colonial heyday it is not.

But it may be in some kind of a heyday yet; and the Roxy Theater is as good a symbol as any. Despite the absence of a projector, a screen, seats, or even a roof, the derelict place still fills up at least a few times a week. These days, though, its patrons are not moviegoers. They are microcredit clients.

On that particular white-hot morning, Jake was at the Roxy to talk with "Community Leaders," women who had distinguished themselves over years of successful borrowing from an Opportunity International, a major Ghanaian microlender. They were the pillars of the microcredit program. Many had taken a dozen loans or more, and most had served as executives of their borrowing groups. And there was one thing they all had in common: None had missed so much as a single payment. They were perfect clients.

Jake had been briefed before he got to the theater, but still didn't know exactly what to expect. He wondered as he climbed the uneven cement stairs to the balcony where everyone was seated: What will these women look like? He half imagined a corps of pants-suited business mavens. Pumps, pinstripes, and shoulder pads; seriousness and savvy. They were, after all, the cream of the crop.

It was a short-lived fantasy. The stairs gave onto a flat cement balcony with metal folding chairs set in neat rows. You could tell how precisely they had been arranged because they had not been disturbed. Nobody was sitting in them. The women were up and moving and talking. They looked just like anybody else: long skirts of bright printed fabric, rubber flip-flops, secondhand silk-screened T-shirts, head wraps. Big smiles framing white, white teeth. And the sound of laughter.

Levity, Jake learned that morning, was another characteristic shared by all these women. Which is not to say they weren't serious—quite to the contrary. They took their debts very seriously. You don't borrow and repay thousands of dollars over hundreds of months without ample reserves of self-discipline and drive.

Their sense of humor came in where other borrowers were concerned; it's what kept them from tearing their hair out.

The loans these women had taken were group loans, so their obligations to the bank were bound up with those of their fellow group members. And while the women at the Roxy Theater had earned designation as Community Leaders by their exemplary track records, many others hadn't acquitted themselves so well. In their vast experience, the Community Leaders had seen it all: people unable to pay on time, people unable to pay in full, recalcitrant borrowers determined to walk out on their debts, group members who simply up and disappeared. When these things happened, it fell to the rest of the group to pick up the slack. They reached into their pockets and made payments on the delinquents' behalf. Over the years, those payments added up.

It's hard to put a number on these things, but Mercy's sense of humor was worth better than a thousand dollars—or, to put it in context, about one and a half times Ghana's per capita annual income. That, she told me, was how much she had paid during her eight years as a client to cover for other group members when they came up short.

Mercy sold dry goods and canned goods in Makola, one of Accra's largest outdoor markets. She stocked things like spaghetti, matchbooks, instant coffee, tomato paste, and canned herring. When she took her first loan she was a lowly "tabletop" vendor: one of the innumerable women who arrives early in the morning, walks through the market aisles with a collapsible card table and a cardboard box of goods balanced on her head, sets up shop on the sidewalk, and repeats the whole process in reverse at sundown. Now, in the midst of her twelfth loan, she had made great strides. She had upgraded to a cinder-block stall with a metal door and a heavy padlock, so she didn't have to carry her wares to and from Makola every day. No longer limited by the amount she could carry on her head, she stocked more, and more varied, products than before. She bought her inventory in bigger bulk and at lower cost from a distributor.

There was no doubt about it—Mercy had prospered over her career as a microcredit client. Of course, just because her business prospered at the same time that she borrowed does not mean the credit *caused* her to achieve this growth. But regardless of whether or how much the loan helped her, the question remains: Did she really have to pay such penalty (the thousand dollars spent covering for defaulters) for borrowing? Is there a better way?

Up there in the still air of the Roxy Theater balcony, Mercy told Jake she thought this loan would be her last. "As for my own, I don't mind at all. I can pay. My business is coming on. But I won't cover for those ones"—and here she drew the corners of her mouth down into a grimace, shut her eyes, and shook her head, thinking maybe of her thousand dollars—"again."

The Vaunted Group Lending Model

It's no wonder Mercy was ready to quit. If anything, we might ask why she hung around as long as she did. But the big question here is not about her; it is about group lending in general. In the last chapter we saw that, for the poor as much as for anyone else, people's unique needs, priorities, and ways of pursuing happiness are hard to suppress. That's why Oti passed up business opportunities to watch movies with his girlfriend and why Philip spent his borrowed money on a rice cooker. Does it really make sense to bind up all these diverse strands, all pulling in separate directions? Aren't some people—particularly the good eggs, like Mercy—bound to get burned and drop out? Where is the sense in a lending program that effectively penalizes the best clients by making them cover for the deadbeats?

Strange as it seems, this has been a feature of modern micro-credit since Muhammad Yunus, the godfather of the movement, made his first loan to a group of Bangladeshi bamboo crafts-women in the late 1970s. In the intervening three decades, most of the thousands of microcredit organizations that have sprung up around the globe were cast in the mold of Yunus's Grameen Bank. Instead of lending to individuals, they grew by lending to groups.

In the standard arrangement, the group as a whole is liable for each member's loan. So, for instance, when ten clients borrow a hundred dollars each, the microlender sees it as a single group loan of a thousand dollars. The group swims (or sinks) together. If the group makes its payments on time and in full, then every-one is eligible for another loan once the current one has been repaid. If they fall short, then all the members—the good apples along with the bad—are barred from further borrowing. (Or at least it's supposed to work that way. Many microlenders threaten to bar the entire group when only a couple members default, but relatively few follow through. It is a common practice to pull aside the well-behaved borrowers from a defaulting group and continue lending to them.)

This setup might seem like a raw deal for good clients like Mercy, but in reality it's a compromise. In theory, group liabil-ity is the reason why microlenders can operate at all. The group lending model solves three problems that historically kept banks from serving the poor. Think of these problems as questions that a bank has to answer for lending to be viable.

First, who is this person who wants to borrow? Second, how

can we be sure she will make her payments? And third, what can we do to get our money back if things go sour?

In most developed countries, vast information networks and powerful legal mechanisms help address these questions. But potential lenders in the rest of the world have so few resources to draw on that they often simply refuse to operate. The great innovation of the group lending model was to bridge these gaps by harnessing the knowledge and power of the borrowers themselves.

One way to see how this works is to put on a credit officer's hat and compare the process of reviewing a loan applicant in the United States with the same process in a developing country— let's say at Mercy's bank in Ghana.

Who Is the Borrower?

For a bank in the United States, answering the first question is simple. A social security or tax identification number, for instance, illuminates a constellation of reliable information, from addresses to vehicle and voter registrations. Beyond that, credit reporting agencies like Experian, Equifax, and TransUnion compile detailed histories of our lives as consumers and distill them into a simple three-digit number—a credit score. A credit score lets a bank know how attentive a prospective borrower has been to her financial obligations in the past, and is a powerful indicator of how she'll behave in the future. All of this, of course, appears instantaneously when the bank officer enters an applicant's name into his computer.

Now let's see about Ghana. A bank starts by asking an applicant's name, but what's in a name? Not much, if that name is not unique, consistent, or verifiable. Most Ghanaians actually have four names: a family (last) name, a Christian given name, a local given name, and a nickname for the day of the week on which they were born. Spellings and order vary, even on official documents—*if* there are any official documents in the first place. Addresses are even harder. Instead of a house number, street name, and zip code, how about: "Go to Agona Junction, walk about four hundred meters toward Tema, turn right opposite Ebenezer Church. Go on the dirt path behind Quincy Chop Bar near the football field. Find the house with a white compound wall and a green gate." Good luck.

Knowing a name or address wouldn't get you very far, anyway, since it doesn't link you to a web of relevant information. The single biggest gap is the lack of credit reporting agencies. Ghana, like most developing countries, has none. It is virtually impossible to learn about a person's economic history. And when a bank can't learn about its potential clients, it can't screen out the bad seeds. Then lending at all means running the risk of choosing untrustworthy borrowers.

The group lending model addresses the problem by passing the burden of screening onto the borrowers. Since the group (and not the bank) pays the penalty when members act up, they are the ones who have an incentive to learn who is trustworthy. In some sense, they are better equipped to do the job anyway, given the dearth of information available to the bank. As neighbors, relatives, parishioners, and friends of fellow group members, borrowers know more about each other than the lender ever could.

How Do We Know the Borrower Can Pay?

Suppose we manage to convince ourselves that a potential borrower is genuine. How can we then be sure she will make her payments once she gets the money?

In the United States, loan applicants have to put their money where their mouth is. People secure loans with collateral like houses, cars, and jewelry. Or, without putting existing assets at risk, a pay stub or a tax return can prove that an applicant earns enough to cover her payments. At the very least, people seeking entrepreneurial loans are often required to submit a detailed business plan that shows how borrowed funds will be used and how the business will generate enough money to enable repayment.

Meanwhile, collateral is unlikely to be an option for a Ghanaian credit applicant. Most people don't have many sizable assets to begin with, and weak property laws hamstring those who do. In a common scenario, an inherited piece of land is offered up to secure a loan. When the bank investigates, it finds half a dozen claims on the little parcel. That's half a dozen people who also believe they own the land—half a dozen people who'd probably stand in the way of a repossession, if it came to that. Understandably, banks usually avoid such entanglements.

Verifying income is no easier than proving ownership. Since most employment in Ghana is informal, people usually get paid in cash. This is especially true for microcredit clients, who tend to be self-employed. So most applicants cannot present a pay stub to demonstrate earnings. Precious few people keep detailed records of their enterprises' purchases and sales, so business plans and projections about future profitability are usually rudimentary if they exist at all.

All this adds up to a lot of consternation among lenders. What they would really like to do is look over clients' shoulders—that way, they could ensure that people are putting loans to good use and exerting sufficient effort to make their payments—but they can't. They just don't have the manpower to keep a close eye on everyone. And so some people wind up doing things their creditors wouldn't approve of. Like Philip's buying a rice cooker instead of paying his rent, for instance.

Group lending offers an organic solution to this problem. As it was with screening, the key here is that clients know one another better than the bank knows any of them. Group members can monitor one another because they buy from the same distributors and sell at the same outdoor markets and they see one another at church. So they hear about it when someone spends her loan money on a new TV (or a rice cooker). They know if someone suddenly starts taking days off from work. And since they *all* have something to lose (namely, the possibility of borrowing again in the future), each member has a material incentive to keep all the others in line.

Even without active prodding by other members, group lending clients feel pressure to perform because they risk damaging their social standing if they miss payments. Business relationships with suppliers and customers become strained. Access to community assistance in times of need can wither quickly and irreversibly. Earning a reputation as a deadbeat often proves very costly in the long run. People usually do their best to avoid it.

By backing formal financial arrangements with social currency, the group lending model finds leverage to keep borrowers on track.

What If Things Go Badly?

American banks resolve the third issue—how to claw back lent money if the borrower fails to pay up—through legal action. Regulations vary from state to state, but in general lenders are well-protected against default. They are empowered to seize collateral, garnish wages, and recover other assets if need be.

If laws are the teeth of the system, then credit bureaus are the jaws. It's hard for delinquent borrowers in developed countries to drop off the map and escape their obligations. Our records, both good and bad, follow us as surely as our shadows, held there by our names, social security numbers, and addresses—things that are hard to shake off.

By comparison, it is very easy to disappear in Ghana. Jake once tagged along with a loan officer who went out to track down a client who had missed two payments. It was a dispiriting trip. They went to the stall in the market where the woman had worked. All they found was an empty plywood table. Then they trekked across the city to her home, which was locked up. A neighbor said the woman hadn't been around for a couple weeks. "She might be at Cape Coast for a funeral," the neighbor offered; but that was all the information they could get.

The loan officer said he believed that, with some sleuthing, the woman could be found. But would it be worth the effort? Her loan was only a few hundred dollars to begin with, and she had paid off most of it. A trip to Cape Coast, three hours away by bus, or more days spent zigzagging around Accra would leave him with less time to deal with the rest of his roughly four hundred clients. Getting the police involved wasn't very appealing, either. It would take even more time, was not much more likely to succeed, and would be quite frustrating to boot. Had the bounty been bigger, he might have bothered, but in the end he couldn't justify it. He let the woman go.

Microlenders around the world face the same situation. Delinquents are hard to track down regardless of where they live or how much they've borrowed; but because microloans are usually fairly small, individual microcredit clients typically don't owe very much. Chasing down a single delinquent may not be worth a loan officer's time, and even if the client is found, the loan officer has limited muscle to recover money. In a group, though, as long as the threat is credible that *everybody* will be barred from further borrowing if *anybody* is late without good reason, the bank can likely get the group to take up a small collection to make up the missing payment.

Again, this just amounts to passing the enforcement buck down to the borrowers. Upstanding clients don't want to take a hit any more than the bank does. When they cover for one of their own, they do everything they can to collect. The beauty of it is that clients are often more effective collectors than loan officers. Not because they are necessarily more tenacious, but because, living and working side-by-side with their debtors, they are in a better position to do it.

Other Advantages of Group Lending

Beyond giving lenders in developing countries a way to answer the three big questions above, group lending also makes credit a more appealing business proposition by controlling lenders' costs. Where meeting with individual clients is time-consuming and expensive, banks benefit by meeting with entire groups—or groups of groups—at once. It is not uncommon for a loan officer to hold a single biweekly repayment meeting for ten groups of a dozen borrowers each. The whole thing might take two hours, or one minute per client.

One reason why the repayment process can be streamlined so much is that the bank does not need to keep detailed records about each individual client. Since it cares mainly about group-level repayment, it can leave the members to sort out exactly who gave how much each week. That's what typically happens at the big groups-of-groups repayment meetings: The group treasurer records each member's payment in her notebook, then presents a single payment to the loan officer on behalf of everybody. The officer might ask to see the individual records if the group's payment is short; otherwise he usually just moves on to the next group. In the aggregate, loan officers save a lot of time—and manage to serve a lot more clients.

Microcredit advocates tout (at least) two more benefits of the group model: the opportunity to integrate complementary interventions into lending programs, and client empowerment. A hundred-plus clients attending a biweekly repayment meeting is a captive audience. As long as they're stuck sitting there, why not give them some business training (like FINCA Peru, whom I mentioned in the last chapter) or a class on nutrition? Some banks have successfully piggybacked auxiliary programs onto their credit programs.

The empowerment angle comes from the simple fact of clients coming together on a regular basis. They talk about their work and home lives, share knowledge, and help one another deal with problems. They inspire one another. Some microlenders—most notably, Yunus's own Grameen Bank—use the social dynamic among borrowing groups to pursue an empowerment agenda explicitly. Grameen does it by having clients commit as a group to a list of sixteen life-affirming behaviors, from subsistence farming to children's education. When the group signs on together, the reasoning goes, they will work hard to honor their commitment, not just out of respect for the behaviors themselves, but out of solidarity with one another.

The Problem with Group Liability

So, in a nutshell, that's the good news about the theory behind group lending. It solves the three basic problems facing lenders (problems that, before Yunus's bold experiment in Bangladesh thirty years ago, had proved intractable in the developing world), gives banks a way to streamline their operations, and serves as a vehicle for other socially beneficial endeavors.

Now for the bad news. For all their merits, these defining features of group lending are really just compromises—trade-offs that ease the burden on lenders so they can operate. Those burdens don't just disappear. When banks cast them off, clients end up shouldering the extra load.

The most obvious way group loan clients pick up the slack is by covering one another's late payments—as Mercy did, to the tune of a thousand dollars. But there are other, subtler ways that individual clients are taxed by the system.

One is simply a time issue. As we saw, holding big repayment meetings is a great boon to the bank, as it allows one loan officer to process scores of clients' payments in a couple hours. It's not so hot from the client's perspective. Instead of making your payment at a teller window, which might take five or ten minutes, you have to wait two hours while your credit officer meets with other clients. Add in the travel time to and from the meetings, and you might be missing half a day of work every week or two. Over the term of your loan, that amounts to a lot of wasted time.

Another disadvantage of the group lending system is the fact that it quietly encourages the clients with modest needs to borrow excessively. Here's why: Suppose that each client applies for her ideal loan amount. Now think about the group member whose loan request is smallest. Because everyone else is more indebted than she is, she's often taking on more than her fair share of risk by committing to cover for them. In the extreme, imagine a group with just two members—one borrowing ten dollars and the other borrowing a hundred. If the ten-dollar borrower is liable for the hundred-dollar loan, she's getting a bad deal. Borrowers level the playing field by taking larger loans than they need, which leads to overindebtedness and, in the long run, trouble. (One potential solution is to make each borrower's liability proportional to her share of the group's overall debt. Some microlenders actually do this, but the vast majority that I have seen do not.)

When trouble does strike, a borrowing group becomes a precarious chain of dominoes. As more members miss payments and disappear, those left behind sink deeper and deeper into debt. Nobody—not even the best client—wants to be the last sucker standing. Eventually even the best borrowers owe more than they can give, and everybody stops paying. The result is a loss for the bank, which might have recovered at least some of the outstanding loans, and a loss for the good clients, whose reputation is ruined through no fault of their own.

Of course, some clients take a more proactive approach. Rather than waiting around for their coborrowers to put them in a bad situation, they pay off one last loan and get out. That's what Mercy was doing. Some people go a step further and avoid microcredit altogether.

The irony is that these folks—the ones who don't borrow for fear of being dragged down by the bad apples in their group—are precisely the people who *should* be taking microloans! By their very refusal to sign up, they demonstrate how much more confidence they have in their own ability to repay than in that of their fellow clients.

Less Is More: Simple Individual Loans Could Be the Answer

A version of microcredit that punishes or scares away people like Mercy isn't ideal for banks. More important, it isn't the best way to help the poor.

Ironically, the major obstacle to fixing microcredit is that, in the eyes of many, it doesn't appear to be broken. Thousands of microlenders around the world, working exclusively within the classic model, have all the business they can handle and see almost no default. Influencers of global thinking from the UN to U2 have stamped it with their seals of approval, which sends money pouring into lenders' coffers from governments, philanthropic foundations, and private donors.

Ask a microlender to change and they might reasonably fire back: Why mess with a good thing?

You mess with it because, if you're losing clients like Mercy, it still isn't quite right. The microcredit world is slowly coming to this conclusion on its own. The past decade has seen many variations on the plain-vanilla group lending scheme. Most visibly, the original architect of (and great advocate for) group-based microcredit himself, Muhammad Yunus, started tinkering.

His idea was to build a new version of microcredit that retained the benefits of group lending—the social dynamism of the borrowing group and the cost-saving practice of large repayment meetings—without overburdening good clients. In 2002 Yunus unveiled his creation and dubbed it Grameen II. On the surface, it looked a lot like its predecessor: Clients formed groups, took loans, and met weekly to make payments together. But behind the scenes there was a very big difference. Grameen II made only individual-liability loans. Clients were no longer forced to cover for one another.

There were concerns that the whole thing would flop. After all, group liability was, in theory, the glue that held the group lending model together. It provided a powerful material incentive for clients to screen, encourage, monitor, prod, and ultimately help one another to make their payments on time. What would happen without it?

As it turned out, there was no need to worry; Grameen II

was a hit. Borrowers liked the new look of microcredit, and they proved it by signing up in record numbers. The bank's client base, which had taken about twenty-five years to reach 2.1 million borrowers in 2002, jumped to 3.7 million by 2004.

Grameen's makeover was an important and visible step, but it has not singlehandedly transformed the microcredit landscape. To make a global change, thousands of banks have to be on board. And while microlenders worldwide draw inspiration and encouragement from Grameen's success, they still have legitimate doubts. They operate in vastly different settings and face different challenges; why should they assume that Grameen II, a solution tailored to the realities of Bangladesh, will work for them?

The Evidence

Fortunately, they don't have to bank on an assumption. The success of Grameen II demonstrated that individual-liability microloans *could* work; that was enough to get people excited. Soon, microlenders began partnering with economists to nail down the important questions and pursue them in the field.

Could individual-liability loans attract more, or better, borrowers than group-liability loans? Would the loans have different default rates? Would clients behave differently under the different regimes?

These questions had to be answered before anyone could say what kind of lending was best. So in 2004 Xavier Giné of the World Bank and I went looking for a partner organization to put individual-liability loans to the test. Actually, we had been hunting for some time already, but hadn't found any takers. It had surprised us how divided the world was. Lenders either did it one way or the other, and very few were interested in finding out rigorously which system worked better for them.

There was one potential partner in the Philippines who I thought might be game. Omar Andaya, president of the Green Bank of Caraga, a family-run bank in Mindanao and one of the fastest-growing rural banks in the Philippines, is a remarkable entrepreneur with an uncanny knack for charging ahead on growth and expansion. He is also an inveterate tinkerer. He is constantly intrigued and motivated by learning what really works and what doesn't, both for his business and for his clients.

Sure enough, Omar was interested. We got to work on an RCT that would put individual- and group-liability loans head-to-head. It helped to break down the comparison into the three big questions that group lending was supposed to answer in the first place: (1) Will group liability attract better clients? (2) Will it ensure that clients use the funds how they said they would and put enough effort into their businesses? (3) Will it help us recover from clients in any case?

All three questions are essential, but they don't come into play simultaneously. To get a good look at each one, we had to compare group- to individual-liability loans at a few different stages in the lending process. So the RCT we designed with Green Bank of Caraga was really two experiments rolled into one.

First, we worked with 169 existing borrowing groups on the island of Leyte in the central Philippines. We randomly selected half the groups to convert to individual-liability for future loans, and had the other half continue under group liability as usual. Whether they were selected for conversion or not, the day-to-day process of borrowing remained the same for everyone. Clients still met once a week and made a single payment as a group, even if the members were no longer forced to cover for one another.

Second, we marketed loans to potential new clients on the island of Cebu, some fifty miles west of Leyte across the Camotes Sea. When the study began in 2004, Green Bank was not yet lending in Cebu, but it had already identified sixty-eight communities where it planned to open operations the following year. We piggybacked on its expansion plan and had it advertise different types of loans in different areas. A third of the communities got plain-vanilla group-liability loans; a third got individual-liability loans; and the remainder got a hybrid—the group's first loan would be group liability, and all future loans would be individual liability. As in Leyte, the individual-liability loans in Cebu didn't look, on the surface, much different from the standard offering. Clients formed groups and made their payments at group meetings. The motivation for this setup, similar to Yunus's in creating Grameen II, was that the social support of other borrowers and the operational benefits of group lending could still be beneficial, even in the absence of group liability.

After months of monitoring, the basic story that emerged was simple: Dropping group liability lifts a burden off clients' shoulders. Clients like that; their patronage proves it. In Leyte, the groups that converted to individual liability attracted more new members and had fewer dropouts than the ones that continued with group liability.

The move to individual liability also strengthened the social ties between group members in two ways. First, since members no longer had to dig into their own pockets to cover for delinquents, borrowers began to cut one another some slack. Clients were less likely to force one another out of groups. Second, the prospect of having to prod and even punish fellow borrowers, which had long dissuaded clients with strong social ties from signing up together, disappeared. People started inviting their close friends and relatives to join Green Bank.

As expected, individual-liability clients did less monitoring, less hounding, less collecting, and less meting out of discipline than their group liability counterparts; and there was some evidence that loan officers picked up the slack. Individual-liability borrowers were more likely to be thrown out of the group by bank staff, and loan officers in Cebu reported that weekly repayment meetings with individual-liability clients took about ninety minutes longer.

For their part, Green Bank's loan officers were understandably apprehensive about the switch. First and foremost, by abandoning group liability they were giving up their first line of defense against client default. Second, it looked as if individual-liability loans would mean doing more dirty work. So it makes sense that they were reluctant to open individual-liability lending operations. Anyone who has lent money to someone for his rent, only to learn that he went out and bought a rice cooker, can sympathize.

But here was the big surprise: It turned out that Green Bank of Caraga had no reason to be afraid! Individual-liability and group liability groups had the same repayment rates across the board. In fact, thanks to the randomized study design, we can say something even more encouraging. Even if our observation was a fluke and there truly *is* a difference in repayment rates, that difference is almost certainly very small.

The view from the bottom line is pretty good too. Even in the worst case, if clients really *are* more likely to default on individual-liability loans, the ability of individual liability to attract (and retain) more clients still means a net gain for the bank overall. Money lost to any realistic increase in delinquency would be easily offset by the revenue generated by additional borrowers.

So what can microlenders learn from the Green Bank's experience? What can anyone learn who wants to do something about world poverty?

First, microcredit has outgrown the stock image that we've become used to—women in brightly colored saris, sitting in a circle and talking about their vegetable stands. An accurate portrait of microcredit would include a cast of characters from Philip to Mercy, and everyone in between. To serve such a vast spectrum of ambitions and needs, we need variations on the theme. We in the United States have a smorgasbord of credit options to choose from—mortgages, car loans, student loans, lines of credit for business, credit cards, cash advance on credit cards, and payday loans, just to name a few. Why should we expect a single type to meet the needs of the billions of poor people around the world?

Which brings us to the second point: We need to be curious and relentless. We need to develop new programs, tweak existing ones, and find out what makes them tick.

For microlenders, that might mean making changes to classic group lending, or offering different products to some clients, or trying something completely new. While they experiment, they need to monitor and respond to the results: Does a new approach serve them better than the one it replaces? More important, does it serve the poor better? If we want to make real progress against poverty, we must get used to improving things in quantifiable, proven ways—and then going through the same steps to improve on our improvements. It is, and will always be, an ongoing process.

The good news is that we don't need to be fatalistic. We can improve microcredit—dramatically!—without demolishing it and rebuilding from scratch. Some parts of the time-tested group lending model work well; let's find out what they are and hold on to them. As for the parts that don't, let's fix them or cast them aside.

What Makes Group Lending Tick? A Game of Trust

So let's try to get to the heart of it: What really fuels the group lending model? In our project with Green Bank of Caraga, we saw people continuing to borrow and repay responsibly, even after the legal tie that bound the group together was severed. That suggested there was more to the group dynamic than the lender's contract terms. And, as we saw in the last chapter, when outside rules come up against people's personal priorities, the rules often take a backseat. So maybe success really has less to do with the rules and more to do with who we are as individuals, or how we interact socially.

It struck me that, if personal integrity and natural social dynamics could induce borrowers to do a good job of screening out risky types up front, there would be no need for group liability. Trustworthy clients would make every effort to repay on time, even without the aid of peer pressure. Right?

I would have liked to ask borrowers point-blank: Are some of you defaulting because you're just not trustworthy? But you can guess how valuable that would have been.

So instead of asking a loaded question, I set up an experiment with some of FINCA Peru's loan clients. In each of the group meetings, I asked clients to play a game. First, every person in the room was given three soles (about a dollar). Then the borrowing group was divided randomly into pairs (some people were paired with members of other borrowing groups too), and each person got a letter (A or B). As soon as they saw the identity of their partner, the Bs were sent into another room.

Then I explained the game to the As: "You can keep the three soles, or you can pass one, two, or all three of them to your partner in the other room. I will double anything you give, so if you pass two soles, for instance, your partner will receive four. Then your partner will choose to pass back however much she wants out of what she received."

Since partners had no opportunity to talk, the game required some implicit trust and trustworthiness. Would A trust B, and pass all three coins? Would A expect B to send back at least as much as was given, and maybe even more? And would B exploit A's generosity by sending back nothing? Or would she prove trustworthy by playing nice?

Traditional economics can tell us exactly how Econs will play the Trust Game: Regardless of how much she receives, B will not pass anything back, because that is the "profit-maximizing" move. And knowing this, A will not pass anything to B. In spite of this tidy, rational explanation, Humans don't always play that way. Some people pass because of social norms; others may pass because they fear retribution after the game is over. About three-quarters of the As in the experiment passed at least one sole to their partners, and more than three-quarters of the Bs who received any soles sent at least one sole back.

I wanted to know whether acting trustworthy in the game translated to *being* trustworthy in real life. Would Bs who sent back more money to their partners be more likely to repay their loan to FINCA Peru one year later?

In a word, yes. After a year had passed, those Bs who had chosen to return more of As' generosity also repaid more of their loans to FINCA Peru. In fact, I saw something even stronger.

Trustworthiness, as far as it was measured by B's action in the game, appeared to transcend the boundaries of the borrowing group. B's actions in the game predicted real-life loan default equally well whether A was a member of the same borrowing group or not. That suggests that the game wasn't just capturing a dynamic between the members of particular borrowing groups, but getting at real and substantive personal characteristics.

But default hinges on many things, not just borrowers' innate trustworthiness. Though clients' screening of one another goes a long way in keeping groups free of deadbeats, even the best of us have bad moments. Everyone is susceptible to unexpected shocks. The strength of the group matters when individuals are stretched to their limits.

So even if intrinsic virtues like trustworthiness keep a borrower constantly on her best behavior, there may still be weeks when her business struggles, when her child falls ill, or when she just makes a mistake. To stay on course through those weeks, the group needs to know how to help. Sometimes people need a break; other times they should be called to task.

Like trustworthiness, the group's unique social dynamic doesn't stem directly from the liability clause in the loan contract. It arises naturally from the way people interact. If we can understand what social factors make some groups stronger and others weaker, then maybe we can build strong groups without sticking them with group liability. With that in mind, let's look at a couple studies that explore what makes groups tick.

The Importance of Hats

In the spring of 1999, immediately after finishing my exams at MIT, I got on a plane to Peru to go see the Lanao family. Iris

Lanao was the executive director of FINCA Peru (the organization I would eventually work with on the Trust Game study we just saw, and Business Training projects discussed in chapter 5). Her parents ran the Ayacucho branch, which serviced most of FINCA Peru's clients. The Lanao family cared deeply about their clients and their community, and they were deep thinkers themselves, constantly questioning the way they did things, looking for ways to improve. They were curious, in the best sense of the word. So when I arrived, they gave me the best possible marching orders: Explore.

I had visited the Ayacucho branch before, during my stint as a consultant to FINCA before graduate school, but back then I'd spent my time hunched over an ancient computer, programming a software system. I had noticed group repayment meetings taking place, but spent very little time in them. This time, I dove into the group process, observing, attending meetings to learn how they worked, and talking to clients about what they thought.

I could tell: There was something about the hats.

I played over the meetings in my head and thought about the hatted and unhatted women. They sat and talked in separate circles. Then I imagined a meeting of only hatted women, all sitting in one big circle and carrying on. Would a completely hatted (or completely unhatted) group get along better than a half-hatted group? Would members be more supportive of, or more attentive to, one another? And if so, would they be better borrowers?

In fact, my question was about more than millinery. Hats were just felt and ribbon, but they stood for the very blood of the people who wore them. The hatted women were *indígenas*, native Andeans. They wore long, thick skirts and plaited their black hair in long, thick braids; and though they could get by in Spanish, they spoke Quechua in their circle. The unhatted were *mestizas*, women of mixed or European ancestry. They spoke only Spanish, wore blue jeans and makeup, and had modern hairstyles.

Though they sat in separate circles, the women got along just fine. They were always civil to one another. But I wanted more than civility—I wanted to see how social connections made the group tick. It seemed to me that groups whose members were "close" (in some hat-related sense of the word) might have an advantage. If they sat in one big circle together, maybe they would know more about one another, and be able to push each other more effectively toward making payments.

FINCA Peru had an unusual way of combining borrowers that made it the ideal partner for answering this question. It had a kind of randomization built right in. Instead of forming groups on their own, like most microcredit clients, people who wanted to apply for loans simply came to a branch and added their names to a list. When the list got long enough, FINCA Peru broke off the first thirty names into a new group. That meant people were thrown together based solely on when they happened to register—not on their relationships with one another. Consequently, the level of social connectedness among groups varied more or less randomly. This is what economists call a "natural experiment," or an RCT by dumb luck.

The remaining challenge involved quantifying and capturing information on both social connections and borrowing behavior. The latter was easy: FINCA Peru already kept track of clients' repayment records. But grasping social connections was not so straightforward. What does it mean in practical, empirical terms to say people are socially connected, anyway?

I settled on two types of connectedness. The first, a culture index, was really inspired by the hats. It was a number between 1 and 8 that captured the "Westernness" or "indigenousness" of each person, based on a few simple observations—language, clothes, and, of course, headwear. A client's culture score was the portion of group members who shared her culture index. The second, a geographic measure, was the portion of group members who lived within ten minutes' walk of the client's house.

The question was whether these kinds of connections between group members led to better performance as clients. After tracking some six hundred clients for almost two years, the answer was clear. Social connections did matter. Clients with higher culture and geographic scores were more likely to make their payments on time and significantly less likely to drop out (or be forced out) of their groups, even if they had missed some payments.

Apparently the improvement didn't come from tough love alone. Well-connected groups were more likely to forgive delinquents than poorly connected ones. Surveying a year into the project, I found clients were more likely to know the circumstances surrounding a default in the group if they were culturally similar to the defaulter in question. That suggested that clients in a well-connected group were monitoring one another more effectively—specifically, they could tell when a delinquent had a good excuse for missing a payment, and they cut the offender some slack. Of course, too much leniency could have been an invitation for bad behavior; but given that well-connected groups had higher repayment rates, it looks like the clients had it right.

Now, the simple fact that socially connected groups tend to behave better may not be earth-shattering, but knowing *how* it happens is potentially very valuable. If a lender knows, for instance, that culturally similar clients monitor one another particularly well, then it could actively promote monitoring by constructing culturally similar groups.

Meetings Matter

Even if intrinsic and unchanging characteristics like trustworthiness or hat preference play a significant role in the success of borrowing groups, one of the big reasons for the world's excitement about microcredit is its promise of personal and group transformation. Clients, whether they arrive hatted or un-hatted, are supposed to *learn* to thrive together through the process of borrowing—through talking, sharing knowledge, covering for and monitoring one another. Indeed, fostering close relationships within the group is one of the purported benefits of—and is frequently a justification for—the time-consuming practice of holding group repayment meetings as often as once a week.

Do frequent and mandatory interactions between members really lead to success for borrowing groups, no matter who their members are? Weekly repayment schedules dominate the microcredit landscape—but what is so special about weekly? Why not every two weeks? Why not once a month? The answers have big implications for the design of group lending programs. If a different repayment regime could still generate acceptable repayment rates, spacing out the schedule might be an attractive option: It would save valuable time for both clients and loan officers, and would give clients more financial flexibility by reducing the number of occasions for which they need cash on hand to make payments. The critical question is: How does the frequency of group meetings actually impact the group's success?

This is exactly the kind of relationship that can and should be tested in the field. But, as with the choice between group and individual liability, in practice most microlenders make a decision about repayment schedules (often with little or no information guiding them) and stick with it. The irony is that if lenders choose unwisely, they're unlikely to realize it: Since most opt for a conservative, labor-intensive weekly schedule, they're most likely erring on the side of too much caution. Such errors sometimes go unnoticed.

This was the scenario when two development economists, Erica Field and Rohini Pande of Harvard University, approached the management of Village Welfare Society (VWS), a major microlender in Kolkata, India, in 2006. Based on its year-end report, VWS was doing quite well. In eleven years of lending it had grown to serve some forty thousand borrowers—all women—with loans of up to three hundred dollars. Its 22 percent interest rate was competitive in India's microcredit market. But the most remarkable figure you could find in the annual report was the clients' repayment rate of 99.1 percent. That's impressive by any standard; by comparison, the repayment rate for American small business loans in the same year was about 94 percent. (If anything, one could argue that VWS's repayment rate was *too* high, a sign that the bank was not funding risky businesses that, on average, could have been profitable and good for growth.)

Still, Field and Pande suspected there might be room for improvement. They also saw an opportunity to understand *how*—and not just whether—frequent group meetings led to success. With everything running smoothly, VWS could easily have told the economists to keep walking, but happily it heard them out.

VWS's credit product at the time was based closely on Yunus's Grameen model: Women borrowed in groups, were liable for one another's loans, and repaid in equal installments at forty-four weekly meetings. Field and Pande, with Benjamin Feigenberg (now a graduate student at MIT and J-PAL), designed an RCT to explore the relationship between meeting frequency, group dynamics, and client default. They set aside a hundred new borrowing groups and randomly assigned each to a schedule: Thirty groups got the standard weekly package, and the remainder got monthly meetings. Over the following two years, during which time most clients repaid their initial loans and took at least one more, they tracked individuals' repayment records and surveyed to capture group dynamics as well.

The differences didn't pop out immediately, but they were there. Over the course of the initial loan, it looked like monthly meetings were a free lunch. There was no difference in default or dropout rates between weekly and monthly repayment clients. But over time it became clear that the more frequent meetings had slowly but surely built stronger groups. Five months in, members of weekly repayment groups were 90 percent more likely than their monthly repayment counterparts to know other members' family members by name, and to have visited them in their homes. After more than a year, members of weekly repayment groups were more likely to socialize together and more likely to say they'd help one another in the case of a health emergency.

The social closeness of the weekly repayment groups was also reflected in their economic choices. About a year after the initial loans had been repaid, the economists set up a game with real money, a lottery experiment, to see how the group members felt about one another. It was a carefully designed lottery, with a nice twist to try to see whether clients simply felt more *altruistic* toward their fellow group members, or were actually more able to *trust* them, to share risk.

Clients were presented each with a ticket to a two-hundred-rupee (about five-dollar) raffle. They were told that the raffle had eleven tickets in all, ten of which had been given to people in other groups. Clients could keep their tickets and participate in the raffle as described (with a one-in-eleven chance of winning), or they could give up to nine *additional* tickets to other members of their own group (which would reduce their individual chance of winning all the way down to one in twenty, but would increase the odds that *someone* in their group would win).

Then the twist: Some clients were told the lottery would pay out a single two-hundred-rupee gift card to be used in a store, while others were told the lottery would pay out four fifty-rupee gift cards, which could easily be shared. So a client in the fifty-rupee-card lottery could give out tickets to other group members, and hope to get a gift card in return if one of them won. On the other hand, the two-hundred-rupee gift card was indivisible (and was intentionally designed to require that the recipient be the one to redeem it at the store), and was thus less likely to be shared.

So if the weekly meetings led people to be more altruistic in general, then weekly repayment clients should have given out more additional tickets to fellow members than their monthly repayment counterparts, regardless of the denomination of the gift cards. On the other hand, if the weekly meetings led people to share risk better, to trust one another more, then weekly repayment clients should still have given out more additional tickets than monthly repayment clients overall—but the increase in giving should be concentrated around the fifty-rupee-card lottery (where ticket givers could more easily be compensated for their generosity in the event of a win).

In fact, that is exactly what the lottery experiment found.

In a basic way, the economists were getting at groups' tendency toward risk sharing and economic cooperation. For the poor, who have the meagerest of economic cushions to absorb shocks, the ability to cope with risk is critical. That underscores the tremendous importance of the lottery result: An outside force (the lender) coming in and requiring weekly, rather than monthly, meetings had a noticeable effect on clients' ability to share risk!

Sure enough, the effects of economic cooperation trickled all the way down to the lender's bottom line: After the initial loans were repaid, clients from the weekly meeting groups were significantly less likely to default on future loans than their monthly meeting counterparts.

Feigenberg, Field, and Pande's study provided some hard evidence that frequent group meetings led to repayment, and, in the process, shed light on one of microcredit advocates' biggest claims—that borrowing can engender real social transformation (here in the form of increased risk-sharing) among clients. That hardly closes the discussion of how each particular microlender should shape its policies, but it's a step in the right direction.

The Next Step(s)

Microcredit has already succeeded in one important way: It has captured the world's attention. Millions of people are engaging for the first time in the fight against poverty, thanks to the support of everyone from Ban Ki-moon to Bono, and to the abundance of moving, true stories of personal transformation through microcredit. Witness the countless clicks at Kiva.org, the $2 million in one-dollar donations to microlenders at the checkout lines of Whole Foods grocery stores. Enthusiasm and participation are themselves a big step forward, and they will provide the power behind any effort we make. The question is: Are we using the right tools?

What if we could do twice as much good with the goodwill

we've already got? What if we're sawing at the prison bar with a butter knife when we could be using a steel file?

Microcredit has a strong foundation in Yunus's group model. It works in some important, fundamental ways. But it's far from perfect, and there are simple ways to make it better. Find out what really drives good behavior, and push it. Find out where the fat is, and cut it. This won't happen on its own. We have to fill in the gaps and chip off the excess by tweaking, tinkering, and testing. Until we have a lending system that can serve both Mercy and Philip—*without* forcing one to pay for the other—microcredit still needs work.

Refining lending practices is only one part of the evolution of microcredit. Another is lenders' expansion into offering a broader range of services to their clients. Most of the talk in development circles is about micro*finance*—it's often glossed over that micro*credit* is just one piece of the puzzle. When we think about the role banks play in our lives in the United States, we don't think only, or even primarily, about loans. We also think about ATMs, savings and checking accounts, money orders, and wire transfers. Though these are not credit, they are no less valuable tools. They make our lives easier.

It wasn't so long ago that we had to make do without these conveniences, but it is increasingly difficult to imagine what the world was like then. As a teenager, I attended a summer program at Duke University to take math and writing courses (and, unbeknownst to me, to meet my wife, Cindy). My second year in the program I signed up for three weeks, but once I was there I decided to stay for seven. That meant I needed more cash for pizza and soda to make it through the summer. I still remember struggling to figure out how, in North Carolina, I could access money from my savings account in Florida. It was a long, drawn-out ordeal involving some research, numerous phone calls, a friend's father driving me to a bank an hour away, and finally a face-to-face meeting with a branch manager.

Of course, the ubiquity of ATMs makes such a scenario unthinkable today in most developed countries. But for the poor it is not so. For the few who have bank accounts at all, simply making deposits and withdrawals still often requires significant travel and waiting time. Money transfers are mostly done face-to-face and in cash—which means they're not just time-consuming, but risky too.

It may well be that the biggest impacts from microfinance will ultimately come from its mundane side: speeding up everyday transactions, giving people the ability to move money from place to place quickly and securely, and, most broadly, providing a safe and reliable way to earn money at one point in time and space, and spend it at another. When the spending happens before the earning, that's credit. But when the earning happens before the spending—which is the case for most people, most of the time—it's savings. Yes, good old-fashioned savings, like our parents and grandparents taught us. In the next chapter we will round out our discussion of microfinance by looking at some innovative approaches to helping the poor save.

7

TO SAVE

The Unfun Option

Vijaya was beautiful, and she was surrounded by beautiful flowers. She sat in the shadow cast by the crumbling east facade of the Koyamedu Market in Chennai, India. When Jake met her she was sitting at her table making garlands. It was repetitive work. She reached in front of her to pick out a single white jasmine bud from a pile of thousands, then she looped a piece of white nylon cord around its tiny stem and cinched it into a knot, sliding it down to join hundreds of others already tied. It was a growing strand of ancient DNA, pairs of opposing buds spiraling around a central axis. The finished portion lay coiled on the table like a wonderful and gentle snake.

The whole place smelled of wet flower petals and sweet incense, but nothing else about it suggested a luxury spa. Nor were the great ropes of fresh flowers destined for opulent hotel lobbies or the dining tables of the rich and famous. They were to be bought and disposed of by common people, who laid them at the feet or hung them around the neck of a religious icon in any one of the thousands of Hindu temples around the city. It takes some getting used to, but it is a fact: You will see a man walking barefoot, wearing a ripped and threadbare lungi, face dirty with soot, and he will be carrying half a yard of fresh roses. He might have spent his last twenty rupees on them.

Vijaya and her neighbors, who sat at similar tables making

similar garlands, were hardworking women. They had something to show for it. Hidden in the folds of their dusty saris were small wads of crumpled, sweaty bills. Ten rupees, fifty rupees. The rupees were usually not plentiful, but that made them all the more important.

Each morning Vijaya arrived at Koyamedu and bought three hundred rupees' worth (about $6.50) of flowers from a wholesaler. She set her table upright, laid down her spool of white cord, and propped a wooden crate on its end for a stool. Then she dumped out the day's flowers on the tabletop and got to work, tying them automatically and efficiently. As long as Jake watched her, she never missed a knot or broke a stem. She took a break only when a customer approached her table. He would point to one of the coiled garlands and she would measure out the length he requested against her forearm. Then she would cut it off with a razor blade, take his money in her right hand, and deposit it in the folds of her sari.

By the day's end she might have sold four or five hundred rupees' worth. Jake asked her what she did with the profit. As it turns out, most of it never made it out of the market. Each evening, after all the flowers were gone, Vijaya was visited by a man who had no interest in garlands. He was there to collect a daily loan payment. A few daily loan payments, actually.

Vijaya had three or four loans outstanding at once. She used them for almost everything: to buy flowers in the morning, for the monthly rent on her family's house, for her children's school fees and hospital bills. The loans varied in amount and duration, but they had one thing in common: interest. That meant Vijaya was paying extra—usually about 3 percent extra per month—for most of her family's biggest expenses.

When Jake asked her roughly how much interest she paid in

total on all the loans, she demurred: "Interest?" If it was a consid-
erable burden, she didn't let it show. "I give about one hundred or
one fifty each day to the man who comes. If I have extra, maybe
I give some extra. If I need more money, I ask for it. That is the
rotation." She stressed that word, *rotation*. It suggested a smooth
and continuous cycle, like the coming and going of the monsoon.

The system of borrowing for most big expenses was actually
less like a monsoon and more like a leaky faucet. It meant rupees
were constantly trickling out of Vijaya's sari—and ultimately
out of her family's coffers—and spiraling down the moneylender's drain in the form of interest. Ironically, losing money in
this fashion, day after day, is no mean feat. That Vijaya was even
able to keep up with her loans proves that she was making more
than enough (the *more* being the interest amount) to cover her
expenses.

Therein lies the puzzle.

Why Saving Is Good

Taking small short-term loans over and over is rarely the best way
to operate, economically speaking, but it is exactly the way many
millions of people operate. The *rotation* is churning in the neon-
lit offices of payday-loans outfits in Sioux Falls, South Dakota, as
much as in the flower markets of Chennai.

Wherever it occurs, the borrowers engaged in it are making
a statement: There is something I need, but I don't have enough
cash on hand to buy it. So I will take it today on credit, and eventually I will pay extra for the privilege of getting it early.

But whence the extra? This is an especially important question for a repeat borrower, say, one who takes $50 every Monday
and pays back $55 on Friday. To support this regular borrowing,

she must have found a way to consistently squeeze (at least) an additional $5 from an initial outlay of $50. So she knows how to put her money to work; unfortunately, it is working for the lender. But it is a powerful engine that turns $50 into $55 over the course of a week, and perhaps it could be refitted to serve her instead of her creditors.

Suppose she resolves to save a dollar each week and put it toward the next week's $50 outlay. (For simplicity, assume through-out that her business remains the same size, always requiring a weekly investment of $50 to buy goods to sell.) On Monday after the first week of saving she borrows $49 instead of $50. That Friday she will repay just $53.90 ($49 plus 10 percent interest of $4.90), saving $0.10 in interest. By the end of the week she has also put aside another dollar, now for a total of $2.10. Next time she only needs to borrow $47.90. As the cycle continues, the compounding interest savings and the growing weekly savings combine to eat away at the loan amount. It's all over sooner than you might expect: After twenty weeks she is completely debt-free. Now her powerful engine, which had been supporting the local moneylender, cranks out five dollars for her to keep once each week, like clockwork.

The example above is fairly realistic in terms of dollars, cents, and percentages, but it is also a fable. There is a moral in it. Saving—even a little at a time—can make a big difference.

Why Saving Is Hard

Like so many things right and good, saving is hard to practice. Most of us can find sufficient evidence of this in our own experi-ence; still, it serves to list a few reasons why people in every cor-ner of the world find it difficult to save.

For starters, on first inspection saving is not very attractive. It does not quench thirst, fill bellies, or prevent illness; nor is it shiny or fun to play with. It preaches abstinence and forbearance, always opts for the sensible shoes, and is probably registered with the local temperance union. Compared with the other things calling out to us and to our wallets, saving is just plain boring.

Second, for those who can see past its homely exterior, it still takes discipline to choose saving over buying something to be used right now, especially when the immediate purchase seems essential. One falls into thinking that today's needs and opportunities are really more pressing than future needs and opportunities will be. Procrastination often sneaks in and makes itself at home while discipline is taking a nap. Saving, like a stern old schoolmarm in a gray woolen frock, will always be there tomorrow, so it can wait.

As this happens repeatedly, the hazy future becomes a storehouse for all the good things we'll eventually do, and not-saving becomes a matter of momentum (or, more appropriately, of inertia). This is actually a pervasive phenomenon documented in psychology and behavioral economics. It happens to all of us, and not just with our piggy banks—the story also makes sense if you replace *saving* with *quitting smoking, eating healthier,* or *exercising regularly.*

Even for a person endowed with discipline and foresight, the road to saving is strewn with barriers and hazards. A few of these are transparent and predictable, like account-opening fees, withdrawal fees, and minimum balance requirements; but for the most part the obstacles are a sneaky, poorly behaved bunch. They are the devils on our shoulders, the monkeys on our backs, and the needy people with whom we are bound up. Your husband's weekly card game, a taste for fine wines, those persistent calls from a cousin asking for a little cash—ferocious beasties all, they can devour a hundred times their weight and still be hungry.

Vijaya was grappling with one of these beasties. She said as much when Jake asked her whether she kept any savings at her house. Naturally, she didn't enjoy handing over the better part of her day's earnings to a collector instead of bringing it home to her family; but she didn't see an alternative. She laughed matter-of-factly and slapped the arm of the woman sitting next to her, who also chuckled and shook her head without looking up from the garland in her hand. Vijaya knotted another jasmine bud and said, "Of course we cannot save anything in the house. Whatever I bring home, my husband drinks it up."

She did the international pantomime for drinking. The adjacent flower sellers, who had overheard her comment, concurred. They also knew the pantomime.

Almost as Good as Keeping It Under the Mattress

Facing a steeply uphill battle at home and with limited access to formal banking, many are forced to develop alternative savings solutions. That's essentially what Vijaya was doing with her loans—using the agent's daily collection to stand in for a savings account she did not have.

Other circumstances have bred a great variety of informal savings schemes around the world. West Africa has *susu* associations, in which a collector takes daily deposits from clients in exchange for a monthly fee; and ROSCAs (short for "Rotating Savings and Credit Associations"), in which members get access to a pool of monthly savings on a rotating basis, flourish on six continents.

There are many varieties, but most informal savings schemes have at least one feature in common: a cost to the saver. In developed countries, where interest-bearing savings accounts are widely available at no cost, solutions like these simply do not stack up. But half of the world's population—over 2.5 billion people— use no formal financial services for either saving or borrowing. The informal solutions survive because, although they're costly, they fill gaps that desperately need filling.

Those gaps are exactly where effective development programs can have a big impact. And we can learn a lot about what's needed by studying the way people use costly savings schemes in real life.

Pascaline Dupas of UCLA and Jonathan Robinson of UCSC undertook such a study in rural western Kenya in 2006. They designed an RCT to see whether obstacles to savings were responsible for low business growth among microentrepreneurs. Specifically, could gaining access to a bare-bones savings account make people better off?

First, Dupas and Robinson identified and surveyed a group of entrepreneurs—market vendors, bicycle taxi drivers, barbers, carpenters, hawkers, and others—and had them agree to keep detailed daily logs on their incomes, expenditures, and health status. Then they randomly selected half and offered to open savings accounts for them at the local cooperative, free of charge.

The account they pitched was no great shakes. It did not bear interest, and carried fees for all withdrawals. (Thus, it effectively had a *negative* interest rate.) It stands to reason that anyone who would actively use such an account must be facing some kinds of obstacles to savings; after all, the venerable under-the-mattress approach offers the same (zero) interest rate and no withdrawal fees. So their first question was: Would anybody even use it?

The answer was a resounding yes. Of those receiving offers, 89 percent opened an account, and 55 percent went on to make at least one deposit within six months. Such a strong response suggests that, for many people, an expensive, no-frills account with the village cooperative was really the best thing going. To find out which participants fit that description, Dupas and Robinson looked at the data they had collected in the initial survey. One thing seemed clear: Women made use of the account far more than men did (although the sample of individuals in the study proved too small to say with statistical certainty why this was the case). Maybe, like Vijaya, they faced more savings obstacles at home.

But a less obvious dynamic also stood out. The strongest predictor of account usage was participation in a homegrown savings scheme, like the Rotating Savings and Credit Associations mentioned earlier. That is, people who were already saving (albeit not in a formal bank) at the time of the offer were significantly more likely to become active users of the new accounts. That's sort of a strange finding. Participants in homegrown saving schemes had already found a way to save; why did so many of them rush to sign up for the new accounts? One explanation is that the new accounts were actually better than the existing alternatives. The way to find out was to see how the village cooperative accounts had changed people's daily lives.

And so Dupas and Robinson came to the detailed daily logs, simple foolscap notebooks filled out in ballpoint pen and dull pencil. Despite their unassuming appearance, these were vast treasure troves of information, containing records of everything from purchases of business inventory to payment of hospital bills. Taken together, the logbooks told a coherent story: Saving in the village cooperative accounts, women invested more in their businesses and increased their spending on food and other goods.

There was also evidence that suggested the accounts improved women's abilities to cope with illness, both to themselves and to other household members. Women without accounts in Dupas and Robinson's study reacted to serious illness by working less, drawing down their working capital, and giving away goods on credit (which was likely a tactic to prevent spoilage). This compounds the effect of sickness by interrupting the business—and the income it generates—precisely when it is needed most.

In contrast, women who had been offered accounts did better. They could draw on savings to pay for treatment right away, so they tended to keep their working hours up even during weeks with sickness. As a result, they were not forced to dip into their working capital or give goods away on credit. Those are steps in the right direction. But why did this happen only for the women in Dupas and Robinson's study? That is an open question worthy of further research. Their finding could be a fluke, or it could be a deep and important truth about the differences between women and men—a truth that has implications about how we should design future programs. Replicating their experiment is the best way to find out. To this end, Dupas and Robinson are currently working on follow-up studies in Kenya, and I am also working with them to replicate and scale their work in Uganda, Malawi, Chile, and the Philippines, through the generosity of the Bill & Melinda Gates Foundation.

Pascaline Dupas and Jonathan Robinson's study in Kenya showed us two things. First, aspiring savers were in a bad spot to begin with. That so many signed up for an account with a negative effective interest rate attests to the amount of obstacles they faced. Second, the fact that village cooperative accounts really did improve people's lives suggests that available alternatives were weak.

There is a much more positive way to look at these findings. Through their use of the village cooperative accounts, the people of western Kenya showed they had both the will and desire to save. If such a middling savings solution can do so much good, then how much more could we do with a better product? The impacts Dupas and Robinson found are encouraging. Now we have to look for ways to get more people on board.

Sunny Saves

Even without a drunkard husband like Vijaya's to tear through our pocket money, many of us find ways to avoid saving. I recently performed a substantial feat of not-saving when I took a friend out for a fancy dinner to celebrate nothing in particular. That expense is easily dismissed as frivolous, but often our reasons for spending are, well, reasonable—repairs or improvements to a house, back-to-school shopping, sending money home to support extended family. These are not splurges.

Unfortunately, the view from inside the piggy bank is stark and simple: Either money gets deposited into the slot on top, or it doesn't. The account balance is no respecter of reasons or justifications. Just shake the thing and see how much is jingling inside. *Clink, clink.* The coins are few; their sound is sad and small. Buyer's remorse sets in. We wonder which recent purchases were unnecessary, which could have waited.

So it was with Sunny.

I met Sunny in the Philippines, in Butuan, a city in the north of Mindanao. Sunny had a few goals for her home. She wanted new plaster on her walls. She wanted to build a nice patio. She wanted to fix her bathroom. Each improvement would cost about two hundred dollars.

Sunny wasn't the poorest person on her block, nor was she the richest. She certainly did not have two hundred dollars. What Sunny did have was a savings account at the Green Bank of Caraga. So she set out depositing money into it, with an eye on her goal. She put in five dollars at a time, and slowly but surely her account balance rose. But every time she reached fifty dollars, something seemed to come up. Nothing earth-shattering: One time her kids needed clothes. Another time her husband was agitating for a fancy new TV. What happened? There was a withdrawal, and Sunny went back to zero.

One day something changed.

The Green Bank came along and offered Sunny a new product called SEED (short for "Save Earn Enjoy Deposit"). SEED was identical to her existing savings account, with one exception: It had a commitment feature, which locked away her money until she reached a goal amount of her choosing.

Sunny signed up and set her goal at two hundred dollars. She saved two hundred dollars, withdrew it, and promptly signed up again. When I met her during a qualitative follow-up survey, she was on round three. She had never managed to save so much before in her life.

SEED was new to the Green Bank and to Sunny, but commitment savings is an old trick. In the United States, Christmas Club accounts have long helped people save little by little toward a big goal. What defines a commitment savings scheme is that deposits are locked up, either until a given date or until a specific account balance is reached.

What's surprising, from the perspective of standard economic theory, is that people actually sign up for these things. The reasoning behind the standard view is that having more options—like the freedom to withdraw money whenever you want—is better. After all, you're never *forced* to withdraw from a regular savings account. You are free to save toward a goal, or not. You can do what suits you. On the other hand, a saver in a commitment scheme has given up the withdrawal option. What could be good about that?

For one, it silences the voices of temptation. It snatches at the windpipes of all the things calling out to us and to our wallets. We cannot make impulse purchases when our money is locked away in a vault. That fact alone was enough to solve Sunny's problem. Is the same true for others? Can SEED, or other commitment savings schemes, help improve the lives of the poor?

Getting the Poor to Save

The fact is that most poor people do not have savings accounts, commitment-based or otherwise, and conventional wisdom has a simple explanation for this. They're not saving because they spend every last cent on the bare essentials. (They're poor, remember?)

I'll admit, there is something attractive about that reasoning. It's clean and it makes a kind of intuitive sense. But it leads to a dead end. If not-saving is simply an inescapable fact of poverty, then even if we find ways to help poor people control their impulses and resist temptation spending, we won't fix the root problem. They still won't have anything left after taking care of their immediate needs. So we should not waste time and money finding better ways for them to save.

Fortunately, we need not accept that line of reasoning on faith; we can test it in the real world.

While I was studying at MIT, I met Mary Kay Gugerty, then a Ph.D. student at the Harvard Kennedy School of Government. Mary Kay was writing her dissertation on informal savings clubs that Kenyan women used to overcome self-control problems. I had also been thinking a lot about temptation—not just with savings, but in other areas of life as well. We went to talk with David Laibson, a behavioral economist at Harvard who had done some pioneering research on self-control.

We went into the meeting hoping to find out how we could test his theories, but we walked out with a much more practical question: How can we use these theories to improve people's lives? Specifically, can we design a product that will help solve the temptation problem?

A week later, Mary Kay and I joined up with Nava Ashraf, another graduate student, and started looking for a product to test and a place to test it. We wrote up a brief proposal and blasted it out to our e-mail list. It turned out a lot of people were interested in temptation and self-control. We got dozens of responses.

Nava and I went to the Philippines in August 2002 to follow up on some of them. John Owens, manager of a USAID initiative to assist rural banks, and microfinance guru, set up a meeting with a dozen potential partners. I'll always remember that trip for one simple reason: Nava and I both had temptation on the brain. I thought about it every morning, when I had to fight to pass up a breakfast of French toast and banana bread while Nava effortlessly opted for a healthy bowl of fruit and cup of yogurt. She thought about it when we talked about clothes. It came out that I hadn't spent more than ten dollars on a shirt as long as I could remember (I usually wear tie-dyes and batiks from West Africa or kurtas from India), while Nava had to hide her credit cards from herself to keep from splurging.

So we had a lot to say when we met with the banks we might work with. The very next day we had a strong partner in the Green Bank of Caraga, the same bank I later worked with to study group- and individual-liability loans. They were eager to find and test new ways to mobilize savings.

Nava, Wesley Yin (a graduate student at Princeton), and I worked with the Green Bank to create SEED, the savings account that would later help Sunny make her home improvements. And in the process we designed an RCT to find out whether a self-control product could really work. We wanted to know what kinds of people would sign up, and how SEED would affect overall savings.

We started by surveying about eighteen hundred current and former clients of the bank. Once the survey was complete, we randomly divided the respondents into three groups. Those in the first group were visited by a Green Bank employee, who spoke to them about the importance of saving and invited them to open a SEED account. Those in the second group were also visited by an employee and given an identical marketing spiel about saving, but were not offered SEED accounts. Finally, those in the third group received no visit and no offer. They were monitored for control.

Our initial survey captured more than the usual demographic and household information. It also included a battery of questions that measured "time-preferences": a person's willingness to pass up gains today for larger gains in the future. These are questions like "Would you prefer to get five dollars today, or six dollars a month from today? How about five dollars in a month versus six dollars in two months?" By probing across a variety of time frames and dollar amounts, we can sketch a good picture of a person's preferences for immediate versus delayed gratification. Or, in plain English, we can find out about patience. Impatient people, for instance, choose the five dollars now over the six dollars in a month.

Things get interesting when preferences change over different time frames. Consider people who are impatient now (i.e., prefer five dollars today over six dollars in a month), but claim they will be patient later (i.e., prefer six dollars in two months over five dollars in one month). You know people like this. They are the ones who never have time to begin their new exercise regimen this week, but are sure they will next week. Or who are always going to start diverting a bigger part of their paycheck to retirement savings—next month. They have identified goals and ways to achieve them, but always find an excuse when the time comes to start. If you knew yourself to be such a person, you might jump at the chance to accomplish a goal by locking yourself into a commitment scheme. That is exactly what happened with SEED.

Overall, the product was a hit. More than a quarter of those invited to enroll did open an account. If that doesn't seem like a strong response, consider what the Green Bank was offering: a savings account identical to the normal one (which anyone was free to open), but *without* the option to withdraw. Seen in that light, the 28 percent take-up rate is impressive: It means 28 percent of people wanted to lock up their money where even they couldn't reach it.

We also confirmed our suspicions about the kinds of people who were opting in. Women with impatient-now-patient-later preferences were about 50 percent more likely to sign up as women without. So, on the whole, SEED was reaching the right people.

We were excited to see people signing up, but the big question was about impact. Would SEED really help people save? In a word, yes. We found that simply *offering* a SEED account caused the typical client's balance to increase by 47 percent over six months. That figure rose to 82 percent after twelve months. Keep in mind that this was the average change in savings balances for everyone offered the account—regardless of whether they accepted. In fact, the impact of SEED only on those who actually opened accounts was a remarkable 318 percent. That is, we found that the effect of offering a SEED account to a client *who will open it* is to increase her savings balance fourfold!

The findings from the SEED study are important for two reasons. First, they confirm that Sunny's experience is no mere anomaly: SEED accounts helped many Green Bank clients increase their savings. Second, and more fundamentally, they undermine conventional wisdom by demonstrating that, if given the right tools, the poor *can* save more, even without a boost to their overall incomes. This is a powerful and encouraging result, for it suggests that people can do better with their existing resources.

Maybe all they need is a behavioral push—or, to borrow a term from Richard Thaler and Cass Sunstein's eponymous book on behavioral solutions to everyday problems, a little *nudge*.

Insights from the Home Front

We have seen what's happening in a south Indian market, in the Kenyan bush, and amid the vast, wet checkerboard of Filipino rice paddies. But what about Decatur, Illinois? What about Astoria Boulevard, Queens, New York? Practical applications of behavioral economics are still, relatively speaking, in their infancy even in the developed world—and it's worth taking a look at the kind of nudges and commitment devices that are catching on over here, to inspire new ideas for what might be tried over there. What's more, as we find that behavioral solutions are adaptable to both rich and poor settings, we strengthen the case that they actually respond to something fundamental and shared, something that transcends the poverty line.

Evidence from the home front supports this view. It turns out that, when it comes to savings, even financial types and (gasp!) economics professors aren't immune to biases and shortcuts in their thinking. The behavioral economists Richard Thaler and Shlomo Benartzi noticed that most people—including their fellow academics—tended to approach retirement savings contributions as they would a certain countertop rotisserie oven: Set it and forget it. When first joining a firm, employees chose a contribution level and an investment plan and tended not to change it. Ever.

From the standpoint of classical economics, this is puzzling. One's needs and resources vary enough over the course of a career that it's highly unlikely any single plan would be best throughout. So these people, savvy as they were, were not making the best economic decisions. What's more, they were failing by their own assessment. When surveyed, many said they were dissatisfied with the size and allocation of their monthly contributions. This came as a surprise; after all, they were the ones who originally set those parameters, and they were free to change them anytime.

What was to blame for these mistakes? Thaler and Benartzi could see procrastination and inertia, two behavioral barriers to saving we saw earlier in the chapter, at work. They devised a plan called Save More Tomorrow (SMarT) that turned these barriers on their heads.

Under SMarT, participants agree now to a series of future savings increases coincident with pay raises, so that saving steps up over time without ever decreasing take-home pay. Because savings will not increase until a pay raise, signing up for SMarT is painless now—that's good news for procrastinators. The plan is voluntary, so participants can opt out of the scheduled increases at any time. Of course, doing so requires some initiative and positive action; thus, for participants, inertia helps, rather than hinders, saving.

Thaler and Benartzi suspected they were onto something, so they partnered with a firm that agreed to offer SMarT and track its employees' saving progress. The implementation went as follows:

First, all employees eligible for the firm's retirement savings plan were offered a free meeting with a financial consultant. For those who accepted, the consultant computed a desired savings rate and recommended an appropriate on-the-spot savings increase to get there. Twenty-eight percent of those who met with the consultant took his recommendation; the rest were offered the SMarT plan. An impressive 78 percent signed up. After four pay raises, the picture was striking. Eighty percent of those who signed up were still enrolled in the SMarT program, and signers-up were saving 55 percent more than those who had accepted the consultant's advice.

Since the first implementation, SMarT has caught on. Fidelity Investments and Vanguard, two of America's largest retirement savings plan operators, now offer a version of the plan to their corporate clients. As a result, millions of employees have agreed to Save More Tomorrow.

One reason why SMarT is such a powerful tool is that it allows people to bind themselves (not too tightly—one can always opt out) to doing the right thing. Economically, participants are changing the relative prices of good and bad behavior. Without SMarT, good behavior (like increasing retirement savings) is costlier than bad: It requires visiting the HR office and filling out a form. Once enrolled, the tables are turned. Good behavior is free, and bad behavior (like freezing or lowering retirement savings) is now the time-consuming option.

What if we had a way to change relative prices of other things in our lives?

With this question in mind, I created stickK.com, a Web site where anyone can make commitment contracts to achieve goals of his or her choosing. StickK.com lets users define what they want to accomplish, what's at stake, and who will certify their success (or failure). This way people can change the relative prices of good and bad behavior directly, using dollars and cents. (You can also put your reputation up as the stakes by committing to automatically notify your friends and family of your success or failure.) Suppose, for instance, you wanted to work out at the gym once a week. With a stickK.com contract, you could fine yourself a hundred dollars for every week you failed to show up.

The plot thickens when you consider the recipient of the money you put on the line. When you make a stickK.com contract, you choose whether your hundred dollars will be transferred to a specific person, a charity, or an "anticharity"—that is, a charity you'd rather not support. Would you try harder to make it to the gym if failing meant sending a check to, say, the Bill Clinton or George W. Bush Presidential Library, as opposed to UNICEF? I suspect so! Other pairs of opposing "anticharities" include the National Rifle Association and the Educational Fund to Stop Gun Violence; Nature Conservancy and the National Center for Public Policy Research; Americans United for Life and NARAL Pro-Choice America. For those in England, stickK.com offers charities on both sides of the great, eternally contentious soccer rivalries: the fan clubs of Arsenal and Chelsea, Liverpool and Manchester United.

It has been a fun process to watch. We have seen plenty of contracts for weight loss, exercise, and smoking cessation. But the Internet has a way of bringing out people's creative sides. With the power of incentives at their fingertips, people have used stickK.com to succeed in some unexpected ways. A few "custom" goals are worth noting:

- I will not call him for two weeks
- No more dating losers
- No more porn
- No more afternoon five-dollar lattes

- No cutting my hair
- Spit my gum in a trash can and not out the window

And a few longer ones, complete with explanations:

- I will wake up AND GET OUT OF BED each workday no later than six-thirty A.M. so that I will be at work no later than eight (goal being seven-thirty). I will e-mail my referee each workday morning so she can see that I am in by eight! I commit to taking a shower no longer than five minutes.
- Buy a car to replace the old POS I have. It will be manual transmission and it WILL be by the end of this year.
- Refrain from swearing even when Philly sports teams mess up if Katie is present. . . .
- Porn is destructive, unhealthy, and perverts my view of sex and relationships. It also can become obsessive-compulsive and an unhealthy release of stress. Watching porn also conditions you to the wrong types of women and the wrong kind of so-called physical "intimacy" instead of valuing their authentic feminine nature. So I commit to not watching porn more than once per week. [Note: Based on the vehement opening, I really thought this contract was heading for cold turkey on the porn!]

Gentler Nudges

Like SEED, stickK.com has some serious bite to it. There can be real money on the line, and money is a powerful tool for shaping our choices in the face of temptation. It makes sense: When you're on the fence about going to the gym, the mere thought of losing a hundred dollars (or having to notify your friends that you skipped) is likely to push you in the right direction. Here's a question, though: How far can we go with less bite? What if the problem is less our weakness than our forgetfulness—and what if the solution lies, accordingly, in the *thought* of losing a hundred dollars rather than the actual loss? Then you might change your behavior just by managing your attention. And maybe you could keep that hundred dollars after all.

That's an idea we can test directly in the developing world. Maybe the poor don't need the bite of restrictive commitment accounts (like SEED) in order to behave better. If they could just *think* of saving at the right times, maybe they would do more of it. Maybe a lot more.

Maggie McConnell (a post doc at Harvard and a former research assistant for IPA in Peru), Sendhil Mullainathan, Jonathan Zinman, and I set up RCTs to test this proposition in three countries: Bolivia, Peru, and the Philippines. Replicating experiments in differing contexts helps us address the ever-present question of "external validity"—whether results from one country or project site can be applied to another. If you really want to know, test the idea in a few different environments! Learn when it works, when it does not, and what the driving factors are for success. This principle was one of the central motivations for creating IPA, and we are testing a number of interventions in multiple locations for exactly this reason.

In all three places, we worked with clients who had recently opened "goal" savings accounts and had made plans to save every month for the year. We randomly chose some of them to get a little nudge toward their goals–the simplest nudge we could think of: We reminded them, once a month, to save. In the Philippines and Bolivia, we sent text messages. In Peru, where cell phone use was less widespread, we sent the messages through the physical mail.

In Peru, we also tried what we thought was a neat idea: to give people pieces of a jigsaw puzzle each time they made a deposit, so that after twelve deposits they would complete a picture of their savings goal, such as a vehicle, a home, or a student at gradua-tion. We suspected that the simple act of depositing money was too abstract, and that a jigsaw puzzle piece would make their goal more salient—and thus provide an extra incentive to make the deposits. Every time we told people about this idea, we were enthused by positive feedback. Some early results even made us hope they would work.

But the jigsaw puzzles did not work. They didn't cause savings to increase or make savers any more likely to achieve their goals. Where did they fail? Perhaps they got the timing wrong: The salience of receiving a piece occurred *after* the deposit was made. So if the problem was one of attention—that individuals weren't thinking of their future goals—then the salience-enhancer needed to be done *before* they were to make their deposit, not as a reward for doing so.

Fortunately, the tiny little reminders really did work. Total savings increased by 6 percent, and people were also 6 percent more likely to reach their savings goals. The effect was even bigger for savers randomly assigned to receive mention of their specific goal (versus a vague reference to savings) in their reminder.

These messages cost the banks pennies apiece. It was practi-cally a free lunch.

A practically free lunch is great, but how about an honest-to-God, zero-cost free lunch? Let's look at one more nudge—one that's even simpler (and cheaper) than sending text messages and *still* makes a big difference in people's behavior. This one is right in our backyard, at H & R Block tax preparation offices in St. Louis.

In 2005, economists Esther Duflo, William Gale, Jeffrey Lieb-man, Peter Orszag, and Emmanuel Saez partnered with H & R

Block to see how offering a one-time matching IRA contribution would affect retirement savings. They found, as expected, that larger matching contributions (say, 50 percent versus 20 percent) generate larger contributions from savers. But they also noticed something strange.

The tax code already contained a program called the federal saver's credit, which was economically equivalent to the matching IRA contributions they were studying. But the federal saver's credit was framed as a rebate instead of a match. Since the two were ultimately the same in dollar terms, they were surprised to find that people reacted to them very differently. In particular, an increase in the matching level generated far more savings than an equivalent increase in the rebate.

Emmanuel Saez returned to St. Louis in 2006 to see what was happening. Again, he partnered with H & R Block and designed an RCT on retirement savings, but this one was different. While the first study was mainly concerned with responses to a range of economic incentives (i.e., the different matching levels), this one focused on a single one. The only thing that varied was the way that incentive was presented.

Some tax filers would be offered a 50 percent match on IRA contributions, and some others an equivalent rebate. In the 2005 study, the federal saver's credit rebate was buried deep in the dense, forbidding tax code—so we might excuse filers if they were unaware of it. But this time he laid it out simply. All the offers were direct and transparent. Still, the results were similar: 10 percent of those offered the match made contributions, compared with 6 percent of those offered the rebate, and 3 percent of those receiving no special offers.

The findings of Saez's 2006 study fit into a growing body of evidence that matching is more effective than equivalent credits or rebates at increasing contributions—to charities, to give one example. Knowing that gives us an easy opportunity to shape better products and policies. Just think: It costs nothing to describe a rebate as a matching contribution, but doing so could increase participation by two-thirds!

That's one reason why strong results about the little things are so exciting—because they point to ways in which we can do better without reinventing the wheel. We are harnessing our irrationality to improve lives.

8

TO FARM

Something from Nothing

Farming is all about growth, about making something out of nothing (or very little). But the sad economic reality is that many farmers make nothing out of something. There is an old joke: A farmer wins the Kansas state lottery and is visited by a reporter from his local newspaper. The reporter wants to know what he plans to do with the money. He asks, "Will you buy a fancy car? Build a bigger house? Quit your job and move to Miami?" The farmer thinks for a moment and replies, "No, I think I'll just keep farming until it's all gone."

Like most good jokes, this one contains a kernel of truth. Lots of farmers lose money. In America, where they often have the benefit of hybrid seeds, fertilizer, piped irrigation systems, perfect roads, mechanized equipment, futures contracts, and easy access to export markets, many struggle mightily to stay afloat. So how about their counterparts in the developing world? Armed with the creaky tools of an earlier age, they work the same earth their grandparents worked—often in the same way their grandparents worked it. They trudge out to the fields at sunup just like American farmers, but they push wheelbarrows of cow dung instead of fertilizer spreaders. They carry wooden hoes instead of tractor keys. Is it any wonder that prosperity eludes so many?

In the landscape of poverty, agriculture is far too big a region to ignore. Well over a billion of the world's poor are farmers. If it is tempting to focus on other issues, perhaps the reason is that the challenges surrounding agriculture in the developing world are so numerous, so varied, and so tightly intertwined that the whole thing appears as an intractable knot.

Let's start to unravel it. First, there are the environmental hazards that all farmers, rich and poor alike, face: droughts, floods, bugs, blights, and the like. Second is the technology gap, in both equipment and cultivation practices. When farmers work without drought- and disease-resistant seeds and rich fertilizers, without testing the soil chemistry to choose which kinds of crops to grow, and without sophisticated irrigation and drainage systems, they are more likely to lose harvests to bad weather and pests. Finally, there are structural challenges. Limited information about, and access to, profitable markets, swings in commodity prices, and the high costs of transporting and storing produce hamstring even those farmers who manage to grow a bountiful crop.

Taken together, these obstacles account for one fact we know for certain about farming in the developing world: It's a tough row to hoe.

DrumNet and the Kitchen Sink Approach

The snarl of problems entangling poor farms hasn't proved much more tractable to aid organizations or policymakers than to farmers themselves. But there have been some successes.

One idea is to provide an integrated suite of services that address many challenges at once. On the ground, this means doing more for farmers than just giving training sessions, or just offering loans for agricultural inputs. In some cases it means nudging them toward new cultivation techniques, or even entirely new crops.

DrumNet, a comprehensive agricultural development program

in central Kenya, did just that. DrumNet was the brainchild of PRIDE AFRICA, a U.S.-based microfinance and agriculture non-profit that serves some two hundred thousand clients across East Africa. With all its experience in the region, PRIDE AFRICA had developed the local expertise to impart some useful information to Kenyan farmers; surprisingly, the most valuable fact on offer was that Europeans had a taste for French beans and baby corn.

When DrumNet came on the scene in 2003, many Kenyan smallholder farmers were growing crops that they could use themselves or sell locally, like maize, potatoes, kale, and bananas. Some knew about the rich European export markets, but those who wanted to sell overseas faced significant obstacles.

First, information was a problem. The farmers, living in the rural villages of Gichugu Constituency, Kirinyaga District, at the foot of Mount Kenya, were out of the loop. They didn't have access to current prices in the world markets for dozens of crop varieties. Second, trust was a problem. Relations with exporters—who were scarce in the first place—were fraught with mutual suspicion. Farmers feared that exporters would arbitrarily slap low grades on their produce or find other ways to shortchange them. Exporters, in turn, feared that farmers would refuse to sell at the agreed-upon price or would simply fail to produce an adequate crop. Third, credit constraints played a role. Selling for export in tightly regulated European markets meant paying for certification and grading in addition to the usual agricultural inputs. Without loans, these extra investments were out of reach for most farmers. The final hurdle to exporting was transportation—arranging and paying for trucks to move produce from farm to port.

PRIDE AFRICA saw in all these obstacles the intertwined strands of a single rope binding farmers' hands, and they designed DrumNet to cut all those strands at once. The program would assist recipients with each step of the transition to exporting: training in farming practices and European agricultural standards, liaising with exporters, opening savings accounts, and providing in-kind loans of agricultural inputs. Although DrumNet was a nonprofit program, it was designed to be "sustainable"—to generate sufficient revenues to cover its costs.

Understanding the impacts of such a rich, multifaceted program was a tall (and exciting) order. With so many moving parts, it's hard to see clearly what each one is doing. But sometimes it is good to start off with a kitchen-sink approach, see if the whole thing works, and then zoom in to figure out the value of each component. In April 2004, Nava Ashraf (from the SEED commitment savings project we saw in the last chapter), Xavier Giné (from the group-liability project in the Philippines, discussed in chapter 6), and I partnered with PRIDE AFRICA to do just that, and evaluate DrumNet with an RCT.

Once the program got under way, different kinds of shoots began to poke out of the furrowed fields of the Gichugu Constituency. French beans and baby corn crept in where maize and kale had dominated the season before. Farmers were responding with gusto to the opportunity presented by DrumNet's suite of services. Those who had been invited to join DrumNet were almost 50 percent more likely to grow export crops than those assigned to the control group.

Interestingly, farmers who were already growing exportable produce at the outset tended to stand pat, even if they enrolled in DrumNet. They didn't dedicate any more of their arable land to export crops. Most of the increase in French bean and baby corn production came from switchers—farmers who had actively made the leap to exporting from subsistence farming or local cash crops as a result of the program. In accordance with the proverb, fortune favored the bold: By the end of the year, switchers' household incomes had increased by almost a third compared to the control groups'.

Better Farming Through Chemistry

DrumNet was humming right along, getting money into Kenyan pockets and vegetables onto European plates, until it ran into the economic equivalent of an oncoming freight train. It was a messy and dispiriting crash, of which we will see a full account later. But before we look at that train wreck, let's consider what the program got right: It hit on a viable (at least initially viable) solution to the specific problems Kenyan farmers faced. Its early success was not serendipity but the result of thoughtful planning and extensive local knowledge. PRIDE AFRICA knew, from its prior experience in the area, that famers were up against an information deficit, a tenuous relationship with exporters, and financial constraints. It had also got its hands dirty. It understood the soil of Gichugu Constituency and knew that French beans and baby corn could thrive there.

Had DrumNet been rolled out elsewhere in the country—in the low tropical plains of the coast, in the arid north, or even just on the far side of Mount Kenya—circumstances might have molded a radically different program. Even if those farmers were grappling with the same economic impediments, maybe the soil couldn't have supported French beans and baby corn; maybe PRIDE AFRICA would have encouraged them to grow something else instead.

The point is that what works in agriculture is highly context-specific, and so advocating a single technical prescription—about what to grow or how to grow it—is unlikely to serve everyone well.

But that doesn't keep people from trying. If the DrumNet

farmers of Gichugu Constituency had met with any extension officers from Kenya's Ministry of Agriculture, they might have learned this firsthand. The Ministry had a plan for every farmer in the country. Depending on location, it recommended one of twenty-four specific regimens of fertilizer usage and seed varieties.

In the maize fields of Busia District, four hundred kilometers west of Gichugu along the Ugandan border, the official regimen called for hybrid seeds and two kinds of fertilizer—one to be applied at the time of planting and another as top-dressing when the plants were knee-high. The Ministry was confident in its recommendation, which was based on evidence from testing farms; unfortunately, real farmers' fields didn't always look like the Ministry's test plots. They varied in soil chemistry, water, and sunlight exposure. Those variations were substantial enough that farmers could not always reproduce the high crop yields from the Ministry's experiments.

That might explain why so few of them followed the government guidelines. In a 2000 survey of Busia's maize farmers, Esther Duflo, Michael Kremer, and Jonathan Robinson found that fewer than one in four had used *any* fertilizer in the previous year; fewer still had used hybrid seeds. Why were so many ignoring the Ministry's advice? Had they never heard of the guidelines? Were they just thickheaded? The researchers gave the farmers the benefit of the doubt. Maybe they knew something the Ministry didn't. Maybe, for the farmers of Busia, following the government's advice would have been a mistake.

Duflo, Kremer, and Robinson set out to design a simple RCT to find out. They chose hundreds of maize farmers at random and worked with them to set up three small adjacent plots, each about seventeen feet square, in each farmer's field. Over the next six growing seasons they tested different amounts and combinations of seeds and fertilizers—including the Ministry's recommended recipe—in two of the three plots, always leaving one for comparison. At the end of each season they measured the output for each plot. When all the data was in, they had a pretty clear picture of the relationship between seeds, fertilizer, and crop yields.

As the Ministry had claimed—and as the farmers knew—higher-quality seeds and greater quantities of fertilizer led to greater yields. Then the researchers went a step further, calculating the net profit for each combination by subtracting the cost of the inputs from the sale price of the final product. That's when farmers' choices about fertilizer started to make a lot more sense. The Ministry's recommended package did produce the highest yield of all, but the inputs were so expensive that the fertilizer investment generated a net loss—about *negative* 50 percent annually of the amount spent on fertilizer—for farmers. Now, fertilizer isn't the largest expenditure for the farmers, so losing 50 percent of a relatively small number is not necessarily devastating. But it sure doesn't help.

So the Ministry of Agriculture wasn't getting it right, but then neither were the farmers. Most were using either too much—in line with the government's recommendations—or not enough.

The researchers' test showed that there was a profitable middle way. It found that using just half a teaspoon of top-dressing fertilizer on each plant (the Ministry called for a full teaspoon per plant, plus fertilizer at planting, plus hybrid seeds) increased crop yields by almost half over comparison plots and, most important, made good business sense. A farmer who followed the half-teaspoon regimen would have earned an annual return of 52 to 85 percent on his fertilizer investment. Though it is again important to note that fertilizer represents a small portion of the overall cost of running a farm, this is a *very* high annual return on an investment. (For reference, it's slightly better than the best year in the U.S. stock market in the past eight decades.)

Farmers Are People Too

Many farmers, as though oblivious to these potential profits, continued to till their fields as they had for generations—with little or no fertilizer. The researchers figured that so many people were not simply turning down more money without a good explanation. Why hadn't fertilizer caught on? They probed the standard economic models, testing explanations about risk aversion and variable returns, but the data just didn't fit. In the final paragraph of their paper on the profitability experiment they concluded, "There may be a role for non-fully-rational behavior in explaining production decisions (e.g., how much fertilizer to use)."

Non-fully-rational, perhaps, but still thoroughly human. The researchers were just saying that the Kenyan farmers, like most of us, do not behave like Econs. Their thought processes, like our own, are susceptible to all kinds of shortcuts, biases, and filters.

The specific lessons of behavioral economics—the things we can leverage to help farmers—are truths about the way these quirks function. Though you are probably not a maize farmer from Busia, hopefully you will agree that the quirks we will discuss are common to rich and poor alike. What makes them bite so hard in Kenya is the simple fact that the poor have much less wiggle room to make mistakes.

Flood of Information: Inertia and the Status Quo

Sit yourself down on a low wooden stool in a mud house and let your eyes adjust. Notice how dim it is, though the light outside from the midday sun is so intense that the cutout window appears as a blinding white square. Feel the still, still heat. Now consider: Planting time is fast approaching. What should you grow this season? Maize, sorghum, finger millet, soybeans, or cassava? How much of each, and where should they go in your field? How much fertilizer should you buy, and what kind, and from which store?

The sheer number of choices can be debilitating. They all call out to you at once, each pleading its own case, so that no single voice can be heard above the din. Meanwhile, information comes in from all sides. You can see what your neighbors are growing, and you can ask how they chose what they did. You know what you've grown the past few seasons and you know how it turned out. Maybe you've had a visit from an agricultural extension officer too.

When you're faced with a flood of information, what floats to the top?

Sometimes the abundance of options and directions leads us, ironically, to choose nothing. As we saw in chapter 3, that's what American grocery store shoppers did when they were confronted with too many exotic flavors of jam. They passed on preserves altogether.

American shoppers can simply go home without jam, but Kenyan farmers pretty much have to decide on *something* to grow, even if the options are overwhelming. For them, not choosing usually amounts to not changing, to doing the same old thing.

That begins to explain one of the most widely observed phenomena in behavioral economics: inertia, or the inexorable pull of the status quo. Time after time we see people pass up new opportunities in favor of the familiar. It's one reason why our farmer, poring over planting options in his dim mud hut, is likely to grow exactly what he grew last season—or why, for that matter, he is likely to be farming in the same way his parents and grandparents did.

Our preference for the usual is pervasive and instinctual. It comes from somewhere outside our rational minds. A California electric company surveyed its customers to decide what kind of service to provide. As it stood, customers who lived in areas with good infrastructure had virtually no power outages, and those who lived in bad-infrastructure areas occasionally lost power, but paid about 30 percent less for electricity. The company was considering upgrading the infrastructure in bad areas, and wanted to know whether customers would be willing to pay more for improved service.

The survey they sent out asked customers to list, in order of preference, six different combinations of price and service quality (the actual price/service combinations experienced in both good and bad areas were included in the six). Tallying the results, they found that, while there was no consensus about which combination was best, most people had a clear preference for the status quo. About 60 percent of both good- *and* bad-infrastructure customers ranked their own price/service combination highest.

As we saw in the last chapter, not even economists, whom we have to thank for cataloging the phenomenon in the first place, are immune. When Shlomo Benartzi and Richard Thaler, the duo behind the Save More Tomorrow retirement plan, tracked the activity of hundreds of professors' retirement accounts, they found that the status quo exerted a strong gravitational pull on them as well. Now, if anyone could be expected to adjust his investment portfolio over time to meet changing needs, it's an economist. But the professors tended to choose an initial allocation and stick with it, sophistication and fine-tuning be damned. In fact, the average professor in their sample made exactly zero changes to his retirement portfolio over his entire lifetime! How's that for inertia?

What Stands Out: Recency and Availability

With our behavioral tendencies pushing us to do the same old thing, the odds seem heavily stacked against any kind of change. But each of us, at least on occasion, cuts his inertial ties and ventures out, unfettered, into new territory. Even then, we carry behavioral tics with us. Think back to our farmer in his dim mud hut. Suppose he resolves to do something different, something better, this planting season. How will he decide what changes to make?

If he's like most of us, he will not fire up an adding machine or run out in search of the latest actuarial tables on crop yields. He'll look over the fence at his neighbor's field, or think back to his cousin's experience trying to grow sorghum last year. Despite the insistence of classical economic models that choices should be made systematically, by dispassionately weighing each alternative in turn, we think in anecdotes. We don't always see the big picture, laid across the vast axes of space, time, and experience—we see specific examples. Local, recent, and extraordinary events stand out in our minds and weigh far more heavily in our decisions than they should.

A classic example of this phenomenon is the spike in sales of earthquake insurance in the days following a major earthquake. In reality, the chance that an earthquake will destroy your home doesn't increase after any one incident, but it's easy to see why tremors send people clamoring for their insurance agents. Fresh images on the six o'clock news—or, even more powerfully, seen firsthand—of collapsed overpasses and mangled buildings flood in and quickly obscure the tiny statistical probability of a quake. Suddenly that policy looks like a pretty good deal.

Daniel Kahneman and Amos Tversky, two pioneers of behavioral economics, used a clever and elegant lab experiment to demonstrate how powerfully specific, salient examples can distort our sense of the overall likelihood of an event happening. Subjects were randomly divided into two groups and had to answer a single question. Those in Group A were asked,

"In four pages of a novel (about two thousand words), about how many words would you expect to find that have seven letters and end with -*ing*?"

Those in Group B were asked,

"In four pages of a novel (about two thousand words), about how many words would you expect to find that have seven letters and *n* in the sixth place?"

The average of Group A's answers was 13.4; Group B's was just 4.7. It's strange that subjects in Group B guessed so much lower, because simple logic proves that the number they were looking for actually *must* be the larger of the two: A list of all the seven-letter words with *n* in the sixth place would include at least all the seven-letter words ending in -*ing* and many more. Again, we get it wrong because we think in terms of examples. It is easy to build seven-letter -*ing* words by conjuring up four-letter verbs and tacking on a suffix, but we don't immediately think of that strategy when we hear "seven letters with *n* in the sixth place." Instead we look for words that just happen to have *n* next-to-last, like *harmony* and *lasagna* (that's what I came up with, anyway). Since these are harder to come by, we underestimate.

Using Our Behavioral Tics for Good

Behavioral economics gets interesting when we move beyond explaining our choices and onto improving them. That's exactly the motivation behind innovations like SMarT, stickK.com, and SEED, all of which we saw in the last chapter. We're far from perfect, but if we can identify the places we often slip up, sometimes we can make tools that help us stay a step ahead of ourselves.

Back in Busia, Esther Duflo, Michael Kremer, and Jonathan Robinson were puzzling over the Kenyan farmers, who appeared to be slipping up left and right. The researchers' experimental test plots had left no doubt: Farmers could have made more money by putting more fertilizer in their fields. Standard economic approaches hadn't even identified what was wrong, much less found a solution. The farmers knew about fertilizer and knew where it was sold—so it wasn't an education or information problem. Fertilizer could be bought in small or large quantity, and at any time of year—so it wasn't a storage problem. Finally, farmers themselves often talked about wanting to use more fertilizer in the future—so it wasn't a problem of desire or preferences.

But it was, undeniably, a problem. The facts were plain as day. On the whole, farmers just weren't using enough.

Duflo, Kremer, and Robinson figured that, if farmers already knew about fertilizer and wanted to use it, maybe they just needed a behavioral nudge in the right direction. So they partnered with ICS Africa, an international nonprofit operating in the area, and developed the Savings and Fertilizer Initiative coupon program (some time later, after evaluating the program, IPA took over operations from ICS Africa on this and other projects).

Representatives of the Savings and Fertilizer Initiative visited farmers at their homes immediately after the harvest and gave them a chance to buy a fertilizer coupon. This way they could pay up front for fertilizer that would be delivered (for free) in time for the following season. At harvesttime farmers were flush with money from selling their crop, and they had agricultural productivity on the brain. If there was ever an occasion when they'd be willing to spend on fertilizer, the researchers figured, this was it.

They were right. Fertilizer use surged by over 50 percent for farmers who had the chance to buy the coupons. Farmers, finally making good on their long-standing wishes to buy fertilizer, grew more crops; and vendors sold over 50 percent more fertilizer without lowering their prices by so much as a penny.

This coupon program is a prime example of the kind of everybody-wins solutions we get from behavioral economics. It's subtle, cheap, and incredibly effective.

There are two catches. First, it is not a one-shot deal. The problems it addresses—farmers' tendencies toward procrastination and shortsightedness—crop up season after season. The fix must be equally persistent. That's the thing about our behavioral tics: They're often easy to treat, but can also be impossible to eradicate. So when the Savings and Fertilizer Initiative pulled out after a one-season initial test period, all the fertilizer gains disappeared. The farmers went back to square one.

Second, it can only do so much good on its own. The Savings and Fertilizers Initiative is a prime example of the way small, carefully designed products that take into account our behavioral tics can make big differences in behavior. But translating those changes in behavior to significant and lasting increases in income or living standards sometimes requires a bit more brute force. The problems farmers face are endemic and intertwined. It doesn't do much good to grow more of a crop if you don't have a good place to sell it, roads to get to the market, prices you can rely on, or brokers you can trust. These are precisely the gaps that the DrumNet program we saw earlier in the chapter tried to fill with its multifaceted approach. How about putting programs like DrumNet together with the Savings and Fertilizer Initiative? Now, there's an idea with growing potential.

Viral Pineapples and Social Learning

Maybe the way to make more enduring improvements to our decisions is to piggyback behavioral solutions on things we already do.
For farmers, one of the essential first steps toward choosing what,
when, and how to grow is walking outside and looking over the
fence at the neighbors' fields. They get information and inspiration from the people around them, and then they act, inspiring
others in turn. It's a natural feedback loop; it's trendsetting. Think
of viral videos on YouTube. Or even viral . . . pineapples?

In the hands of Chris Udry, a Yale colleague and mentor to
me, viral pineapples are a conduit to learning about how people
learn. In 1996, Udry and Timothy Conley, a former colleague of
Udry's at Northwestern and guru of spatial econometrics, set out
to study how farmers learn to adopt new tools and techniques.
They set up in the Akwapim South District of Ghana, an hour
north of the capital city of Accra.

It was a good place to work because change was afoot in the
gently rolling hills of Akwapim South. For generations, farmers
there had raised maize and cassava, rotating their fields between
the two crops season by season. But in 1990, the first timid spikes
of smooth, succulent leaves could be seen peeking out of the
soil. A small portion of farmers, less than one in ten, had begun
growing pineapples for export to Europe. As those first intrepid
growers enjoyed success, others caught on. By the time Conley
and Udry surveyed in 1996, nearly half the farmers in Akwapim
South were in the pineapple business.

Those who made the switch had a lot to learn. Compared
with maize and cassava, pineapple is a labor- and input-intensive
crop. It needs to be planted carefully and calls for more fertilizer. Unfortunately, pineapples don't come with an instruction

manual. The specifics of spacing within a plot, and the timing and quantity of fertilizer applications have to be found out by hand. But not necessarily *first*hand—one pineapple grower could spare himself a great deal of trial and error by talking with others, learning from their successes and failures.

Conley and Udry wanted to know: Was this happening? Were farmers actually sharing information? And if so, how did it flow?

Since it has neither size nor shape, nor color, odor, or taste, information is a very hard thing to track. Spoken words, the vehicles for most of the farmers' information, disappear into thin air. But even if we cannot see the thing itself, we can follow its impact. This was essentially Conley and Udry's strategy—to model the spread of information between pineapple growers by monitoring their fertilizer decisions for evidence of learning.

To begin, they had to map the pathways along which information could potentially travel. So they visited the homes of 180 pineapple growers in Akwapim South and asked which other growers they spoke to about farming. The result was a series of interconnected networks—"information neighborhoods"—linking each grower to the people he might learn from or teach.

For the next two years, Conley and Udry checked in on the farmers regularly to see the process at work. Sure enough, the information neighborhoods were crackling with activity. People were learning. When a farmer experimented with a new fertilizer regimen, for instance, his information neighbors took note. If the new treatment led to better-than-average profits, the neighbors were more likely to follow suit. On the other hand, when a farmer saw low profits from a given fertilizer regimen, his information neighbors were more likely to try something different at the next planting opportunity.

Beyond confirming the presence of learning in general, the

fertilizer data also revealed a natural hierarchy. Whom do people listen to the most, and who does the most listening? Farmers new to pineapple growing were the most susceptible to influence from their information neighbors, while veteran pineapple growers had the most clout. The veterans' wealth of experience translated into influence in two ways: First, their information neighborhoods tended to be larger; and second, the people in those neighborhoods paid close attention to—and were more likely to emulate—their actions.

The news that greenhorns take their cues from old hands may not be so surprising, but it is important if we want to design programs that work.

For instance, suppose you had found the perfect crop variety and fertilizer mix, but you only had enough money to fund a dozen demonstration plots. Where should they go? You could choose at random, or space them out evenly across the region, or place them near the biggest village; but there is a better way to get the message out. Just as you would put your ads on the Web sites that get the most traffic, you should put your demonstration plots in the most-watched fields. Given the findings of the viral pineapples study, those fields belong to seasoned farmers.

The Collapse of DrumNet

Because he lived some two hundred years before the concept came into being, the eighteenth-century Scottish poet Robert Burns couldn't have known the first thing about development economics. So he certainly would not have suspected, when he penned them, that his famous lines would be so relevant to the world of antipoverty programs at the dawn of the new millennium. He wrote,

The best laid schemes of mice and men
Go often awry,
And leave us naught but grief and pain,
For promised joy!

Or, to paraphrase: Despite our efforts to anticipate problems and plan ahead, things go haywire, reducing our grand visions to rubble.

Which brings us back to DrumNet, the Kenyan program that encouraged and helped farmers to grow French beans and baby corn for export to Europe. When we left them, the DrumNet farmers were skating right along. In 2004, participants had made a tidy profit selling the first season's harvest to the exporters, who in turn sold it to European grocery stores. When they returned to their fields the following year, the DrumNet farmers faced a new challenge: EurepGAP, a set of food safety standards for agricultural products, adopted by most European grocery stores in early 2005.

If they wanted to continue exporting their produce, DrumNet participants would have to satisfy the criteria for EurepGAP certification. That meant farmers had to have a grading shed, a secure chemical storage facility with flush toilets and cement floors, an arsenal of mechanized sprayers, modern protective suits to wear when handling chemicals, detailed records of the seed varieties and fertilizer treatments for every plant they raised, and professional analysis of their water and soil done each year. Sadly, this extensive laundry list was simply out of reach for most DrumNet farmers, and it was a stretch even for the few who potentially could manage it. Not a single DrumNet participant could have earned EurepGAP certification without making changes to his farm.

So they had a choice: buy in or get out. Invest in sheds, storage, sprayers, and the rest of it, or quit the program. One independent study estimated the cost per farmer of complying with EurepGAP at $581, or about eighteen months' income for a typical DrumNet member. That wasn't much of a choice at all; the vast majority just couldn't afford it.

Something had to give, and that something was DrumNet itself. In 2006, at the end of its second growing season, the program collapsed when the exporters declared they would not buy the produce, none of which had been EurepGAP certified. Without the exporters to take delivery of the crops, the chain broke down. Trucks never came to pick up the bushels of baby corn and great sacks of French beans, so farmers were stuck with them. Some of the harvest simply rotted; the portion they did manage to sell went to middlemen, usually at a significant loss.

By the time another year had passed, the Gichugu Constituency DrumNet program was nothing more than a bad memory. The farmers reverted to growing maize, potatoes, and kale, just as they had a few years before—just as their parents and grandparents had for ages.

Strong Foundations

Though behavioral insights like viral pineapples and the Savings and Fertilizer Initiative program have a great deal to offer, they cannot carry the day all by themselves. The foundation on which development programs are built—the bedrock of open markets, legal systems, infrastructure, and the like—have to be in order too.

Changes to the bedrock can hurt (as when the adoption of EurepGAP export standards demolished DrumNet) but they can also help. They have the power to open up vast new economic

spaces, to push back the boundaries encircling the poor. In the
state of Kerala, on India's southwest coast, a broader economic
horizon meant more people got to eat fish.

Since at least the year zero, the fishermen of Kerala have been
hauling in netsful of the sea's glinting silver bounty and dragging
them ashore to sell in the markets that dot the state's hundred-mile
coastline. For most of the past two thousand years, they steered
their boats into shore each evening by the market closest to their
homes, where their day's catch would be bought by retail vendors.
This system had the advantage of simplicity, but it was far from
efficient. The number of fish hauled into the market on a given
day often exceeded the number of hungry mouths to eat them, or
vice versa. Ironically, towns just a few miles apart often had opposite problems. Looking across the entire state, supply and demand
might have been in balance, but buyers and sellers were being
mismatched—to their mutual disadvantage—by the fishermen's
inflexible custom of selling exclusively at their local markets.

In 1997, Robert Jensen, a UCLA economist (and filmmaker!)
organized a weekly survey of fifteen coastal markets to track the
sales of fish over time. What he saw were a lot of missed opportunities. On a typical day, eight of the fifteen markets had an excess
of either buyers or sellers, which meant hopeful customers went
home disappointed in some towns while surplus product was left
to spoil in others. Prices, working to align supply and demand,
fluctuated wildly from day to day, up and down the coast. Where
there were too many fish, vendors literally had to give them away;
where there weren't enough, buyers paid ten rupees for a kilo of
sardines. The upshot was that the market was an uncertain place
for both fish eaters and fishermen.

That would all change with the introduction of cellular phones
in Kerala between 1997 and 2000. The installation of towers along

the coast wasn't part of any aid program, but an infrastructure investment by a for-profit communications firm. It also happened to be a perfect solution to the fish markets' problem. Now, instead of blindly choosing to sell at the home market each afternoon, a fishing boat could call around to check the prices at nearby markets and set a course for the most profitable one.

In estimating the overall impact of cell phone access on the market for fish, Jensen took advantage of the fact that the cellular network expanded tower by tower, gradually opening new areas of the coast to communications. It created what economists call a "natural experiment"—something that looks and acts a lot like an RCT, except that people are assigned to treatment or control by a natural process (in this case, the construction of cell phone towers) rather than by explicit and purposeful randomization.

When each new region of Kerala came into the cellular coverage area, prices and availability of fish stabilized virtually overnight. The chart of weekly sardine prices across that region's markets, which had looked like the seismograph of a catastrophic earthquake, converged to a steady plateau around six rupees per kilo. Now customers could count on finding reasonably priced fish whenever they went to market. Fishermen could count on selling their catch every day and earning a steady income. The cell phone company must have been pleased with all the ship-to-shore communications, and even economists could take some satisfaction in the elimination of a deadweight loss: Unsold fish were no longer being left out to spoil. It truly was a win for everybody.

Why Fighting Poverty IS Like Rocket Science After All

Harvard economist Michael Kremer is an inveterate optimist and a firm believer that we can make great strides against poverty if we use tools and methods proven to work. That's why, in lieu of vacation, he spends his free time interviewing schoolchildren in Kenya about their exposure to hookworm, and why he thinks constantly about how to get governments and organizations to scale up proven-effective ideas. He is also the first in the triumvirate of MacArthur Foundation "genius" grant winners who are part of this movement (Esther Duflo and Sendhil Mullainathan being the other two). If he really thought economic development was like a space shuttle disaster, he wouldn't invest so much of himself in it. Still, he has been known to lead off a discussion about development with the story of the *Challenger*.

Watching as the shuttle, breaching gently like a great metal whale over the Atlantic Ocean, bursts suddenly into flame and disperses in spidery fingers of white smoke, one's immediate thought is that only a total mechanical failure could be to blame. The voice of mission control crackles in an eerie monotone while falling debris traces the gnarled shape of a bare tree branch across a cloudless sky: "Obviously a major malfunction . . ."

But weeks later, when the wreckage had been recovered from the ocean floor and painstakingly inspected, NASA determined that the culprit was a simple rubber O-ring. It had become brittle in the cold morning air on launch day and failed to hold its seal.

Kremer's point is that the *Challenger*, a mechanical wonder comprising thousands upon thousands of moving parts, millions of horsepower, and three fifteen-story-high fuel tanks, relied completely on a flimsy piece of rubber much like the one found in your bathroom faucet. In fact, it relied completely on innumerable such commonplace and forgettable things. The failure of a single rivet, valve, or circuit could just as easily have caused a catastrophe.

Like space shuttles, development programs are complex systems with many potential blowout points—prices, credit, infrastructure, technology, law, trust, and even weather. The failure of DrumNet shows just how vulnerable they are. Who would have thought that the buying policies of Italian supermarkets could derail Kenyan farmers?

The good news is that every potential blowout point is also an opportunity. O-rings are not hard to fix; you just have to keep testing. After all, who would have thought that a simple fertilizer coupon could change generations of farming practices?

9

TO LEARN

The Importance of Showing Up

In September 2000, the UN launched an ambitious campaign against poverty by announcing the Millennium Development Goals (MDGs), a set of eight development benchmarks that, if achieved, would constitute a drastic reduction in suffering and privation around the world. It was a big plan on a big stage, and a lot of people were enthusiastic about it. The declaration containing the MDGs was adopted by 189 nations and signed by 147 heads of state and governments.

Such a consensus was a watershed moment in the global conversation about development and poverty. At last, the world's movers and shakers were in agreement (not perfect agreement, of course—many griped about their favorite initiatives being left out), if not about the principles that ought to guide development or the broad issues in most dire need of attention, then at least about specific targets and clearly defined indicators to measure them. Now, some argue that support for goals and targets can be too easily won—and means little—when the supporters themselves face no immediate consequences for failure. To quote Esther Duflo, "Nobody is going to come from Mars and say, 'You didn't reach the goals, so we will invade'—there is no onus [on the UN to reach them]."

In any event, one thing everybody could get behind was schooling, an easy rallying point. (After all, have you ever seen a political advertisement that announced a stand against *education*?)

Right near the top of the list of MDGs—second only to "Eradicate extreme poverty and hunger"—is "Achieve universal primary education." There are good reasons for the high ranking, not least of which is the fact that education trickles down into many of the development outcomes we care about. Educated people have better jobs, better health, and greater gender equality. Many also argue that education is an end in itself, that literacy and numeracy are essential to an active mental life that is ultimately its own reward. So, politically, education was an easy win for the UN.

Things were not so clear for Anthony, who lived in a small village in central Ghana. Like the UN, Anthony was convinced that education was valuable, both for its own sake and for the doors it would open in the future, and so he wanted more. Unfortunately, dignitaries' signatures alone couldn't help him.

Had he been asked to, though, he certainly could have appended his name to the UN's landmark declaration; when Jake met him he had just finished practicing his penmanship.

Jake's mom had come to visit him in Ghana during his time as a research assistant there. They had traveled along the pitted highway up to Lake Bosumtwi, a vast silvery disc bounded by the steep crater walls of an extinct volcano. They drove along the water's edge on a dusty track that came over a rise and curved to a stop in a flat dirt basin shaded by tall, wide trees. The village kids must have heard the car coming, for they were on it before it pulled to a stop. They were a motley crew, different shapes and sizes: tall, skinny teenage boys projecting authority, rambunctious younger boys terrorizing one another, prepubescent girls with little brothers and sisters on their hips. You could tell from the commotion that they didn't get too many visitors.

Jake and his mom were swept up in the little crowd and guided by some of the older boys through the trees and a small reed marsh beyond to the shore of the lake, where they were invited to stand and marvel. They did. One teenage boy, who looked to be about seventeen years old, walked up while Jake was looking out over the water and tapped him on the shoulder. He was smiling hugely. He said, "Good afternoon!"

"Good afternoon. Thank you for bringing us to the lake."

"Oh, this lake." He pointed and looked past his outstretched finger over the water and kept smiling. "That is Lake Bosumtwi."

"Yes, I've heard."

"And I am Anthony."

"Hello, Anthony. It's nice to meet you. I'm Jake."

"*Tjchek*?"

"Or Jacob. Jacob is fine too."

"Oh, Mister Jacob! We are very glad to meet you." Anthony was still smiling. He had big, smooth, almond-shaped eyes that darted around and flashed excitely.

"I'm glad too. You can just call me Jacob, though. I don't need to be Mister."

But the die had been cast. To Anthony, Jake was Mister Jacob that day and all the days that followed. When they were leaving the village a half hour later, he said *Mister Jacob* when he asked for Jake's mobile phone number, and when he took it down in his foolscap notebook he wrote "Mr. Jacob" next to it in neat, deliberate print with a blue ballpoint pen. That was when he showed off the pages of penmanship practice. It was mostly his name written over and over, spaced out evenly across the lines so they were arranged in tidy columns. "I did them this morning," he said.

Anthony called Jake a couple weeks later. He said he wanted to discuss something very important, and that he would come to Accra for a meeting. Because coming to the capital would cost him about six dollars (not to mention eight hours in a rickety van), Jake suggested that they should talk it out over the phone, but he wouldn't budge. He would be there on Friday, he said.

Friday came and rain poured down so that the streets rushed like muddy streams in the spring melt. Somehow, Anthony fought his way out of the morass of the capital's central *trotro* station, with its scores of lurching, skidding vans, and up the hill to the General Post Office, where Jake found him sitting under the awning at the appointed hour. His clothes were wet, but not muddy, and he wore the same wide smile under his darting eyes.

They stood beneath the awning, and sheets of water fell on three sides. They almost had to yell to be heard over the rain. Anthony described his predicament. He was just finishing the SSS (Senior Secondary School) exams, which would determine his eligibility for tertiary education—university, polytechnic, or vocational training college—and he was worried. His parents, he explained, had put all their educational eggs in one basket, and the basket was almost empty.

Anthony was not the only child in his family, but he was the eldest—and, for the moment, the only one destined for SSS and beyond. His parents knew they did not have the money to send all their children to school beyond JSS (Junior Secondary School), so they pooled their limited resources and invested in him. His siblings' sacrifice meant that Anthony could continue on, at least for a while. For their part, the parents reasoned that the younger kids weren't dropping out for good; rather, once Anthony finished college and got a job befitting a graduate, he would earn enough to send his brothers and sisters back to school.

The family had recently made a heroic push, scraping and saving to pay the SSS exam fees, and now there was nothing left. High scores on the SSS exam could potentially lead to a scholarship to a tertiary institution, but first he had to apply. Each application carried a $40 fee. That's where Jake came in.

How could he refuse? If $40 (or $80, or $120) was really the missing link in a chain that would pull Anthony and his siblings up the educational ladder, then surely it was a worthwhile expense. But, like any good donor, Jake had some questions. First and foremost was: Where do you want to go for college, and why?

Jake hoped this would be a good conversation starter, but it stopped Anthony dead in his tracks. For a moment his smile fell and he looked out at the rain, still sloshing down in buckets, still deafening. Then he recovered himself and reeled off the names of three prominent institutions: a liberal arts university, an engineering polytechnic, and a college that trained teachers. He said, "I want to attend university so I can get my degree. That way I will develop myself and find better work."

"But those places you named are all very different. One trains teachers and another trains scientists. What is it you want to study? And what kind of work do you want to do in the future?"

"By all means, I will study geography. As for the work, I can be in a company. I would be a manager."

"A manager of what?"

"Oh, any kind of company will be fine. Or a bank."

It was becoming clear that Anthony didn't know exactly what he wanted. The trickiest part, it seemed, was right in front of him. Anthony didn't have a good sense of what tertiary education was about—of what one puts in and what one gets in return. Specifically, he never talked about acquiring expertise or skills that would ultimately find application in a job. But he spoke with great reverence about the college degree (*any* college degree) as if it were a very powerful talisman that would automatically confer wealth and prestige on its owner. His smile came back whenever he talked about it. The particulars—subject matter, educational institution, future employer—faded away. The value of higher education, it seemed, resided wholly in gaining access to the mysterious power of the degree. It was not something he had ever thought to question.

That's not a strike against him; of course, the same is true of millions of high school graduates headed off to college, both in the United States and beyond. Many of us (Jake and me included) didn't settle on a specific career path before we finished high school. We pursued college degrees because we knew they were good to have, even if we were not sure exactly how we would use them. When we got to university we tried new things, stumbled on an interesting field of study, fell into a job—our paths were improvised and meandering. But it seemed that, with so much of his family's resources invested in his education, so much of their future hanging in the balance, and so minimal a cushion for mistakes, Anthony might have done well to have some kind of strategy.

So Jake pressed him on it, little by little. He tried working through it backward: Start with a realistic goal ("to get a job in a bank") and identify the best way to achieve it (study business, finance, or accounting at a four-year university). He tried working through it forward: Start with what you like to do ("play soccer"), now try again ("help my brother with his maths"), and see where you might end up if you followed that path (teaching math at a primary or secondary school).

At no time that afternoon were the contours of Anthony's future revealed in a flash, but he allowed that he had never thought about things in this way before. He was slowly edging toward a plan.

They had been talking for nearly an hour. It was getting late, and although they had stood under the balcony the whole time, they were both wet. Slowly but surely, the splatter from a gutter's gushing downspout had doused them. Anthony said he had to return to the *trotro* station so he wouldn't miss the last van heading north. His big, darting eyes looked out through the rain and down the street coursing with muddy water, all bound for the bottom of the hill and the impossible bog of the station. Jake asked whether he had plans to return to Accra, so that they could talk more and decide how to proceed.

"Talk more?" he asked. "I thought you would help me with the application fees."

"But where are you going to send the applications? Have you already decided after our conversation?"

Here was the smile and the confidence; this was a question he was ready for. "Yes. I will send them to the three"—and here he reeled off the same three names again—"as I said before. So the cost is three times forty, or one twenty."

Jake was crestfallen. "But what about all we talked about? About planning a course of study and planning how it will lead toward a specific job?"

"Oh, by all means Mister Jacob, it will, it will." Smiling, waving his hands. "Anyway I didn't know we were talking about this very application period. I thought it was all in future. But please, Mister Jacob, the application is now, so I'm sure I can count on you?"

Anthony was probably not satisfied walking back through the rain with a measly fifteen dollars to cover his travel and food; and fortunately the story does not end here. We will see Anthony again soon. But we have heard enough already to open a window on one of the most pressing and pervasive problems with education for the poor.

Step One: Adding Students

Honestly, we can't claim to understand exactly how education— real learning—arises. But we do know some things about it. We'll start with the obvious: In schools, education is something that happens between teachers and students. We can be confident about that much. But although students are an essential ingredient in the recipe, at least 115 million school-age children around the world aren't in school. Why not?

One explanation is price: It's just too expensive to send them. In some countries, the government does not provide any free public schooling, even at the primary level, and in these cases the cost of private school tuition alone puts education out of reach for many. But there are fewer and fewer such countries, and they account for only a fraction of missing education worldwide. Much of the problem is in countries where education is readily available—at least in theory. Ghana, for instance, technically provides free public education all the way through the end of SSS (equivalent to high school). So why should Anthony's parents be unable to afford secondary education for their children?

The answer, which is by no means unique to Ghana, is that even free schooling isn't completely free. First, there is the opportunity cost of education—that is, the money a student *could be earning* were he not in the classroom. And there are plenty of regular, explicit costs too. Students need to provide their own uniforms, notebooks, textbooks, pens and pencils, lunch money, and bus fare. Then there are PTA fees, additional charges for exam preparation (even, in the Ghanaian case, when it is conducted during regular school hours), and registration fees for nationwide standardized tests like Anthony's SSS exams.

The burden of these ancillary costs is enough to keep many poor children out of school. This is a dark cloud, but it has a silver lining. It implies that the will and desire for education is already there. Parents might not send their kids to school for lack of resources, but they would if they could. On its own, that's little more than cold comfort; fortunately, it also points the way to a solution. If people want education but can't afford it, development programs could help bring more students in just by making it cheaper.

The other good news is that we can do more than speculate. Dozens of programs around the world aim to get more kids into classrooms by lowering the costs associated with schooling, and a number of them have been rigorously evaluated. These run the gamut of scale and complexity, from programs distributing single uniforms to pupils all the way up to nationwide initiatives with crossovers into public health. Let's look at a few.

Clothes Make the Student

Michael Kremer, the Harvard economist who conceived the space shuttle theory of development we saw in the last chapter, remains convinced that the basics really matter. The O-rings have to work. He and two students, David Evans and Muthoni Ngatia, suspected that simple things—uniforms, textbooks, notebooks, and the like—were the missing link. Maybe students who didn't have these materials were embarrassed to come to school. They proposed to test a simple solution with an RCT. They would give out uniforms for free to some students, and see whether their attendance improved.

They partnered with ICS Africa (the same organization that had worked on the Savings and Fertilizer Initiative we saw in the last chapter), which ran a sponsorship program for primary school students in western Kenya. The program used some of its donors' money to buy one uniform per year for sponsored students and to pay for some schoolwide benefits—a grant for classroom construction and books, several visits per year from a pair of trained nurses, and instruction from an agricultural representative who organized student clubs to grow crops on school grounds. The schoolwide benefits were made available equally to all students, not just those who received sponsorships.

Twelve primary schools were chosen to participate in the RCT, and there were enough sponsorships to cover about half of the students. Recipients were chosen: First, students who had lost one or more parents were identified and selected; then the remaining sponsorships were allocated by lottery. Field officers made unannounced visits to the school to track the attendance of both sponsored and unsponsored children. They also monitored all students' performance on annual standardized tests.

Over the course of three years under the program, those who had received uniforms from ICS came to school more than their classmates who hadn't. At the beginning of the program, the absence rate hovered around 18 percent—so most students had been missing about one day of school per week. Based on the tracking data, the researchers found that receiving a uniform cut that number by 7 percentage points—more than a third.

Breaking down the students into subgroups, they saw another striking result. Among those receiving uniforms from ICS, the gains in attendance were concentrated around students who did not own even a single uniform when the program began. These students' absence rate dropped by 13 percentage points—more than two-thirds!—while the change in attendance for students who had at least one uniform at the outset was small and statistically indistinguishable from zero.

It looked like the researchers' initial suspicion was right. Providing one uniform to a student who had none made a big difference, but giving an additional uniform to a student who already had at least one did not.

Kremer's team and ICS had hit on a commonsense solution—one that many of the students' mothers surely would have applied themselves, if they had had the means. They recognized that kids were embarrassed to go to a school where they stood out, and helped them feel more comfortable. To use Kremer's space shuttle analogy, providing uniforms to students who had none ensured that one of the many O-rings on the line to education held its seal.

Cutting Checks

Providing free uniforms is one way to get kids into classrooms, but it is certainly not the only way—and it may not be the best. What we really want to know is, for each dollar spent, what approach gives us the biggest education gains? We cannot evaluate a single idea and go home. At the end of day we have to choose between many seemingly good ideas. And that's where the uniform result gets turned inside out.

Another approach to making education cheaper is to do so directly, by paying people in return for going to school. Programs like these are called "conditional cash transfers," because they consist of direct payments to participants, conditional on their behavior. One success story of poverty alleviation through education is Mexico's Progresa program (now called Oportunidades), a government-run conditional cash transfer program that pays poor mothers if their children maintain a minimum of 85 percent attendance at school.

When it was begun in 1997, Progresa was one of the largest and most ambitious programs of its kind ever attempted. It came with a hefty price tag, and the government wanted to know just how much good it was doing with all that money. So they partnered with economists and designed an RCT to measure impacts on education and integrated it seamlessly with the phase-in of the program. In fact, the design turned a budget constraint into an advantage: At the outset there wasn't enough money to launch Progresa in all

495 targeted communities, so they randomly selected two-thirds of communities to receive the program right away, and monitored the rest as a control group for a two-year period. At the end of that time, when funds were available, Progresa was implemented in the control communities. Thus, they were able to perform a rigorous evaluation without excluding anyone they wished to help.

Paul Schultz, an economist at Yale University, crunched the numbers on Progresa's impact on school enrollment. It had been a home run. As expected, eligible students in participating communities were significantly less likely to drop out. The decrease in dropouts was spread across grade levels, but was concentrated where it needed to be—among secondary school students, who had had the highest dropout rates prior to the program.

Demonstrating effectiveness on such a large scale also caught people's attention. The Mexican government was rightfully applauded for having had the foresight to integrate an evaluation into its launch. More important, countries around the world started following Mexico's example. Today, thanks largely to Progresa, Colombia, Honduras, Jamaica, Nicaragua, Turkey, and a number of other countries are delivering similar conditional cash transfer programs to millions of families.

From Good to Better

The Subsidios program in Bogotá, Colombia, is one of Progresa's descendants. In the initial planning phase, the government had imagined a program that closely followed the Mexican example: Eligible families would receive monthly transfers if their children maintained 80 percent attendance or better. They also took a cue from Mexico's success and engaged a team of economists— Felipe Barrera-Osorio of the World Bank, Marianne Bertrand of the Chicago Graduate School of Business, Leigh Linden of Columbia University and IPA, and Francisco Pérez-Calle of G|Exponential—to design an evaluation.

The economists saw an opportunity to make a good idea even better. They suggested that the government of Bogotá test out two tweaks that might improve the program's effectiveness without greatly increasing its price. The first variation was simply a change in timing: Instead of collecting the full payment each month, a third of the money would be held in a savings account, payable at the time of year when students reenrolled in school. The second variation actually changed the structure and conditions of payment. As in the first, eligible families received two-thirds of the regular amount each month, but in this variation they received a large bonus if the student graduated. If, after graduation, she matriculated immediately to a tertiary institution, they could collect the bonus early; if she didn't matriculate, they had to wait an additional year before collecting it.

Both of these variations come straight out of behavioral economics. They recognize that people do not make choices based solely on the dollar value of incentives, but that timing matters too. Think back to Vijaya, the flower seller we met in chapter 7, whose pocket money was never safe from her husband's unquenchable thirst. A standard Progresa-style conditional cash transfer program might not have served her family very well (though her drunkard husband probably would have liked those big monthly checks), but timing tweaks like these could have made a big difference.

The timing of the lump-sum bonus payment to coincide with students' reenrollment period was also a potential plus. It lightens the burden of the out-of-pocket expenses necessary at the beginning of a school year, and so increases the likelihood that families will make those essential purchases. Just think how much easier back-to-school shopping seems when you've just cashed a big check.

The researchers rolled the basic program with the first varia-tions into a single RCT so they could be compared side by side, and conducted a second RCT to evaluate the second variation. They tracked both attendance and enrollment for about thirteen thousand students: eight thousand who had each been randomly assigned to one of the three treatments (the standard program and the two variations), and five thousand who were monitored as a control group. After a year of observation it was clear that, on the whole, the incentive approach worked, as it had in Mexico. Students eligible for the treatments had about 12 to 26 percent fewer absences than their counterparts in the control group.

There was also evidence that the variations worked better than the standard conditional cash transfer program—that Bogotá had indeed found ways to improve on the successful Progresa model. Specifically, both variations had bigger impacts on matriculation rates than the basic Progresa-style program. It turned out that stu-dents eligible for the basic treatment were no more likely to enroll for the following year than control students, while those receiving the variations were significantly more likely to do so. What's more, the vast majority of the increase in year-to-year matriculation was driven by students who were predicted most likely to drop out. That means the incentives were reaching the people who needed them most.

But the most striking difference between the standard pro-gram and the two behaviorally motivated variations was in ter-tiary institution enrollment. Here the impact of the basic program was statistically indistinguishable from zero, while the variations increased enrollment substantially. Starting from an enrollment rate of 21 percent in the control group, both variations were big improvements: The first increased tertiary enrollment by almost half, and the second more than tripled it!

We don't want to get lost in the numbers, but it is important to see just how powerful the details—like timing—can be. Like many other behavioral nudges we have seen so far, Bogotá's variations on the basic conditional cash transfer program have me excited. They are elegant and clever. More important, they are attractive to policymakers and practitioners, who understand—and would rather avoid—the challenges inherent in completely overhauling programs or designing new ones from scratch.

Subtle improvements like these, which leverage the importance of timing in household decision making, can have tremendous consequences.

The Surprise Knockout: Deworming

When all is said and done, there is one school attendance program that stands head and shoulders above the rest; and, to be honest, it snuck up on researchers unexpectedly.

Michael Kremer was at work again in Kenya, this time with Edward "Ted" Miguel of UC Berkeley, on the unseemly problem of worms—hookworm, roundworm, whipworm, and schistosomiasis. Many of us know these characters primarily as the villains of travelers' stories, where they usually amount to an annoyance; but they are a far more tragic reality of everyday life for billions, especially in developing countries. They infect one in four people worldwide.

Heavy worm infections can bring on symptoms like severe abdominal pain, anemia, and protein malnutrition, which might put a person out of commission; but the vast majority of cases are milder. Ironically, this is a big part of the problem. Worms can cause a general and persistent malaise—lethargy, slight queasiness—that people get used to. Many live with it all the time.

Biologically, the worms are parasites that live and breed in human and animal feces. They are typically contracted when people come into contact with fecally contaminated water or soil. The particulars of transmission vary slightly from worm to worm, but they're all devastatingly easy to catch. Depending on the species, ingesting motes of contaminated dirt by eating with unwashed hands, playing in fresh water, or even walking barefoot through puddles near where infected people or animals have defecated—any of these commonplace behaviors could result in infection. It doesn't take much imagination to see why worms are a scourge of children in developing countries.

Fortunately, a highly effective treatment exists for these parasites—a single deworming pill that eradicates roughly 99 percent of worms currently in the body and provides protection for about four months. Even better, the total cost of manufacturing, transporting, and administering the treatment to at-risk children is about twenty cents per pill.

From a public health perspective, providing such an inexpensive cure to anybody who wants it is practically a no-brainer, purely on the basis of benefits to the individual, but there is actually a stronger case for giving deworming pills away. The spread of worms is a chain reaction: Worms spread through contaminated soil and water; soil and water become contaminated through the presence of contaminated feces; feces are contaminated only if the people producing them have worms. So when more people in a community are infected, they create a hazardous environment for everyone else. Conversely, when fewer individuals are infected, the rest of the community is safer too.

A case like this, where the general public benefits when an

individual gets treatment, practically cries out for an intervention. We should do whatever we can to get people dewormed—not just for their own sake, but for everybody's. This sound reasoning was one of the factors that led Kremer and Miguel to get involved in evaluating a program that provided deworming pills for free to students in primary schools in western Kenya in 1998.

They partnered again with ICS (the same organization that gave away school uniforms) and devised a simple program. ICS officers would first meet with students' parents at the school to describe deworming and secure their consent. Then they would return and administer the pills to all the students whose parents had agreed. Most parents (about 80 percent) signed their children up.

Kremer and Miguel designed a study to test the impact of the program on both health and education outcomes. ICS had identified seventy-five primary schools to work with, and the researchers divided them into three groups. Twenty-five schools would get the program in 1998, twenty-five schools in 1999, and the remainder in 2001. Like the Progresa evaluation in Mexico, the phase-in design allowed ICS to provide treatment to everybody they wanted (albeit over time), and also generate rigorous evidence about their program.

Given the proven effectiveness of deworming medication, the researchers fully expected to see noticeable gains in students' health. They were not disappointed. The program cut the total number of worm infections in half—not just for those who took the pills, but for *all* the students in the schools where they were offered. It was the story of cascading community benefits, just as they had hoped: Disrupting the cycle of infection made even those who weren't taking the pills better off. There were simply fewer worms around to infect people.

But another result emerged that took them by surprise, at least in its magnitude: Students started coming to class more. A lot more. The absence rate in program schools fell by about a quarter. Much to their—and the students'—satisfaction, ICS had hit on a tremendously powerful way to get kids into classrooms.

Dollar for dollar, it's no contest. The other attendance programs did work, but compared with deworming they cost an arm and a leg. Crunching the numbers, an additional year of school enrollment from Progresa comes out to about $1,000 a head. Generating an extra year of school attendance with the uniform-giveaway program costs roughly $100 per student. An additional year of attendance from deworming costs $3.50. Yes, you read that right.

Sure enough, the remarkable results of Miguel and Kremer's initial study made their way around the development world. Soon there was interest in school-based deworming far beyond the Kenyan bush. Miguel and Kremer were confident in the research they had done, but they weren't ready to recommend school-based deworming always and everywhere. They recognized that a single evaluation could only tell them so much.

At the end of the day, they had a sizable piece of hard evidence to support a simple theory: Where school absenteeism and worm infection rates are high, school-based deworming can be a powerful attendance driver. As with any scientific theory, the only way to add credence to theirs was to put it to the test again.

They didn't have to wait long. In 2001, just as the Kenyan study was wrapping up, Miguel, along with Gustavo Bobonis of the University of Toronto and Charu Puri-Sharma of India's Niramaya Health Foundation, designed an RCT to evaluate a deworming program for preschool students in Delhi, India. Here they were up against more than intestinal worms, which afflicted about one in three students. The other problem was anemia, another bane of children in developing countries that can be reliably treated for pennies (in this case, with iron supplements) but rarely is. A staggering 69 percent of preschool students in their study suffered from the disease.

The program ran much like the Kenyan one: Program officers sought permission from students' parents, then administered deworming, iron, and vitamin A pills three times per year at schools. Sure enough, absence rates fell by about 20 percent—about the same amount they had fallen in Kenya.

Replicating the initial Kenyan result greatly strengthened the case for scaling up school-based deworming around the world. With a sensible theory—that school-based deworming can work in settings where worm infections are common—and mounting evidence to support it, advocates were soon beating the drums and calling from the hilltops. Their arguments were further bolstered by research by Hoyt Bleakley at the University of Chicago on historical data from the American South, where the Rockefeller Foundation's efforts to eradicate hookworm in 1910 led to higher incomes in the long run. Evidence still rolling in from Kenya corroborates this story. Follow-up surveys with participants from Kremer and Miguel's original deworming study found that, a decade later, students who had been assigned to the early treatment groups (and had thus received two or three additional years of school-based deworming treatment) were working 13 percent more hours and earning 20 to 29 percent more income than their late-treatment counterparts. Those are big, long-lasting gains from a few twenty-cent pills.

Happily, all this good news has grabbed people's attention. School-based deworming has been one of the great recent success stories of evidence-based decision making in development, with upward of twenty million students in 26 countries dewormed in 2009 alone.

Anthony Again

When we left Anthony he was walking through the rain down the hill toward the *trotro* station, hurrying to make it there in time for the last van heading north out of Accra. He had no free uniform, no merit scholarship, and no conditional cash transfer bonus waiting for him; but he did have aspirations and a potential benefactor, and these were better than nothing. Some weeks later, after more discussion (this time, thankfully, by phone), Jake agreed to pay the fees for two applications. One went to the four-year liberal arts university, and the other to the two-year training college for teachers. Anthony was on tenterhooks waiting for his admissions letters.

In mid-June he called to say he had been accepted to the training college, and a few weeks later came the news that he "might have a chance" at the university. He sounded excited. When Jake asked what "might have a chance" meant, he explained that some applicants are accepted outright, others rejected, and still others offered "a chance" to matriculate—meaning they can bribe an admissions officer to get a spot. Apparently it would have been gauche for the officer to name a specific price, but Anthony figured a couple hundred dollars would do the trick.

Now the picture was becoming clear, and it looked lousy. Jake told Anthony he was willing to cover tuition, but not a bribe. But Anthony was adamant that it wasn't really a bribe per se. This was how things worked. Still, Jake was disgusted just thinking about it—a big, smiling man closing his meaty hand around a stack of bills in some sweaty back office while Anthony stood nervously, also smiling, his eyes darting so as not to fix on the money. Besides, where would it end? Anthony conceded that students who slip in through the back door are sometimes called upon for more palm greasing later.

So Anthony settled for his second choice, the teacher training college. The good news was that simply being enrolled there gave him the opportunity to begin working right away, as a part-time teacher at a private elementary school. He found a job in a village not far from the college and began working that summer. He caught up with Jake some months later when he called to ask for a loan to cover his rent. He had been keeping a single room in a boardinghouse near the school.

Jake was confused. "Anthony, why can't you pay it yourself? Haven't you been earning money from teaching?"

"Yes, Mister Jacob, yes. I have been earning money from teaching. But it is just that I have not been getting it."

"Not getting what?"

"The money."

"I don't understand. Have you been paid?"

"Yes. No. That is, the school proprietor, the one who is owing us money. He said he wanted to pay us, the teachers, but he is not having anything."

"Oh. How can he do that? How can he ask you to work if he doesn't have money to pay you?"

"Yes, that is our challenge. As for the payment, he said he cannot give us what he himself does not have."

"Well, when was the last time you received a paycheck?"

"I am still waiting on that one."

Anthony had been working four months and hadn't seen a dime. He and the other teachers had a plan, though, and their plan made sense. If the proprietor couldn't pay, they wouldn't work. It was that simple. The only loose end, it seemed, was the students.

Step Two: Getting Teachers into Classrooms

As was said earlier, though we cannot claim to know the whole recipe for education, we are sure of at least two ingredients: students and teachers. So far in this chapter we have visited a number of innovative programs that helped to fill up classrooms. But there is a question on the lips of all those kids—in Anthony's school, for instance—who look up from their desks at an empty blackboard. Where is the teacher?

If you listen closely, you might hear this question being asked in Hindi. India has about a quarter-billion school-age children, many of whom suffer from teacher absenteeism on a regular basis. A series of unscheduled visits to rural schools across the country found that a quarter of teachers were missing, and that fully half of those who were in their classrooms were not teaching! That probably helps to explain some dismal facts about the state of learning in the country: A nationwide 2005 survey found that 65 percent of public school students in grades 2 through 5 couldn't read a simple paragraph, and 50 percent couldn't do basic arithmetic.

Those are bad numbers and they reflect grim realities for those children who do make it to school on time. Why should the teacher be an adversary, and not an ally, in the fight for education? Of course, teachers aren't *supposed* to skip school, but the fault is not entirely theirs. Some of the blame belongs to the principals and administrators who either fail to check that their classrooms are staffed, or, worse, who tolerate teacher absenteeism. Which is not to say that their jobs are easy either: Even with the right rules in place, monitoring teacher attendance in small rural schools is tedious and time-consuming.

A Picture Is Worth a Thousand Rupees

Seva Mandir, an Indian NGO, knows a thing or two about these problems. It runs about 150 small schools in the remote, hilly country outside Udaipur, a beautiful and ancient city in Rajasthan, a state in western India. The schools are one-room affairs in tribal villages with a single teacher each. Seva Mandir's response to the problem of teacher absenteeism was to innovate.

Working with Esther Duflo and Rema Hanna, an economist at Harvard University, they hit on a potential solution in a combination of monitoring and incentives. Since checking attendance directly was too cumbersome, they devised a clever way for teachers to do it themselves, using disposable cameras that cost a couple dollars each. At the beginning and end of each school day, a student was chosen to photograph the teacher and the rest of the class together. The cameras marked each photograph with a tamperproof time and date stamp. This way Seva Mandir administrators at the head office could verify weeks' worth of teacher attendance all at once by reviewing a roll of film.

Having cameras serve as their eyes in the field solved the monitoring problem, but they still needed to give teachers a reason not to get caught playing hooky. The program needed teeth. So Seva Mandir decided to tie teacher salaries to their attendance records. Under the old regime teachers were paid a thousand rupees (about $23) per month, provided they showed up at least twenty days, and warned that they could be dismissed for skipping. In practice, though, firings were very rare, even when it was clear they were well-deserved. The new plan was to pay a flat five hundred rupees ($11.50) per month for teaching ten or fewer days, plus an additional fifty rupees ($1.15) for each day over ten. The cameras were exactly the tool they needed to enforce the new incentive structure.

They thought they were onto something, but they would not be content with a hunch. As an organization, Seva Mandir is as serious about evaluation as it is about innovation. Its management firmly believes that the best way to help the poor is by drawing resources toward programs that have been proven effective, and repairing or abandoning programs that haven't. Duflo and Hanna coordinated an RCT and randomly assigned half of more than a hundred Seva Mandir schools to switch to the new system. The rest were monitored as a control group.

It didn't take any subtle analysis to see what was happening. The combination of cameras and incentives caused teachers to show up more—a lot more. Absences were halved, from 42 percent in comparison schools to 21 percent in the ones using the new system. Although student attendance rates didn't change in response to the program, the increase in teaching days alone meant that students were getting almost a third more instruction than under the old regime. Further, a series of unannounced field visits to the schools confirmed that teachers were actually teaching during these additional days, and not just showing up.

Everything came together at test time, when students at the camera schools performed markedly better than their counterparts under the old system. Encouraged by the hard evidence from the evaluation, Seva Mandir made the program standard policy for all its schools. The gains in teacher attendance persisted, and children continue to reap the benefits today.

When You Need More Than Attendance

In Mumbai, the issue was not that teachers were missing school; it was that schools were missing teachers. There were just more students than could be effectively taught.

Pratham, an Indian NGO, took a commonsense approach to the problem. If we don't have enough teachers, they figured, let's get more. In partnership with the government schools, they developed a program that pulled the lowest-achieving students out of class for two hours each school day to work on basic competencies with an instructor hired and trained by Pratham. The instructors were called *balsakhis*—Hindi for "the child's friend."

Esther Duflo, with fellow MIT economist Abhijit Banerjee, Shawn Cole of the Harvard Business School, and Leigh Linden of Columbia University, set up a study to find out whether, and how, the *balsakhi* program affected students' learning. They tested by monitoring test scores over two years for about 350 schools, roughly half of which had been randomly assigned to receive the program. As expected, the struggling students in *balsakhi* schools who were pulled out for remedial instruction did better. Even the optimists were surprised by the size of the improvement, though receiving instruction from a *balsakhi* produced just as big an increase in test scores as half a year of regular schooling.

On the Right Track

Clearly, the students targeted by the *balsakhi* program benefited from the extra attention they received. But one might have expected to see impacts across the board—even for students who never needed remedial instruction—since pulling out the low achievers effectively cut class size in half for two hours per day. Proponents of small classes have long argued that fewer pupils per teacher leads to more learning through increased individual attention, and instruction tailored to meet the needs of each student.

When smaller classes are created by dividing students according to their ability, the technique is known as tracking. Advocates contend that tracking allows teachers to more effectively tailor their instruction to the level of the students. In contrast, when faced with a wide range of student ability, they are forced to "teach to the middle," leaving the struggling students overmatched and the stronger ones underserved. The opposing argument is that everyone benefits from sharing a classroom with the best and brightest, and so dividing classes by ability robs weaker students of a valuable resource.

The jury is still out on the value of tracking in general, but we can say one thing about it: In many contexts, it's a viable alternative. For a school already hiring additional teachers to reduce class size, tracking—by grouping students according to their grades on a prior year-end test, for instance—is cheap and easy. It can also be very powerful.

The *balsakhi* program in Mumbai was essentially a part-time tracking scheme. For two hours each school day, classes were effectively tracked when the weaker students were pulled out for remedial instruction. But students who didn't meet with the *balsakhis* appeared not to benefit much. In fact, the researchers couldn't rule out the possibility that the program had no effect on them at all. As we saw, there were some significant positive impacts from the program in general, but the evaluation can't say whether tracking in particular was an important part of the explanation, since it looked at the whole package: two hours' daily instruction from a specially trained *balsakhi* for some students, plus smaller classes and part-time tracking for all. To say more, we need an RCT that isolates the impact of tracking by itself.

Unsurprisingly, Esther Duflo, Pascaline Dupas, and Michael Kremer were hot on the trail, this time in Kenya. They partnered again with ICS Africa, now familiar from the uniform giveaway and deworming programs, and designed another RCT. ICS was rolling out a program that identified primary schools with just one first-grade teacher and gave them grants to hire an additional one, effectively dividing each first grade class into two sections.

It was a golden opportunity to test tracking directly. In half the schools, students were assigned to sections based on their grades in the previous term. In the remaining schools, students were randomly assigned to sections. So the only difference between schools was the method of assignment into sections—by rank versus by chance—which gave the researchers just what they wanted.

The program was a success. In tracking schools, students' test scores in *both* sections improved more, on average, than those of their counterparts in nontracking schools. So, unlike in the *balsakhi* program, benefits seemed to accrue to all students—not just lower achievers. Another powerful piece of evidence came from students near the middle of the ability spectrum: They improved similarly, whether they were assigned to the higher or lower section. The top students in the lower sections and the bottom students in the higher sections fared equally well. That was a big win for tracking, as it suggested no students were losing out.

Which is not to say that opponents' arguments don't hold water; in fact, the study found evidence that smart kids *do* positively affect their classmates' learning. Presumably, students in the low sections of the tracking schools were missing out, but it appeared that their losses were overshadowed by the gains from teachers tailoring instruction to the level of students. The test scores supported this story: low-section students improved more in basic competencies, while high-section students improved more on advanced topics.

This approach is now one of IPA's scale-up efforts, with

a recent launch of a large pilot in Ghana under the leadership of research director Annie Duflo. If it proves successful in this context, the groundwork has been laid for a nationwide scale-up and for replication in other countries, with the generous support and enthusiasm of the Children's Investment Fund Foundation in the United Kingdom.

Another Surprise Knockout

Most education programs—and all the ones we've seen thus far—focus on getting teachers and students into schools. It does stand to reason. As I said at the beginning of the chapter, those are two ingredients virtually everyone can agree on.

Mark Twain was always an oddball, and, were he alive today, he might not be part of the consensus. He famously admonished, "Never let your schooling interfere with your education." Maybe he knew something others didn't about the elusive key to learning, or maybe he was just talking about the importance of life experience. But he probably wouldn't have guessed how apposite his comment would be to some corners of the world a century after his utterance. If he could see the decrepit schoolhouses of Uttar Pradesh, India, I bet he would have some even stronger things to say.

The school system in Uttar Pradesh was broken. There were spectacular failures of education across all subjects and grade levels. A 2005 survey of children aged seven to fourteen produced some dismal figures: One in seven kids couldn't recognize a written letter, one in three couldn't read numbers, and two-thirds were unable to read a short story written for first-graders. The survey also found that students' deficiencies went largely unnoticed by their parents. In the most severe cases, where children couldn't recognize written letters, only a third of parents knew the extent of the problem. Most thought their children could read just fine.

This was in spite of a government program that sought to get local communities involved in making schools better. The vehicle for participation at the local level was the Village Education Committee, made up of three parents, the head teacher of the village, and the head of the village government. As the primary bridge between the villagers and the district-level education administration, the committees served many functions, from monitoring and reporting on classroom activities to hiring and firing teachers and allocating federal funds to schools. There seemed to be opportunities for regular people to make a difference in education, either by working through committee members or simply by joining.

Maybe those opportunities were mirages, or maybe people were just apathetic. Maybe both. Whatever the case, it is no surprise that parents were also neglecting the Village Education Committees, given the extent to which they were misinformed about their own kids' schooling. Ignorance about the committees was almost universal, with fewer than one in twenty parents aware of the their existence.

Incredibly, this ignorance extended to the committee members themselves! When asked which organizations they belonged to, barely a third of members mentioned the Village Education Committee; when specifically prompted about it, one in four still had nothing to say. What little awareness members had about the committees was mostly superficial. Almost nobody understood the roles and responsibilities of the committee. Only one in five members knew that they were entitled to government money at all, and just one in twenty-five knew they could request funds to hire additional teachers. The upshot was that Village Education

Committees were utterly ineffectual, and students were deprived of a valuable advocate.

Pratham, India's largest educational NGO, wasn't content to let the children of Uttar Pradesh suffer. They believed that if the villagers (including committee members) learned about the powers and duties of the committees, maybe they would respond. So Pratham partnered with researchers Abhijit Banerjee, Esther Duflo, and Rachel Glennerster, and with Stuti Khemani of the World Bank, to test three programs designed to kick village education into gear.

In the first and most basic program, Pratham organized a series of neighborhood-level meetings that culminated in a village-wide meeting to discuss the state of education, the role of the Village Education Committee, and the educational resources available from the federal government.

The second program had all the elements of the first, plus training on a testing tool that let villagers assess the level of students' learning. The assessments were conducted in each neighborhood and compiled in "report cards," which were discussed at the village-wide meeting. Villagers were also trained on a monitoring tool that allowed them to track progress in students' achievement over time.

The third program had all the elements of the second, plus training in Pratham's "Read India" program, a group-based reading skills curriculum. Once trained, villagers were encouraged to set up reading camps for local students and run them as volunteers.

Pratham chose 280 villages in Uttar Pradesh and randomly assigned a quarter to receive each program. The remaining quarter were monitored as a control group. After the programs had been running for a year, they surveyed to see what had changed.

Their first finding was encouraging: Across all three programs, the village meetings had been well-attended, with over a hundred villagers participating on average. On closer inspection, though, it looked like the meetings might have been a waste of time. There was a marginal increase in awareness of the Village Education Committees, but it was tiny relative to meeting attendance figures—so small, in fact, that it actually implied that many of the villagers who showed up never even learned of the committees' existence.

Whatever the impact on awareness, the functioning of the committees and the schooling situation—the real objects of the initiatives—were unchanged. There was no increase in the hiring of teachers, no change in parents' engagement with schools (e.g., visiting, volunteering, donating), no evidence of children switching schools, and no change in student or teacher attendance. It is hard to conclude anything except that the meetings had failed.

Fortunately there were some bright spots in all the darkness, and perhaps a key to the secret ingredient in the recipe for education. While the committees remained utterly useless, reading camps thrived. Of the sixty-five villages that had been offered training in Pratham's Read India program, fifty-five had started camps, serving an average of 135 children per village. The camps were tremendously successful, especially for the people who needed it most. Children who, at the outset, couldn't identify written letters, got a huge boost from the reading camps—they all learned to do so. By comparison, less than half of comparable children from non-reading-camp villages made the jump.

The wild success of the reading camps gives us reason to be hopeful. Even where schools are practically useless, and where parents are at best unable to coordinate their noble efforts at improvement (and at worst utterly apathetic), there are still ways to help. We just have to think outside the box—or, in this case, outside the schoolhouse.

Finding the Secret Ingredient

Students and teachers are easy to agree on; the pixie dust that makes the whole thing work is not. Some of the most promising results come straight out of left field.

We have to cast a wide net for solutions in education. The incredible impact of deworming on students' attendance and the power of reading camps to boost reading levels is proof positive that routes to learning don't all start and end in the classroom.

We in developed countries feast on quality education all the time, but in some sense we don't know what we're eating. One reason why it's so hard to identify the secret ingredient(s) is that school systems in rich countries typically have a great many things that their poorer counterparts lack, from well-appointed classrooms to healthier students to functioning PTAs. That means teasing out the effect of any one input alone just by looking at a well-functioning system is often impossible. (Indeed, the same difficulty also applies to research about improving farming, banking, health care, and other areas of life that touch us all, rich and poor alike.)

What we *can* do is go to the field and test. Little additions and changes, one or two at a time, to find out what makes education tick. We have touched here on some innovative ideas—but this is only the beginning. For starters, millions of schools around the world are still in dire need of the two most basic components: students and teachers. How many stories like Anthony's are out there?

Of course, questions also remain about textbooks, school lunches, classrooms, desks, and countless other inputs. The more we learn through rigorous testing and evaluation, the more of these we start to get right, and the closer we come to a recipe for education that nourishes everybody.

TO STAY HEALTHY

From Broken Legs to Parasites

For just over a year, Jake lived in a tidy compound house on Ring Road in Accra, Ghana. On a friend's recommendation he hired a housekeeper to clean and do laundry twice a week. Her name was Elizabeth, and in January 2008, she hurt her leg.

Jake found out about the incident a few weeks after it happened, when he called Elizabeth to ask why she hadn't been coming by the house to clean. He said, "Elizabeth, I haven't been seeing you recently."

"Oh, Brother Jake. I'm sorry I haven't been coming. I broke my leg."

"Elizabeth! What happened?"

"I was at market and I fell inside a ditch."

"Oh! I'm so sorry. Have you seen a doctor?"

"Yes, I went to hospital."

"And the doctor told you your leg is broken?"

"Yes. He said I have twisted it. Near the foot."

"Oh, so it is twisted. But is the bone itself broken?"

"Yes. The bone is not broken."

They had reached the limit of their ability to communicate over the phone. It was clear they would need the benefit of hand gestures to get the point across. Elizabeth said she was well enough to come the following Monday to clean. Then she would tell him the whole story.

When he came home from work the following Monday he found her sitting on the front porch. Her left leg was extended awkwardly in front of her, swollen below the knee and wrapped tightly in a ratty Ace bandage from the shin down to the foot. She wore her usual wide smile and greeted him kindly.

As they talked she described the accident. She had been at an outdoor market, crossing a ditch on a wide plank that had been laid as a bridge. The plank broke under her and she fell a few feet onto the gravelly dirt below. Her two-year-old son, Godswill, cinched tightly to her back by a fabric wrap in the typical Ghanaian fashion, was lucky not to be crushed. A few days later she went to the hospital, where the doctor suggested a few possible courses of treatment.

Elizabeth chose the most traditional. She went to see an herbalist. He put her on a regimen of daily applications of a topical cream and weekly checkups. The whole package cost sixty cedis (about sixty dollars) per month, half her salary. But for all that money, Elizabeth couldn't be sure exactly what she was getting. Herbal clinicians in Ghana rarely let their patients know the contents of the balms, salves, poultices, and tinctures they prescribe, because the ingredients can usually be found at the local market for pennies. Whatever it was, Elizabeth liked it—at least enough to keep taking it. When the first month was up, she signed on for a second.

Unfortunately her leg was not so convinced. After two months of treatment, there were still good days and bad days. Sometimes it felt completely normal and there was no pain or soreness; other times, when it was swollen, she had to walk on it very tenderly, or not at all. She would unwrap it and rewrap it tighter. The pain on these days came "from inside," she would say, pointing to the area above her ankle.

It was a dismal situation—two months gone by, pockets half empty, and leg still a mess—but, one must concede, not a completely surprising one. If her leg was actually broken, then the herbalist's ointment by itself couldn't be expected to do much good.

Whatever was happening under the skin, it was painful just to watch her. She did her level best to carry on, coming to clean on most of the appointed days, often limping while she swept, sitting at the laundry basin with her leg puffed up and jutting out to the side. Jake told her she had better go back to the hospital for an X-ray and a consultation.

Nobody said it would be easy. Elizabeth went to Korle Bu Teaching Hospital Monday morning, signed herself in, and waited. Around midday she was told by a nurse that the doctor wasn't coming in; she should come back Wednesday. So she was there again Wednesday morning, name on the sign-in sheet, sitting in the folding chair. She sat there through lunch. In the afternoon a woman came out from behind the reception counter and told Elizabeth she had seen her name on the sheet with "X-ray" written next to it, and had watched her sitting all morning. Didn't she know she was at the wrong hospital? X-rays were done at Ridge Hospital across town. By now it was too late to go to Ridge, though, so she should go tomorrow morning, first thing. She did. Thursday at Ridge the doctor should have been in—he hadn't called in sick—but nobody could find him. Surely, the receptionist said late that afternoon, he would come tomorrow. (As we will see, this is not a freak occurrence. As with teachers, simply getting doctors and nurses to show up is a big part of the problem with health care in developing countries.)

In fact he did come on Friday, and Elizabeth was there waiting for him. It must have been an exciting moment, as the anticipation had been building for about twenty hours in various waiting rooms over the course of the week.

The doctor took an X-ray of her lower leg and reviewed it with her. What had been a hairline fracture in January had, in the intervening two months, opened into a wider fissure, which helped to explain why the swelling and pain persisted. He was adamant that a plaster-of-Paris cast was now the only option. Anything less might earn Elizabeth an amputation somewhere down the line. This proved to be a convincing argument. She agreed to the cast then and there, though she would spend another sixteen hours over three days in the waiting room before it was put on.

Sorry, We're (Always) Closed

Jake felt let down when Elizabeth first told him she was seeing the herbalist. It seemed she was being duped, half her salary for a jar of ancient paste; it was superstition. At best, witchcraft. In any event, it was no cure for a broken bone. He was sure of that.

But hearing the story of her return(s) to the hospital, the dozens of hours waiting, the utterly indifferent employees, it was easier to sympathize. When she visited the herbalist for her weekly checkup, she walked right into his office, sat down, had her appointment, and left. Whatever can be said about his medieval treatments, he obviously knew how to attend to a patient.

Relative to its neighbors and to other developing countries, Ghana actually has a pretty good public health care system, with extensive coverage, even in rural areas, and fairly well-trained staff. But clearly customer service is not its strong point. When Jake told some Ghanaian colleagues about Elizabeth's weeklong odyssey to get an X-ray, they didn't bat an eyelash. One said, "When you go to hospital, then that is it. You will wait. And when it is only your leg paining you, you can wait even two or three weeks. When you want to see a doctor fast, for anything, then you should go see a herbalist."

Why could the herbalist provide such efficient and attentive service, when the hospital could not? We see this across all facets of life in developing countries. People settle for second-best because first-best is inconvenient. They borrow from moneylenders at high rates because microfinance banks have inflexible repayment schedules. They save their money in non-interest-bearing clubs because the clubs offer deposit collection at subscribers' businesses. They send their children to more expensive private schools because private school tuition can be paid in installments. And they treat their broken bones with herbal salves because they don't have to endure a week in the waiting room—and give up a week's earnings in the process—to do it.

Halfway around the world, in the mountains of rural Rajasthan, India, patients were facing the same problem. When they visited public clinics they, too, were met by interminable waits—if they got in at all. A 2003 survey of health care facilities in the area found that the clinics, which were supposed to be open six days each week for six hours a day, were closed a staggering 54 percent of their scheduled operating hours. The doctors and nurses just weren't showing up. Over time, people had learned to take their health problems elsewhere, to more expensive private facilities or traditional healers. Less than a quarter of doctor visits took place at public clinics.

Seva Mandir, the Indian NGO that had conducted the 2003 survey, saw in these findings a lamentable waste, both of the government's resources and the people's time. It also saw a potential solution. If you want staff to show up, they reasoned, you have to make it worth their while. Conversely, if you want to reduce the number of absences, you have to make missing work a costly proposition. In short, clinic workers' salaries had to be tied to their attendance records.

This was not the first time Seva Mandir had found a way to fight absenteeism with incentives. As we saw in the last chapter, their scheme involving disposable cameras and attendance-based pay proved incredibly effective in getting schoolteachers to come to work. They hoped clinic workers would be equally susceptible to the power of the rupee.

While it was surely encouraged by its earlier results—and rightfully so—Seva Mandir is not an organization that likes to stand on conjecture. It is committed to rigorously testing many of its programs.

It partnered with local government (which employed the clinic workers) to implement the incentives package, and it worked with Abhijit Banerjee, Esther Duflo, and Rachel Glennerster of J-PAL to design the specifics of the program and evaluate it with an RCT. The program was to be rolled out in about fifty clinics, so Seva Mandir identified one hundred clinics to study, and the researchers essentially flipped a coin for each. They assigned forty-nine to the incentives program and monitored the remaining fifty-one for control.

The incentive scheme itself was similar in design to its educational predecessor. Workers received full pay for the month if they worked at least half of the days. If they worked fewer than half, they had to pay a penalty for each day they had missed. Two consecutive months of poor (less-than-half) attendance would result in a summary dismissal.

To back up all the tough talk, Seva Mandir needed a reliable way to track attendance. Instead of using disposable cameras to monitor, as it had in the schools, it provided the forty-nine selected clinics with machines that punched paper cards with a tamper-proof time and date stamp. Each employee had her own card and was instructed to clock in three times each workday—once in the morning, once at midday, and once in the afternoon—to earn an attendance credit. At the end of a month, employees' salaries were calculated by tallying their attendance credits.

Workers reacted to the incentives quickly and with gusto. Attendance, observed in a series of unannounced visits to the clinics, spiked. During the first three months, employees at the forty-nine program clinics showed up about 60 percent of days, compared with 30 to 45 percent in the control clinics. It looked like Seva Mandir had succeeded again. But the response began to sag as the months wore on. By the time a year had gone by, the picnic was clearly over. Attendance in all one hundred centers had settled in a dismal plateau around 35 percent. The incentives, like the employees themselves, had stopped working.

The deterioration was more troubling than it was puzzling, but Seva Mandir was puzzled nonetheless. While it was clear from the unannounced visits that employees were missing a lot of work, it was equally clear that they weren't suffering the consequences. Paychecks—and the clinics' internal attendance figures, from which salaries were calculated—were as high as ever.

Seva Mandir went looking for answers, thumbing through the stacks of time cards. Sure enough, something stunk. Cards from some clinics had long stretches of days without time stamps, which, according to clinic supervisors, corresponded not to staff absences but to periods when the stamping machine was out of order. Consulting their records, Seva Mandir found that the machines had often sat broken for weeks before being discovered by visiting auditors. Some even appeared to have been deliberately damaged—a few "looked as if they had been hurled into a wall." Instead of calling Seva Mandir to request repairs, the clinic supervisors were treating these equipment failures like attendance holidays. They would manually sign the cards to verify that their workers were showing up, even if they weren't.

Further investigation revealed that the equipment-failure scam was just the tip of the iceberg. Supervisors had another ace up their sleeves—the power to excuse an absence. This prerogative had been built into the incentive system to answer concerns that it was too rigid. Why should an employee be penalized if, for instance, she was attending to work-related duties outside the clinic? So supervisors were allowed to grant "exempt days"—and you can guess how that turned out. Across the forty-nine program clinics, workers had an excused absence about one in every six days. It is unclear whether the supervisors were actively covering for their subordinates or just failing to investigate excuses the workers brought to them, but from the standpoint of attendance it didn't really matter. Like aggressive dentistry, the exempt-days loophole pulled the teeth of the incentive system right out. From there, the clinic workers' response left no doubt: They weren't afraid of a pair of gums.

Seen alongside the success of its incentives program with teachers, Seva Mandir's experience in the Rajasthani health clinics underscores one of the big themes in the story of development, which is also a central motivation for the IPA's research: context matters. Sometimes we talk about development initiatives as giving people tools to improve their lives, but it's not like handing out screwdriver sets. Think of it more as a transplant. Sometimes the graft and host are compatible, sometimes not. In this case the public health system was so weak that it could not support a seemingly effective tool to fix it.

Indeed, even for programs designed on seemingly universal principles like incentives, success and failure are situational. All the more reason to test them—repeatedly, and in a variety of contexts—in order to learn what types of hosts will accept what types of grafts. In medicine, we know something about the theory (e.g., that the blood type matters), which helps us understand when the host and graft will match and when they will not. In economics, we can take the same approach. And sometimes the answer is remarkably intuitive: Incentives only work if the monitoring tool for administering them is corruption-proof.

Paying Patients to See the Doctor

It's easy enough to see why the sick were not flocking to Rajasthan's rural public health clinics. When Seva Mandir started working there, a patient arriving during scheduled business hours was more likely to find the place closed than open. That had changed, albeit briefly, for the few months at the beginning of Seva Mandir's incentive scheme, but people did not seem to notice. Despite the period of increased staff attendance, the average number of visits per day to the clinics stayed the same throughout the project. Had the incentives survived and staff attendance persisted, maybe the public would have responded over time by visiting more often; unfortunately, we cannot know. But it's possible that the clinics would have been underutilized even if they managed to stay open during business hours.

In the view of the Mexican federal government, this was among the problems facing the country in 1997. There was a functioning nationwide network of health clinics ready to provide care and counseling in a variety of areas, but not enough people used them. Easily preventable and highly injurious conditions like low birth weight and child malnutrition were widespread. So the government folded doctor visits into its landmark conditional cash transfer program, Progresa. We heard about Progresa in the chapter about education, where it was used to encourage school attendance. In that part of the program, poor families were eligible for a cash payment if their children went to class. In the health component, poor families could earn money by making use of the public clinics.

It was a pretty good deal, all things considered. In exchange for accepting free preventative care, immunizations, pre- and post-natal care, and nutritional supplements, and for attending health, hygiene, and nutrition education programs, families could receive a cash payment of about a quarter of their monthly income. The program targeted low birth weight and child malnutrition specifically, so mothers and children received the most attention. But since all family members had to commit at least to annual preventative checkups, there were gains to be made across the board.

Of course, the whole thing would likely have ground to a halt if it encountered an obstacle like the one Seva Mandir found in the Rajasthani supervisors. Health clinic staff could have undermined the Progresa incentives by saying participants had attended education programs or appointments when they hadn't. For that matter, any number of other elements of the program, administrative or substantive, could just as easily have failed. Aware of all the potential weak links, the government set aside the first two years of Progresa's implementation as an evaluation period.

They were also concerned about politics getting the best of the program. In Mexico there is a long history of new administrations (even from the same political party) shutting down all prior social programs and creating new ones. This process is costly and wasteful, but it appears to be inevitable—unless the prior programs garner great critical acclaim. With Progresa, the administration sought to conduct a rigorous evaluation that would be above the political fray. This way, if the program worked, it would be hard for the next administration to get rid of it.

Evaluations are usually designed and staffed by people with experience in the country. The idea is that local expertise helps improve the quality of the evaluation. But that's not always how it works. In 1997, Paul Gertler, a professor of economics at Berkeley, received a call from a Mexican government official. Do you speak Spanish? No. Do you have any experience working in Mexico? No. Perfect! They wanted someone completely new to Mexico, so removed from Mexican politics that he did not even speak the language, much less know anyone. Then there could be no suspicion of partisanship or foul play by the evaluator.

It was an ironic selection process, but it proved to be tremendously effective. To this day Progresa—and Paul's study of it—remains one of the shining lights that guides both the politics and practice of evaluation. In many meetings I've attended in Latin America, the mere mention of "doing something like Progresa" piques practitioners' interest and pushes the conversation forward.

The full version of Progresa, which by the year 2000 reached 2.6 million Mexican citizens, was so ambitious in scale, and carried such a hefty price tag, that the government was dead set on demonstrating its impacts on recipients' health. If nothing else, being able to show conclusively that improvements were due to Progresa could help justify the expense. An RCT would be essential to establishing whether the program was a cost-effective tool. This was a dream assignment for a development researcher—a rigorous study on a massive scale (about eighty thousand people in 505 communities) that would provide hard evidence about the program's impacts.

It turned out to be a boon for Progresa's advocates too. When the results came in, one thing they could say without a doubt was that the public liked the program. In the 320 communities that were offered Progresa during the study, 97 percent of eligible families signed up. More impressive, 99 percent of those who enrolled ultimately got paid, which meant they had satisfied all the health care requirements. Unlike its counterpart in

Rajasthan, Mexico's health administration proved strong enough to enforce the incentives. There was no evidence of systematic fraud by doctors or patients—those check marks in the clinics' records actually stood for real patient visits.

As the program's designers had expected (and hoped), health outcomes followed close behind the increase in usage. Follow-up surveys conducted during the two-year pilot found big impacts on children: Enrolled children saw a 23 percent reduction in illness overall, an 18 percent drop in the incidence of anemia, and a 1 to 4 percent increase in height. The program might have been declared a success on the strength of these results alone, but happily there was more good news to report. Beyond requiring doctor visits to receive payment, Progresa actually had a second mechanism for improving health—the cash transfer itself. A separate study looked at the ways participating families spent their extra money and found that, on average, 70 percent went toward increasing the quantity and quality of food available to the household. That meant more, and more nutritious, food for everybody. No doubt this dynamic contributed to the program's success in improving children's health; it also rubbed off on other family members. The follow-up surveys found that enrolled adults across all age brackets saw a decrease in the number of days they had difficulty doing basic activities due to illness, and an increase in the distance they could walk without fatigue.

Everybody was benefiting; manna seemed to rain down from the sky. The biggest winners were the program participants, but they weren't the only ones to get a slice. The Mexican government came out just fine, too, and with them the researchers who had designed and run the evaluation and, in the process, established the gold standard for government-researcher collaboration to help learn what works.

It was not the first time a country had mounted a successful nationwide antipoverty campaign, but it was the first time one had used an RCT to rigorously demonstrate impacts on so large a scale. The world took notice. In the years that followed, Progresa-style programs have sprung up in a half dozen other countries, and now serve tens of millions of families worldwide. Many of them are being rigorously evaluated. For advocates of effective development practice everywhere, this is a landmark victory and a great example of research-driven policymaking. We *can* make progress in the fight against poverty if we use tools that are proven to work.

Make Your Own Incentives

Progresa's strategy of paying patients to see the doctor proved to be an effective tool to drive people's health choices—so effective, in fact, that the social benefits from the resulting improvements in health justified the government's expense. It was a big win for a big—and costly, and initially controversial—social program. But imagine: How much easier would it have been to pitch Progresa if people had been lining up to create their own monetary incentives for better health choices?

This is exactly the idea behind stickK.com, the commitment contract Web site I started and mentioned in the chapter on saving. StickK.com gives anybody with an Internet connection and a credit card a way to push himself toward a goal of his own choosing by raising the stakes (many actually do not put money on the line, but rather put their reputation on the line by naming friends and family who will be informed of their success or failure). When there's money (or reputation) on the line, slipups become an expensive proposition, and we work harder to avoid them.

Since its inception in 2007, thousands of people in the United

States and elsewhere have used stickK.com to achieve health goals like losing weight, exercising more, and quitting smoking. For many, these were long-standing ambitions. They had tried other approaches and come up short. StickK.com gave them the nudge they needed to succeed. Could a similar commitment approach help the poor get healthier?

You could raise the commonsense objection that, even if they wanted to, poor people simply don't have money to cut themselves checks for good behavior, or to penalize themselves for making bad choices—precisely because they're poor. But we've seen this kind of thing happen before. In chapter 7 we met Sunny, who tied her money up in a SEED commitment savings account so she could make improvements on her house. It turned out that Sunny was not alone. SEED ultimately helped hundreds of people resist the temptation to spend and instead save up for much-needed expenses.

Encouraged by the success of SEED, I went back to the Philippines in 2006, this time with Xavier Giné and Jonathan Zinman, to see if a similar product could work for health too. We worked again with Green Bank, our partner from the SEED study, to develop CARES (for "Committed Action to Reduce and End Smoking") and test it with an RCT.

CARES was a simple, no-nonsense commitment savings account. Clients started by making an initial deposit of fifty pesos (about a dollar) or more. Once a week for the next six months, each client received a visit from a Green Bank deposit collector and had a chance to add to his account. At the end of six months there was a one-time urine test for nicotine. If the client passed, he got all his money back (with no interest); if any nicotine was found, the entire balance went to a local orphanage.

From the perspective of traditional economics, CARES should have been even less attractive than SEED. The worst that would happen with a SEED account was that you'd have to wait to spend your money until you reached the balance or time goal you had set. With CARES, the best-case scenario was the same— you just cashed out the money you had put in—but you could actually *lose* your savings if you slipped up!

We usually cannot get the free market to increase the price of things that we'd rather avoid, like cigarettes or fatty foods. But, all other things being equal, it's much easier to resist our temptations when giving in to them is expensive. The simplest way to explain CARES, and stickK.com, is that they provide people a tool to change the relative prices of good and bad behavior—making their vices more expensive, or their virtues cheaper.

Our study left no doubt that at least some of the poor were ready to lay down such a gauntlet for themselves. Of 640 smokers approached on the street by Green Bank staff, 75 (about 12 percent) opened accounts when given the chance. That's a pretty impressive figure, I think: More than one in ten smokers not only wanted to quit, but wanted it bad enough to put money at risk on the spot.

People were willing to sign up, but would CARES really help them kick the habit? Maybe smokers who were serious enough about quitting to wager their hard-earned money in a CARES account would have been successful even without the aid of a commitment device. To find out, we had to compare. So in addition to the 640 CARES offers, we monitored about 600 more smokers (without offering them accounts) as a control group.

The upshot was that CARES worked. Six months after the marketing, those who were *offered* CARES—including those who turned it down!—were about 45 percent more likely to pass the nicotine test than the control group. Now, two things are worth noting. First, quitting wasn't easy for anybody. Only 8 percent of the control group smokers passed the six-month test; even more striking, just a third of those ambitious enough to put money on the line with a CARES account wound up recovering their savings. Second, one could argue that the six-month test was an unfair comparison anyway. Unlike those in the control group, people who opened CARES accounts had a lot riding on that nicotine test. Maybe they were just staying on their best behavior to recover their savings, and would relapse when the pressure was off.

So we waited another six months to see whether the results would stick. A full year after we had begun, we approached all the smokers again and asked them to take another nicotine test. This one was on-the-spot and equally unexpected for everyone. And all the CARES accounts were closed, so there was no incentive for anyone to stay smoke-free just to game the system. Here again, the clients who had been *offered* CARES—including those who turned it down—did markedly better. It looked like they truly had managed to quit.

Of course, CARES didn't work for everybody. The 88 percent of people who passed on the offer to open an account probably didn't benefit much from it, and even those who did sign up were hardly guaranteed success in quitting. But there are two important lessons here. First, CARES *was* a powerful motivator for those who opted in, and, compared with health incentive programs like Progresa, it's cheap to offer. All CARES really provided was a lockbox, a deposit collector, and a nicotine test. Those cost something, but they're much less dear than the essential ingredients—willpower and financial incentives to harness it—which participants brought to the table themselves.

And that is the second lesson: The developing world is ready for these kinds of solutions. There are, among the poor, countless people who stand on the cusp, who genuinely want to improve their lives and will go to great lengths to do it. All they need is a vehicle, a tool. No single tool is a universal cure-all. But if we can make one that's proven to work for some—and if we can get it to those people—then it is a step in the right direction.

Malaria

Four days out of five, Davis P. Charway came to work in a three-piece suit; and even when he didn't, his shirts were always impeccable. They were that kind of thick, soft, textured cotton you see on the front table at Nordstrom's, woven with a tiny herringbone design. As a rule, he wore a French cuff. His cuff links, like the exotic beetles at the Smithsonian, were shiny and came in every color. They always matched his necktie. Davis looked sharp sitting at his desk and he also looked sharp sitting behind the wheel of his car, a black Mercedes E-Class sedan. When it came up in conversation, he never failed to poke fun at himself. "It is only an E-Class," he would say. "When I am *really* a big man, then I will upgrade to the S."

By any reasonable standard, Davis already was a big man. From a typical childhood in the Ashanti region of central Ghana, he had made it to the Ivy League and beyond, ascending finally to a vice president's office high above lower Manhattan in the headquarters of a major credit card company. After a few years he made good on a growing desire to return home and became an executive manager of a Ghanaian microfinance bank based in Accra, the capital city.

That was the capacity in which Jake knew him. IPA had partnered with his organization to study its microloans, and Jake was a research assistant on the project. Once, after only a few weeks in the country, he went to Davis's office for a meeting and found the place locked up. His secretary said he was out sick. Jake asked whether everything was all right, and she said, "Oh, don't worry about Davis. He's just having some small malaria. I'm sure he will be back by Friday, or else next week."

At the time, Jake's knowledge of malaria was limited to what he had read in travel advisories and in news items that invariably characterized the disease as a great scourge of the developing world—none of which had led him to believe that it was something for bank executives to worry about. It conjured up images of dense tropical jungles, rural villages, thatch-roofed huts with unscreened windows, and squalid slums full of standing water. It was hard to see how a malarial mosquito could even have bitten Davis. In his office, his car, and his house, he always kept the windows shut so he could run the air-conditioning.

Over the following twenty months, as he watched dozens of bank employees lose weeks of work to similar flare-ups, Jake got to know better. Malaria respects neither rank nor social standing. It afflicts businessmen, farmers, and beggars alike. (And my eight-year-old daughter, Gabriela, got it this past summer in Ghana. Her case illustrates the mixed blessing of expensive drugs: Even for more than a dollar a day, the prophylactics do not always prevent getting malaria—but they do soften the symptoms significantly. She was quite a trouper.)

The standard depictions that informed Jake's initial impression were incomplete, but they were not inaccurate. The poor and defenseless *do* suffer the most, and the most acutely, when malaria strikes. In the summer of 2009 he visited Port Victoria, Kenya, on the shores of the great lake from which it takes its name. Approaching the town, he came over a rise and saw the place spread out below, a cluster of buildings beside the glittering lake, and big rectangular fields of sorghum and finger millet marching off into the distance.

For residents, living where they do is both a blessing and a curse. Being so close to the lake, fish like tilapia and Nile perch are plentiful, but large areas of the low-lying town flood frequently and for weeks at a time, creating a perfect environment for parasites and mosquitoes to breed. When this happens, the population writhes quietly in the grip of a bitter pestilence. People contract malaria and other parasitic diseases, and they fall sick in droves. Some make it through and some succumb; scores and scores die, leaving behind orphaned children and empty houses. Of the eight hundred students at Port Victoria's Lunyofu Primary School, three hundred had lost both parents. Both.

But Jake didn't know any of that when he first arrived. He had actually come to Lunyofu on behalf of IPA, hoping to learn about the school's experience with the tremendously successful deworming program we saw in chapter 9. The headmaster, Michael, was happy to oblige. He registered his satisfaction with the program in no uncertain terms, and even invited a group of students from the eighth grade class to talk about their impressions of deworming day. Most of the students had vivid stories to tell, but a few girls stood quietly at the back. Once the others had finished, Michael called them forward. The six of them formed a line by the side of his desk and cast their eyes down. They seemed embarrassed.

Michael looked them over, turned his attention to Jake, and began: "I want to make a compassionate plea." The girls, he went on to explain, came from small, remote islands in the lake, far from shore. Their parents had sent them to Port Victoria for schooling, but without relatives on the mainland, they had no place to stay. Michael had done what he could, which was to offer them the schoolhouse. It wasn't much, but it was their only option. At night, hours after the other students had returned home, the girls pushed the long wooden desks to the edge of their classroom and slept on the floor. They had little more than the roof over their heads. With their ill-fitting doors and without screens on their windows, the rudimentary buildings were hardly an obstacle for the mosquitoes.

Every morning the girls woke up to find new bites, and they were often stricken with malaria. Bed nets would have provided the protection they needed, but the school couldn't afford them. There was, after all, no budget for housing. Had they been expecting mothers, or under five years old, the girls could have acquired the nets for free at any government health clinic. (In Kenya those groups are eligible for fully subsidized bed nets.) Being neither, they would have to pay. And since they couldn't pay, they would continue to come into the headmaster's office when they were called; they would stand bashfully, averting their eyes; and they would wait for Michael's compassionate plea to fall on sympathetic ears.

Fighting Malaria: Selling Versus Giving

Biologically, malaria is the same everywhere—the same five protozoan parasites, carried from person to person by the female *Anopheles* mosquito. A mosquito becomes a carrier when she bites an infected person. Then she has to stay alive for two weeks (which is hardly a given; most *Anopheles* mosquitos' entire lives last about two weeks) while the parasite gestates in her abdomen. Only then can she pass it to other humans, which she does when she bites them to feed.

Which particular people she bites makes all the difference. For Davis P. Charway, malaria is an inconvenience; for the people of Port Victoria, it's a plague. While the particulars vary widely, all malaria stories are sewn together with the thread of needless suffering, which is reason enough to work toward eradication. So what's the best way to fight?

The first step is to keep the enemy at bay. During waking hours, a wave (or slap) of the hand is usually sufficient defense, but at night—which happens to be peak biting hours for the *Anopheles* mosquito—people need help. The most effective preventative measure developed thus far has been the bed net, a simple fabric screen, impregnated with insecticide, which hangs over a bed and tucks under the mattress.

Beyond protecting those who sleep under them, bed nets (much like the deworming pills we saw in chapter 9) also confer indirect benefits on the broader community by breaking the chain of transmission. As more people are directly protected, fewer opportunities exist for mosquitoes to become carriers, and consequently the risk of infection decreases for everybody. You could argue for providing free bed nets to the poor on a purely humanitarian basis; but these cascading social benefits make the case even stronger. A number of influential economists, most notably Jeffrey Sachs, have recommended just that. Their arguments have found traction in the aid community, which has distributed millions of free nets in the developing world over the past decade.

But others contend that it's not as simple as setting up a card table in an impoverished community and doling out nets to all the passersby. Getting nets into the hands (and bedrooms) of the poor is, after all, only the first step. To be effective, the nets must be used properly; and this is where some economists raise a concern. They argue that blind giving is wasteful, that it ignores the preferences of those we intend to help. Think, for instance, of the coupons slid indiscriminately under windshield wiper blades in the parking lot of the grocery store. How many of them end up littering the ground? For whatever reason, some people might have no interest in sleeping under an insecticide-soaked screen; surely any bed net that fell into the hands of such a person would only collect dust. In his book *The White Man's Burden,* William Easterly, NYU economist and former senior adviser at the World Bank, reports, "a study of a program to hand out free nets in Zambia to people, whether they wanted them or not . . . found that 70 percent of the recipients didn't use the nets."

This camp proposes to address the issue of waste with a market solution—by selling nets for a nominal price instead of giving them away. Requiring people to pay *something*, they argue, achieves two goals. First, it filters out those who don't want, or don't need, the product; second, it creates a sense of investment for those who do choose to purchase. Having sunk hard-earned cash into the nets, buyers should want to get their money's worth.

Ever buy tickets to a show, and then when the night comes you don't really want to go—but you still feel obligated? Behavioral economists call that the "sunk cost effect." It is the phenomenon that makes you feel like you should go to the event, just because you paid for it, or that you really should finish that lobster dinner you ordered, even if you're already full.

Now, an Econ would stop eating his lobster: He knows he's already bought the meal, and that he's going to pay for the whole thing, no matter how of it much he eats. So he'll just eat the amount that makes him happiest. We Humans don't always think that way. We force ourselves to get out of the house and go to the show. We finish our lobster dinners.

The idea of the market solution camp is to keep protection within reach for everyone—hence the big discounts—while using insights from behavioral economics to ensure that the nets go to people who will use them. Among practitioners, the market-based approach also has its adherents. Population Services International, a leading international health NGO that sells discounted nets in dozens of countries (but doesn't give them away), claims that its programs prevented nineteen million episodes of malaria worldwide in 2007 alone.

What can we make of these conflicting stories, each with its cadre of supporters and its battery of compelling statistics? Amid the assertions and invective, there are a few pieces of hard evidence to guide our thinking. One comes from Jessica Cohen of the Brookings Institute and Harvard School of Public Health and Pascaline Dupas of UCLA and IPA, who worked together on an RCT to learn how the method of distributing bed nets impacts the way they are used. They snatched the debate between free and cost-sharing out of the realm of abstraction and put it down on the dusty ground in western Kenya. In their study, pregnant women who had come to public health clinics for prenatal care were offered bed nets at randomly assigned prices. Some women were offered nets for free, and others for a nominal price between fifteen and sixty cents apiece.

What they found was simple supply and demand, the bread and butter of classical economics, at work: Fewer people bought nets when they were more expensive. While this discovery lacked the power of revelation, the intensity of the women's responses to price was remarkable. Cohen and Dupas calculated that increasing the price from zero to seventy-five cents (which was the going rate for a discounted net from Population Services International) would drive off three-quarters of customers!

Of course the drop-off in demand might have been acceptable, maybe even desirable, if the people being filtered out were less likely to use, or to need, the nets (that is, after all, the advocates' reason for charging something in the first place). But it was not so. When the nets were distributed, clinic workers measured each recipient's hemoglobin level, a strong indicator of malaria, and found that those who paid more were no more likely to be sick than those who paid less or nothing. So the invisible hand of the free market was not doling out protection to those who needed it most. Higher prices also failed to screen out people who wouldn't use the nets effectively. Surveyors visited the homes of recipients a few weeks after the nets

had been distributed to see whether they had been installed properly and to ask how they were being used. If, like those in the market
solution camp, they were expecting to find most of the free nets still
in their wrappers, they would have been disappointed. Roughly the
same portion of nets—just over half—were found hanging in all
the homes, regardless of the price that had been paid.

Since prices didn't change the kinds of people who got nets
or the way they were used, the difference between cost-sharing
and free distribution could be easily summarized: A lot fewer
people ended up protected, and the providers of the nets saved
some money. Unfortunately, they weren't saving much. Each net
cost about six dollars to produce, so when Population Services
International sold nets to Kenyans for seventy-five cents, according to their prevailing policy, they were already bearing the vast
majority of the cost. Covering the last seventy-five cents would
have increased their cost per net by about 13 percent, but then
they could have served four times as many people!

In fact, given the indirect social benefits of protection (i.e., breaking the chain of transmission), spending a little bit more to boost
demand for the nets probably made economic sense too. Cohen and
Dupas crunched the numbers from the providers' perspective and
determined that, on average, it was likely cheaper to save a life by
giving the nets away than by selling them.

The Most Important Drops in the Bucket

Malaria isn't the only global health scourge that has the attention of
the development community. Diarrheal diseases claim two million
lives (mostly children's) each year worldwide—a loss that is doubly tragic because it is so needless. There are cheap, highly effective
ways to treat and prevent diarrhea, but they are woefully underused.

Back in chapter 3, I mentioned Sendhil Mullainathan's discussion of oral rehydration salts as an example of the "Last-Mile Problem": We have a perfectly viable solution, but we've failed to get it into the hands of the people who need it most. Chlorine—dilute chlorine solution for drinking water, to be precise—is a very similar case.

When human and animal waste collects near a water source like a spring, a well, a borehole, or a stream, water drawn from that source is susceptible to contamination by *E. coli* and other diarrhea-causing bacteria. Even water drawn from a clean source can become contaminated if it is stored in a dirty container. But a few drops of chlorine will reliably eradicate diarrheal bacteria from ten to twenty liters of water, even in a dirty container. It's powerful stuff.

Most of the people of Busia, Kenya (the same village with the school uniform giveaway program we saw in the last chapter), know a thing or two about chlorine. If you asked, 70 percent of people would tell you that dirty drinking water can cause diarrhea. Better yet, closer to 90 percent would tell you that they had heard about WaterGuard, the brand of dilute chlorine solution sold at more than a dozen shops in town. This broad awareness of both the problem and a solution was largely due to the efforts of Population Services International, which introduced WaterGuard in 2003 and has advertised it widely ever since. Just as it does with bed nets, Population Services International sells WaterGuard at a nominal price rather than giving it away. A month's supply for a household in Busia is sold for about thirty cents, or roughly a quarter of a day's wage for a typical agricultural worker.

The only problem is that this cheap, well-known solution to a pervasive problem has failed to catch on.

People still fall ill frequently with diarrhea; some die. Michael Kremer, the Harvard economist whom we last saw searching for the best way to get Kenyan kids into school in chapter 9, decided to try to tackle the diarrhea problem as well. There were a lot of ways he could dream up to get people to use more chlorine— from simply giving it away, to community education programs, to cajoling individuals—but it wasn't obvious which would work best. So he tested them all.

Kremer, along with Sendhil Mullainathan, Edward Miguel, Clair Null of Emory University, and Alix Zwane from the Bill & Melinda Gates Foundation (and a former board member of IPA), designed a series of RCTs to find out how different inducements to use chlorine stacked up against one another.

First, they tried lowering the price by distributing free bottles of WaterGuard to some houses and half-off coupons to others. Cutting the price in half did increase the portion of houses that used chlorine from about 5 to 10 percent. But giving it away was an obvious choice from the public health perspective. Houses receiving free chlorine saw a huge jump in usage, to roughly 70 percent.

The researchers suspected that prices might not tell the whole story. They had ideas from behavioral economics too—ideas that had to do with social learning, attention, and trust. They tested the effectiveness of one-on-one and village-wide encouragement of chlorine use by NGO workers, the importance of social networks in getting people to adopt chlorine, and the impact of paying local promoters to pitch the product within villages. There were some things to say about the first two—village-wide marketing worked slightly better than one-to-one, and community leaders' chlorine usage appeared to influence other people's decisions somewhat— but they only led to small and short-term increases in overall usage. Having a local promoter drawn from the village itself, on the other hand, drove up usage both immediately and persistently.

In some sense, the most powerful local promotion device is the example of others in the community. Maybe the way to drive usage, the researchers thought, is to make chlorine use public and visible. So they also designed and tested a chlorine dispenser: a stand with a (free) bottle of WaterGuard locked inside and a special spigot that delivers exactly enough chlorine to disinfect a standard twenty-liter jerry can of water. Instead of adding chlorine at home, as one would with retail WaterGuard, the dispensers were located right at water sources. You add the chlorine when you fetch the water, and it does its work as you walk home with your jerry can balanced on your head. This setup also has the benefit of a natural attention mechanism: The chlorine is *right there* when you are preparing your water, begging you to put a dollop inside the jerry can. This is akin to selling fertilizer coupons at harvesttime, right when cash is in hand. Capturing people's attention at the critical moment is one of the many reasons that timing matters.

Dispensers were the best approach of all. They were at least as effective in driving usage as providing free WaterGuard directly to households, and they didn't require costly door-to-door distribution. Better yet, the dispensers appeared to engender real, lasting changes in behavior. People in dispenser communities appeared to be disinfecting more, and more consistently, as time went on. In communities where free WaterGuard was provided to households, chlorine usage peaked just weeks after distribution and slid down thereafter; in dispenser communities, usage continued to increase for months after installation, and remained high even a year and a half later.

Beatrice and Agnes

It looks like chlorine dispensers might be the answer to the Last-Mile Problem for chlorine—or at least part of the answer. But there are still big unanswered questions. First and foremost, who's going to pay? We saw that charging even a nominal price (fifteen cents per family per month) for retail WaterGuard drove away most people; but with a shared community dispenser, maybe the cost could be split among many families, or maybe people would be more willing to pay because of social pressure.

One morning in the field was enough to show that there's probably not a tidy answer. In the summer of 2009, Jake went with staff from the IPA office in Busia to talk with some of the "refillers," who had volunteered to maintain the chlorine dispensers by checking regularly that they had enough WaterGuard and reporting problems to IPA staff.

The first dispenser they visited was in a rural area. They drove out of town, turning after some time into what looked like a wall of maize but was actually a narrow path between two fields. Soon they came to a cluster of five small mud buildings, where they parked. Then they were led out of the compound, down a narrow dirt path, and onto a gently sloping hillside where young maize and sorghum grew shoulder-high on either side. They came upon a spring, next to which a chlorine dispenser had been set in the ground on a pole.

After a few minutes, a woman in a bright blue polyester blouse emblazoned with a wild silver design came down the path and introduced herself as Beatrice, the refiller. She explained that she had been nominated for the position because she lives close to the spring, is literate, and has a mobile phone. She said that, since the advent of the dispenser, the community had put together some collective initiatives of its own, namely chicken-raising groups. Everyone could agree the dispenser had done a lot of good, both health- and economics-wise, the latter because of the money saved on treating cases of diarrhea and typhoid.

When Jake asked where she saw the dispenser program going in the future, Beatrice said that IPA should continue to provide free WaterGuard for a long time so that they could enjoy their health. But, he asked, what if the subsidy stopped? Would the community pull together and pay full price to keep the dispenser stocked? She seemed doubtful. That would mean hitting up people for contributions, a job nobody was keen on doing. No, Beatrice sighed, an end to the subsidy would probably mean an end to the dispenser.

About a half hour later, and just a mile or two back on the main road toward town, Agnes strode through the metal gate of her compound, confident and self-possessed, and introduced herself. She was another refiller. Agnes smiled a lot, was not timid, and had funky teeth. She told Jake that she and her husband, the owner of the compound and landlord to a number of tenants, had constructed a well in the compound's courtyard some years ago. They offered the water for free to their tenants, and sold it to other households in the neighborhood. As it turned out, initially the water was no good. People fell sick—and complained—regularly. Agnes had tried disinfecting the well by sprinkling chlorine crystals into it, and she had tried advising her clients to boil the water, but neither tactic worked.

When IPA came along with the chlorine dispenser, she saw an immediate improvement. There was less sickness, both in and outside her immediate family. Her tenants and clients were happier, and they became more numerous. When Jake met her she was serving twenty-three neighborhood compounds besides her own.

Asked what she would do if they began charging for the WaterGuard, Agnes didn't hesitate. She knew the chlorine was a worthwhile expense, and she would be prepared to go on buying it. Never mind her tenants' and clients' satisfaction; the money she saved on treatment for her family members alone, she said, would justify paying full price.

No Size Fits All

Beatrice and Agnes, living just a couple miles apart, were in different worlds as far as the chlorine dispensers were concerned. Agnes would have been ready to press on without subsidy on the spot; Beatrice would have needed to do some serious organizing and political maneuvering. In the same vein, the problems posed by malaria are as different as Davis Charway and the girls of Lunyofu Primary School.

The solutions are likely to be just as varied.

Rigorous testing showed that pregnant Kenyans would likely be better served by free distribution of bed nets than by cost-sharing, but that doesn't mean we should abandon market-based solutions altogether. They have their place as sure as Agnes does; what we need to do is figure out *when* and *where* the different solutions work, so we can apply them just when conditions are right. We can't write global prescriptions about specific program designs until we do that figuring. And that's exactly why IPA continues to test different ways of running the chlorine dispenser program, both in and beyond Busia.

As far as general directives go, I agree with Sachs that nobody should be priced out of protection, and with Easterly that resources—and the will it takes to mobilize them—are both too valuable and too scarce to waste. What's essential is that we pursue effectiveness in our campaigns with the same vigor and tenacity as we pursue the ultimate goal of eradication. If we do any less we will fail on both accounts.

11

TO MATE

The Naked Truth

While I was studying for my Ph.D., Paul Gertler, a professor at UC Berkeley (who we saw in the last chapter working with the Mexican government to evaluate Progresa), visited MIT for a day to give a seminar. This is a common process at many universities, for an outside professor to come and give a ninety-minute talk based on one of his or her current research papers. It's a way for economists to keep current and get feedback on projects or papers before they are published. Aside from the talk, the visiting professor usually schedules appointments throughout the day to meet with faculty and, occasionally, graduate students.

I had never had such a meeting before, but Esther, my adviser, e-mailed me and said, "Get on Paul's schedule." I did. As I walked to our appointment I was a bit nervous, having no idea how these conversations really proceeded. Paul did, of course. He asked me what I was doing, and I told him I was about to leave for South Africa to set up an experiment to measure the impact of microcredit. (The experiment totally failed, and I learned an early and now-obvious lesson: The staff of the partner organization really should want to be evaluated, otherwise they will find any one of a hundred ways to ruin an RCT.)

He said—and I'm fairly certain this is an exact quote— "Great! While you are there, how about finding out the price of whores with and without condoms?"

I laughed but never did follow up on this. I didn't fully absorb that hookers' prices could be a topic for serious economic research.

I was wrong. Turns out Paul wasn't joking. He was talking about a new way of looking at an issue that affects almost every person on Earth—man and woman; black, white, and brown; rich and poor alike. It's sex.

Sex is a great equalizer—first because practically everybody does it, but more important because it strips us down to our naked selves. I'm not talking about clothes. Sex is a primal activity. It's in our biology. In some sense, we are most definitively Humans—and most definitively not Econs—when we're doing the deed. In that space of urge, impulse, and heavy breathing, a lot fades into the background. There are really not so many differences between rich and poor in between the sheets.

Which helps to explain why we all make mistakes about protection, no matter where we live or how well-off we are. In the heat of the moment, the probability of contracting a disease or having an unwanted pregnancy—the downside of unprotected sex—is not salient, if it is known at all; the upside, meanwhile, is beating down the door. The throes of passion simply are not the best setting to run through a cost-benefit analysis.

But someone who faces the decision regularly, and who doesn't do it for the passion, might learn to do better. After all, practice makes perfect, right? If anyone should know, it's the professionals. Prostitutes, that is.

So that's what Paul was really talking about when he asked me to talk to hookers in South Africa. Fortunately he marched ahead with his idea even though I missed my chance to participate. He got together with Manisha Shah, also of UC Berkeley, and Stefano Bertozzi of Mexico's National Institute of Public Health, and went to Mexico City. They leveraged the expertise of local pimps, police officers, taxi drivers, medical workers, and bar owners to find and interview about a thousand sex workers near Mexico City in 2001. They asked the women about the details of their last few "transactions." It turned out the women knew all about safe and unsafe sex—their sliding prices proved it.

Condom use was the standard, but it wasn't a hard-and-fast rule (no pun intended). According to the interviews, prostitutes protected themselves nine times out of ten. And the tenth time, when they agreed to go without, they charged extra—about 23 percent more, on average. Here was the evidence that they knew about the relevant hazards: They were demanding more money for taking additional risks.

Professional as they were, these women didn't have anything as simple or direct as a menu with options and prices. Agreements were born out of a bargaining process.

Most of the time, the prostitute suggested he use a condom and the john agreed. In the other cases, the john usually asked to have unprotected sex. Knowing that she had something he wanted, the prostitute now had a chance to extract something in return. It reflects the bargaining nature of the transaction that women identified as "very attractive" made the most from this opportunity, capturing a 47 percent premium for unprotected sex—more than double the average.

So the prostitutes knew about the risks they were taking. They also evidently knew about supply and demand. All other things equal, they would have accepted a lower price in return for protected sex; but when they discovered that the customer actually preferred that, too, they were more than happy to make him pay extra for it. In cases where the john was the one to suggest condom use, prostitutes managed to extract an 8 percent premium for agreeing. That's just plain savvy.

Bad Information, Bad Choices

So that's the view from the trenches, where these battles are fought night in and night out. But, of course, most sex on Earth is not had by sex workers; so to address issues of reproductive health more generally, we need to see what the amateurs are doing. Do they know the risks of unsafe sex? If so, how are they being compensated for those risks when they take them? And if not, could learning the relevant information lead them to behave differently?

On the whole, public knowledge about sexual health in developing countries is limited. It suffers both from a lack of information, and also from a frightening amount of *misinformation*. I'm not just talking about the fine points here. Dr. Manto Tshabalala-Msimang, South Africa's minister of health from 1999 to 2008, was famously off the mark on AIDS. During her tenure she warned against the use of antiretroviral drugs (she contended they were toxic) and instead advocated a strictly nutritional approach to prevention and treatment, earning the nickname "Dr. Beetroot."

She spoke with conviction, but her program was straight out of medieval times: "Shall I repeat garlic, shall I talk about beetroot, shall I talk about lemon? These delay the development of HIV to AIDS-defining conditions, and that's the truth."

Fortunately, in most developing countries, the highest cabinet position on health is not occupied by a Dr. Beetroot type; nonetheless, bubbling springs of misinformation abound. They are amorous potential partners, extension officers for rural clinics, parents, pastors, and teachers charged with delivering health curricula. Jake once attended a church service in Ghana where the preacher testified that the Devil himself, manifest now as AIDS, wishes to infect us all, but that we can protect ourselves—"slam the door in that Devil's face" was the direct quote—by singing praises to God. There was no mention of sex, safe sex, or even abstinence. Those unlucky enough to be downstream of such contaminated springs usually drink foul water, and so it comes to pass that millions are confused or ignorant about the issues.

Adolescents, especially young girls just beginning their sexual lives, have the least personal experience to draw on and the longest road ahead. If anyone could benefit from a shot of the straight dope, it's them.

Sugar Daddies

Girls in Busia, Kenya, grow up fast. They always have. By tradition, women become marriageable once they reach childbearing age—usually around fourteen—at which point many are snapped up by eager suitors, often in some version of an arranged marriage. In recent years, the tide has begun to turn. Girls are spending more time in school before entering domestic life, and some are continuing to university and starting careers. More marriages are voluntary, fewer arranged by parents. But the girls of Busia are still confronted early and often with decisions about sex.

They might look to their mothers for advice, but their mothers grew up in a simpler time. Vying for the girls' affections today are not just men from the village, but also hotshot businessmen from town and boys from school. The sheer variety of partners available would be surprising enough to the older generation; the notion that a girl could choose freely among them, a real shock.

Of course, the limited number of women means competition between suitors, and this plays out in Busia much as it does in America, or in Archie comics. Those who can afford it buy the girls presents or take them for rides in their sports cars. Those who can't find other ways to impress, like scoring the winning goal in a football match, or sending florid text messages.

In general the girls are not sharks; they're teenagers. But they can see which side their bread is buttered on. In private they refer to older, wealthier suitors as "sugar daddies." For an adolescent girl, choosing a sugar daddy as a partner is like buying reproductive insurance. Should she become pregnant, he is prepared—and expected—to marry her and support the child.

But there is a catch. Being older and wealthier (and, in many cases, more lecherous), sugar daddies have had more past sexual partners, and now they have more diseases—HIV in particular—to show for it. Among Kenyan men ages fifteen to fifty, the highest incidence of HIV is about 8.5 percent, in the thirty-five-to-forty-four group. By comparison, the girls' peers in the fifteen-to-nineteen cohort are practically harmless, with only 0.4 percent infected. So, whether she knows it or not, a girl who chooses a sugar daddy is making a trade-off.

A strictly dollars-and-cents view of the situation is that financial security in case of pregnancy, along with all the sports car joyrides and the courtship gifts, is effectively compensation for two things: First, the girl is being paid for her companionship, a scarce and sought-after commodity. Second, she is being compensated for the risks she has to bear as a companion, like the possibility of getting pregnant or of contracting a sexually transmitted infection. If girls already know about the different rates of HIV infection for older and younger men, then standard economic theory would assume they are extracting a fair price from sugar daddies for taking one additional risk of infection.

And if this really is the case, then simply providing girls with information about HIV incidence by age group shouldn't change anything about who they choose as partners or how they get compensated. It should be old news. But if they don't already know, telling them might make a difference.

To see whether it would, IPA researcher Pascaline Dupas, then as part of her Ph.D. dissertation, set up an experiment in 328 government schools near Busia in 2004. Seventy-one of the schools were randomly chosen to participate in the Relative Risk Information Campaign, in which a program officer met once, for forty minutes, with the eighth-grade class. At the beginning of the meeting, students completed an anonymous survey to determine how much they knew about the prevalence of HIV among Kenyans. Then the program officer screened a short film about partnerships between girls and adult men, which led to an open discussion on the issue of cross-generational sex. During the discussion, the program officer presented a detailed breakdown of HIV incidence in Kenya by age and gender.

At the same time and in the same 328 schools, the Kenyan government was reviewing its own HIV education program. During the previous year, half of the schools had been randomly selected to receive additional teacher training on the national HIV curriculum (which they were supposed to be teaching already). The curriculum included information on a range of topics from biology and transmission, to caring for infected persons, to the impacts of the HIV/AIDS epidemic.

Where Dupas's program presented information but stopped short of telling people what to do, the government's curriculum did not hesitate to give advice. It also featured a module on prevention, the spirit of which was captured in its message to students: "Say NO to sex before marriage," and, even more succinctly, "Avoid sex."

By piloting in half the schools, the government hoped to

determine whether training teachers would ultimately help students. It was a perfect opportunity for a horse race, pitting Dupas's information campaign against teacher training on the standard HIV curriculum. Comparing results of follow-ups across all 328 schools, they could see which program had bigger impacts on students' choices about sex.

Deciding how to track those choices was a thorny issue in itself. The real item of interest was HIV status, easily determined by a blood test—but screening each student was not feasible. A first alternative was to ask students about their sex lives directly. About eight months after the programs had run, field teams administered a short survey on sexual activity, condom use, and demographics of sexual partners. There were legitimate doubts about the value of girls' responses to the survey. They knew they weren't *supposed* to be having sex—let alone unprotected sex. Why should they be expected to tell the truth on a questionnaire?

Another strategy was to monitor pregnancies as an indicator. Granted, it is an imperfect measure—only a fraction of unprotected sexual encounters lead to pregnancies—but the number of pregnancies is at least a lower bound for the amount of unsafe sex girls were having. Student pregnancies were also easier to observe because they were talked about by classmates, and, unlike surveys, were not susceptible to reporting biases. A big lump is difficult to hide.

The results on pregnancies were clear: The Relative Risk Information Campaign worked. Dupas's program cut the incidence of childbearing by about a third. This suggested a significant decrease in the overall amount of unprotected sex, which was encouraging. Most of the reduction in childbearing, it turned out, was due to a 60 percent decrease in out-of-wedlock pregnancies. On the whole, that meant girls in the Relative Risk group who did get pregnant were much more likely to get married too.

Meanwhile, training teachers on the national HIV curriculum had no significant impact on overall rates of childbearing or on the likelihood of marriage for pregnant girls. Which is not to say it didn't accomplish anything—quite to the contrary. There were big academic impacts. Teachers taught more about HIV, and students learned more, as measured by their scores on HIV knowledge tests. But the impacts on real-life choices about sex, captured in the follow-up survey, were harder to tease out. Girls in the teacher training schools reported having about 25 percent less sex overall, and about a third less unprotected sex too—but this is hard to square with the persistence of pregnancy rates. The girls in these schools might just have been underreporting the extent of their sexual activity to the surveyors.

For students in Dupas's Relative Risk program, it was just the opposite. In the follow-up survey, *more* girls reported being sexually active. That's right: *more* sex with *fewer* pregnancies, and presumably fewer infections too.

The girls achieved this satisfying result by changing their partners and their habits. They began to choose younger men over sugar daddies, a solution that allowed them to lower their risk of HIV infection without giving up sex altogether. But how does the increase in the girls' sexual activity jibe with the significant drop in childbearing we saw above? The key is protection. Most of the students who had more sex were using condoms. This is perhaps the most encouraging result of all, because the Relative Risk program didn't have anything to say about condom use. Students were making the right choices on their own.

Just as Dupas had suspected, girls, armed with the relevant information, made better decisions. Either they extracted more compensation from sugar daddies in return for the higher risk of contracting HIV (as evidenced by the drop in out-of-wedlock pregnancies), or they found ways to lower the risk of infection—by choosing younger partners or practicing safe sex.

Paying for Testing

The Relative Risk program succeeded not just because it gave the girls of Busia valuable and relevant information about their prospective sexual partners, but because the girls took that information and put it to use. That's an important distinction. The fact is that you can lead a horse to water, but you can't make it drink.

Some portion of the bad decisions about sex can rightly be attributed to misinformation—thanks to scourges like Dr. Beetroot and the Ghanaian preacher Jake encountered—and in these cases, information-based approaches like the Relative Risk program can be the answer. But a big part of the problem is that we're just stubborn horses. Most people around the world (and virtually everyone in developed countries) actually know enough about HIV and other sexually transmitted infections to protect themselves and their partners—if they want to. In that sense, information is not the issue. The issue is that, even though we know we *should* use protection, we don't.

From a public health perspective, that's just not good enough. People who know better but continue to make bad decisions don't just endanger themselves; they pose a risk to the wider community. In that sense, HIV and other sexually transmitted infections are like the worm and malaria infections we talked about in chapters 9 and 10. Because individual protection redounds to the good of all, there are strong arguments for governments to step in and actively promote it.

Now, the most effective thing would be to have public health officials on the scene at the moment of truth, tearing open the foil wrapper and handing you a condom. Thankfully, that's out of the question. Until we invite them into our bedrooms, they will accede to the demands of propriety, keep a respectful distance, and try to influence our decisions indirectly.

How? The sex ed class you took in high school was one way. Giving away condoms at the health clinics of many U.S. colleges is another. A third is advertising. A few of our favorites: (a) A billboard in Accra, Ghana, where naked cartoon silhouettes, coupling in an impressive variety of positions, cavort across the width to spell out "WEAR A CONDOM." (b) Another billboard in Accra, Ghana, where there is a picture of a smiling couple and a slogan in big print below: "Just because you can't feel it, doesn't mean it is not there." (What is "it"?!? I still wonder whether the advertisers intended this to be a triple entendre, double entendre, or no entendre at all.) (c) A billboard in El Salvador that translates to "Be faithful to your wife, or wear a condom." (d) A video that shows a scene in a grocery store with a father and his child, who is throwing the worst temper tantrum you've ever seen, tearing cans off of the shelves and screaming at the top of his lungs. And then a simple tagline: "Use Condoms." And a fourth way to influence decisions is to pay people in exchange for learning their HIV status.

Many HIV researchers and policymakers, both in and outside government, believe that people who learn their status will act accordingly. That is, those who are infected will protect others, and those who aren't will protect themselves. This belief is the rationale for programs that emphasize testing. If it is true, then convincing people to learn their status is a viable, if indirect, route to the bedroom, a way to influence the important decisions that would be made in private. But that's a big "if."

Rebecca Thornton, an economist at the University of Michigan and IPA researcher, wanted to know for sure whether learning HIV status really did cause people to behave differently. So in 2004 she went to Malawi to find out. Thornton designed an RCT that offered participants free HIV tests and an opportunity to buy condoms. If participants who learned their status decided to buy more than those who hadn't, there would be some hard evidence in favor of the connection between testing and decisions about sex.

The question is: How do you randomly select, for the sake of an evaluation, which individuals learn their status? Barring some people from testing altogether, or forcing tests on others, was unrealistic and, more important, unethical. But Thornton saw an opportunity in people's general tendency to drag their feet about getting HIV test results. To be fair, there are good reasons for avoidance, not the least of which is fear, plain and simple. Jake remembers literally shaking in his seat at the Columbia University Health Services office while he waited to hear the result of an HIV test, even though he was quite certain it would be negative. (It was.) People in the Malawian context, where 12 percent of adults are HIV-positive (compared with 0.6 percent in the United States), had much more reason to fear bad news; but they could also have been inclined to stay in the dark for reasons far more concrete than existential trembling. The prospect of losing a day's work, or a five-mile round-trip walk to the clinic, might have been enough.

Being an economist, Thornton had incentives on the brain. (It's true—economists think about them a lot.) Figuring that more people would take action if it was worth their while, she built a reward into the HIV testing program, giving people money in exchange for learning their test results. And in order to see just how much encouragement was needed, she randomly varied the reward amounts, from nothing to three dollars. In a country where

the average daily wage in 2004 was about a dollar, these were substantial sums, presumably big enough to impact people's choices.
That's precisely why randomly assigning the rewards was so clever:
The reward amount acted as a proxy for the likelihood that an
individual would learn his or her status. Voilà—randomization
without forcing anybody into or out of testing.

In the end, the program worked as follows: Health workers
went door-to-door in 120 villages, offering participants free HIV
tests. Each person who agreed to be tested gave a saliva sample on
the spot and received a randomly chosen voucher redeemable at a
mobile health clinic. If an individual went to the mobile clinic to
learn his test results, he received the voucher amount in cash, and
researchers recorded that he had learned his HIV status. About
two months after results became available, participants were visited at home by surveyors who had no part in the testing portion
of the program. They administered a short questionnaire about
recent sexual behavior, gave the respondent about thirty cents
in appreciation for his time, and then offered condoms for sale
at a highly subsidized price. A package of three cost five cents; a
single was two cents.

The study's findings shed light on two questions. First, are
incentives a good way to get people to learn their HIV status in
the first place? Second, and more important, does learning one's
status really lead to better choices about sex?

There could be no doubt about the first: The incentives
worked. Participants who received vouchers for any positive
amount were more than twice as likely to get their results as
those who got vouchers for nothing. Interestingly, the size of the
reward—as long as it was greater than zero—seemed to matter
less. For the nonzero vouchers, each *additional* dollar did increase
the likelihood of learning results, but only marginally so. In fact,

a voucher worth ten cents produced more than three-quarters the effect of one worth ten times as much. This is an important finding in its own right, as it gives us valuable information for designing policies and programs. If each additional dollar generates an increasingly weak responses, then there is a limit to the amount we can boost participation simply by throwing more money in the pot.

Incentives worked well enough in Malawi that 69 percent of people who were tested went to learn their results. But the critical question was whether those 69 percent would act differently once they knew—and here the results were mixed. On one hand, learning status had a substantial impact on HIV-positives who were sexually active. (It is worth nothing that these were only about 4 percent of all the participants.) Those who got their results were more than twice as likely to buy condoms as those who didn't, which was a step in the right direction.

But, on average, those individuals bought only two more condoms than their counterparts who hadn't learned their results. That's not a whole lot of extra protection. For HIV-negatives—who made up about 94 percent of the participants—the results were dishearteningly bland. Those who learned their test results were no more likely to buy condoms than those who didn't. The follow-up questionnaire about sexual behavior, administered when the condoms were offered, was also a wash. It found no difference in behavior among sexually active participants, whether they had learned their test results or not.

Thornton had to conclude that the program didn't stack up. Door-to-door testing is expensive, and despite the boost from incentives, it appeared to generate only a small change in behavior—and only for HIV-positives, who made up just 4 percent of the participants. Resources could be better spent on other programs proven to have bigger impacts.

Beyond a verdict on this cash-for-test-results program, there are some general lessons to take away from Thornton's study.

First, it strengthens the case for incentives, which proved again to be a powerful motivator. Second, it's a prime example of the value of finding out what *doesn't* work. As I said way back in the introduction, new ideas are essential. Rather than being discouraged that this particular approach wasn't a home run, we should be gladdened that we can now rule out some ideas. Thanks to Thornton's creativity and insistence on testing, we know more now than we did before, and future efforts will be better for it. Maybe the next HIV program will continue to use incentives to encourage the retrieval of test results, but will find a better way to sell condoms.

Third, and most important, this project highlights the importance of understanding exactly *how* programs work, of tracing the links between the behaviors we can see and influence and the outcomes we care about. Sometimes those links are tenuous; frighteningly often they are altogether unexplored. The most obvious and ubiquitous figures that charities and development programs advertise—dollars spent, people enrolled—are only signposts. If we don't understand how those things lead to the welfare of recipients, we are losing sight of what matters—helping people make real improvements in their lives. In the big picture of poverty, that just won't cut it.

12
TO GIVE

The Takeaway

I hope that, by this point in the book, you've been inspired by some of the ideas we've seen that work to fight poverty. If you're like me, you might also be struck by the daunting challenge of figuring out what to do.

Odds are you don't work for an aid organization, and you most likely won't be called upon to design or deliver a development program. For most people, the "what to do" is about giving. As I touched on briefly in the introduction, we have more ways to give now than ever before—not just by putting checks in the mail, but also on the checkout line at Whole Foods Market, by text from our mobile phones, and online through Web sites like Kiva.org. As the avenues for giving have multiplied, individual donations have spread to fill them. In the United States today, individual donations exceed those of corporations, foundations, and bequests by three to one.

So individuals have a lot of clout, and we can use it if we act together. What we have to realize is that every donation really is two things: First, it is a contribution to a particular organization, which helps them to run their programs; second, it is a vote. Giving to one organization means choosing it over another (actually, over thousands of others), and it sends a message. That message gets amplified whenever we discuss our favorite causes with friends, families, and co-workers; or when we talk about them on Facebook, Twitter, or MySpace.

The development world is listening. Indeed, given that individual donations account for the majority of funds available to charities (not to mention the fact that Americans' private giving to other countries exceeds the U.S. government foreign aid budget), it really doesn't have any other choice. And that means that we have a unique opportunity to make our voices heard.

The question is: How should we choose what to say, whom to support? This book has been mostly about ideas that hold promise for the poor. But ideas don't just happen; someone—usually some organization—has to go out and *make* them happen. That means that when we consider contributing, we really need to know two things: First, is there good reason to think this idea will work to solve this problem in this setting? Second, will this particular organization implement this idea effectively and efficiently?

This book has had a lot to say about the first point, but has not talked about the monitoring of organizations to determine which are efficiently run and which are not. I will leave you here with some thoughts and recommendations, and will continue the conversation through the Proven Impact Initiative Web site (about which more below), as well as through partnerships with groups that focus on aid effectiveness.

First, one important note of caution. Discussions about aid effectiveness often hinge on the issue of administrative costs: Put pejoratively, what proportion of each dollar donated gets sucked away to overhead and fund-raising expenditures? Organizations with low administrative costs are generally thought to be better, as they spend more of their money on delivering products or services. But, truth be told, this is a really bad metric. Based on the evidence, it's unclear whether administrative costs have *any* correlation at all with aid effectiveness. Some interventions simply cost more to manage than others.

More important, administrative cost figures are fairly arbitrary; many items can be counted either as overhead, or as program services. The gray area of nonprofit accounting is just that—gray. So rewarding those with low administrative costs often amounts to rewarding those with aggressive accounting practices, nothing more.

The question we should be asking when we give is simpler and more focused on what actually matters: For each dollar donated, how much good will be done?

In the hopes of coordinating our voices behind that question, I want to leave you with seven ideas that have me particularly excited. These are some of the programs and products we've seen in this book that stand out. Each of them has been subjected to at least one rigorous evaluation, and has stood up well compared to some alternative solutions to the same problems. That does not mean they are all conclusively proven and above reproach. Some are closer to "proven," while others are still "being proven," which is just to acknowledge that the spectrum of evidence is wide. It's a long journey from having no concrete knowledge to making confident prescriptions, ready to scale up without further testing. The ideas below are all somewhere along that path, but they're not all at the end of it.

I also want to be clear about what is *not* included here: a lot of promising ideas—many of which we have encountered in this book as well—that also have evidence behind them. The list below is not intended to be exhaustive.

Finally, funding should not be confined exclusively to "proven" (or even "being proven") ideas. We do need to take risks. As I said in the introduction, there is always a need for creativity, for trying brand-new and unproven tactics. That is the essential process that keeps us moving ahead. Organizations that innovate—and innovate thoughtfully, testing their new ideas rigorously—also deserve our support. That said, innovation without evaluation does not help the world as much as innovation with evaluation. I'd much prefer to give to an organization that conducts rigorous evaluations of its own programs because that gives me the confidence that in five or ten years they will likely be making better choices. They will adapt better to new contexts, technologies, and ideas. Many of the groups discussed in this book—notably Pratham (remedial education), Seva Mandir (teacher and nurse attendance), and Freedom from Hunger (microfinance)—are shining examples of organizations that continuously strive to improve through rigorous evaluation, that learn from their failures and their successes, and that publicize both so the world can learn too.

Enough caveats. Here are the seven:

Seven Ideas That Work

Microsavings

In chapter 7, we began with Vijaya, who was stuck in the borrowing "rotation" (and losing money hand-over-fist in the process) because her husband made it impossible to save at home. Then we saw women in Kenya signing up in droves for a costly barebones savings account—and improving their lives as a result. In fact, while claims of gender empowerment have long been made by micro*credit* advocates, the evidence suggests that women's status and authority is elevated by saving, whereas credit has yet to exhibit such impacts. The need and the desire for savings are already in place; now we need to provide people with options. How many borrowers (like Vijaya) might be better served with savings products than with credit products? In all the enthusiasm over microcredit, we seem to have forgotten that basic lesson we learned from our parents and grandparents: Saving is important!

Reminders to Save

Saving is good, but it doesn't come easy. We all know that. With all the things we have to spend on, saving rarely grabs our attention. There always seem to be more pressing—or more tempting—options. Ultimately, most of us save less than we say we'd like to. As we saw in chapter 7, little reminders, like the text and direct-mail messages banks sent to their clients in Peru, Bolivia, and the Philippines, help cut through the cacophony of voices calling out for our money. They have proven to be cheap and effective ways to mobilize savings among the poor.

Prepaid Fertilizer Sales

Of all the efforts to increase fertilizer usage—subsidies, outreach from agricultural extension officers, demonstration plots—this simple solution is a no-brainer. For a vendor, selling fertilizer costs roughly the same no matter what time of year you do it. But, as we saw in chapter 8, timing can make a huge difference to customers. Kenyan farmers who had a chance to pay (full price!) for next season's fertilizer at harvesttime, when their pockets were full from selling this season's crop, bought 50 percent more. That's a huge boost in productivity and agricultural output, practically for free.

Deworming

Sometimes the numbers really say it all. In chapter 9 we saw that deworming at Kenyan primary schools generated an additional year of attendance for about $3.50; the next best solution, providing free uniforms, cost about twenty-five times that much.

And that doesn't even consider the simple health benefits of being worm-free—they're icing on the cake. In areas where intestinal worms are prevalent, fully subsidized deworming at schools is a dirt-cheap and tremendously powerful intervention. No wonder it's catching on. Efforts by Innovations for Poverty Action and its partner organizations have led to millions of children being dewormed, but much more remains to be done.

Remedial Education in Small Groups

The *balsakhi* remedial program and Pratham's reading camps, both of which we saw in chapter 9, are prime examples of a new direction in educational solutions for the developing world. They both found ways to work around dysfunctional school systems—the former by hiring private teachers, the latter by training volunteers—to promote genuine learning. Where existing schools are under-staffed or overcrowded, outside programs like these may be the most effective path to education. Annie Duflo, research director at IPA, is working with the Ghanaian government, local teachers, and the UK Children's Investment Fund Foundation to launch a large replication of this approach in Ghana; if all goes well at a large scale, IPA will march on to see it scaled up in many more countries.

Chlorine Dispensers for Clean Water

Two million people do not need to die of diarrhea each year. But they do—and solutions have eluded us for decades. Treating drinking water with chlorine is a cheap and highly effective pre-ventative measure—so let's get people using it. Despite the ben-efits of protection, distributing chlorine to households, even for free, has not proved effective enough. Yet providing free chlorine in an easy-to-use dispenser at water collection points—like we saw in chapter 10—has. Programs may become even more efficient and self-sustaining as different subsidy schemes are tested, but dispensers are a big step toward solving the basic problem: getting more people to drink clean water.

Commitment Devices

We saw in chapter 7 for savings, and in chapter 10 for smoking, that commitment devices can be an effective tool to help people reach their goals. This applies to everyone, rich and poor alike, although the examples in this book focus mainly on applications in developing countries. The SEED commitment savings account helped women like Sunny make significant improvements to their households. Targeting smoking, a major health problem in much of the world, we saw how a commitment account in the Philippines was strikingly successful in helping individuals quit. The basic principle behind both of these examples can be applied to many facets of life: Commitment devices let people make their vices more expensive and their virtues cheaper. In doing so, they help people make more virtuous choices.

The List Goes On: Proven Impact Initiative

The downside of the Seven Ideas That Work is that they are static. The ink has dried; they're not going anywhere. But solutions in the fight against poverty *are* going somewhere. They are moving and changing all the time, driven by innovation and research. Hopefully these Seven Ideas will someday be eclipsed by Seven Better Ideas. I'll be happy when they are.

But how will *you* know when it happens? Unless you read

economic journals or attend development conferences, it's hard to say. The latest research doesn't always make its way to the general public.

That's why IPA has launched the Proven Impact Initiative. This initiative will help ensure that donors both large and small have access to ideas that work, and an easy way to support them. We are now working with several partners to communicate this information to the general public, in the hopes that we can help donors be as effective as possible.

So stay tuned. We are just at the beginning of our search for the right questions to ask, and for the answers that follow. We look to the countless people working in development for inspiration, but we also remember that good intentions are not enough. To make a difference in the fight against poverty, we need more than good intentions, more than what sounds good, and more than what looks good anecdotally. The answer isn't always what we want it to be, and frankly that does not matter.

We need to think clearly, ask tough questions, and set up objective processes for learning the answers. This book is a glimpse of the work that has already been done, and a mere dent in the work that remains. But the exciting and encouraging fact is that we do have some clear answers, and are on a path to many more.

NOTES

Chapter 1

11 *and a hero of mine.* Peter Singer. 2009. *The Life You Can Save: Acting Now to End World Poverty.* New York: Random House. Singer uses slightly different facts. But his writing, and conversations with him, inspired this directly. I made tweaks simply to rebut a couple of standard objections to the analogy. For instance, Singer traditionally has ruining a fancy pair of shoes as the "cost" of saving the drowning child, but then one may object, "Why don't you just take your shoes off?" For other (funny) challenges to the analogy, watch Stephen Colbert's interview of Singer. It is available online at http://www.colbertnation.com/the-colbert-report-videos/221466/march-12-2009/peter-singer (accessed 4/26/10).

14 *a real Facebook page:* http://failbooking.com/2010/02/05/funny-facebook-fails-texts-cost-money (accessed 3/28/10).

16 *how it really works.* Kiva is clearer now about its inner workings than it used to be, thanks largely to the urging of David Roodman from the Center for Global Development. But the truth is still in the small print. As of this writing (March 2010), the Web site says, "Your funds will be used to backfill this loan." Then three lines below, in much larger type, it says: "Raised so Far" and "Still Needed." Needed for what exactly? To finish the backfilling? The impression they are trying—successfully—to create is that your funds go straight to the person you clicked on. And the interest rate is not called interest rate, but rather "portfolio yield." I wonder how many Kiva investors/donors realize that portfolio yield is the same as interest rate?

16 *over a hundred million as of November 2009.* http://www.kiva.org/about (accessed 3/28/10).

17 *three times as much as the sum of all corporations, foundations, and bequests. Giving USA,* a publication of Giving USA Foundation, researched and written by the Center on Philanthropy at Indiana University.

Chapter 2

28 *here in the United States.* Two of the seminal papers on randomized evaluations of social programs are (1) Ashenfelter, O. 1978. "Estimating the Effect of Training Programs on Earnings," *Review of Economics and Statistics*, Volume 60, 47–57, and (2) Gary Burtless and Jerry A. Hausman, 1978. "The Effect of Taxation on Labor Supply: Evaluating the Gary Negative Income Tax Experiment, *The Journal of Political Economy*, Vol. 86, pp. 1103–1130.

37 *effectively in society.*" http://www.un.org/esa/socdev/unyin/documents/ydiDavidGordon_poverty.pdf (accessed 2/22/10).

Chapter 3

39 *the Slanket was born.* For a discussion of the battle to launch and spread the sleeved blanket, check out the *New York Times* article (among many other Internet write-ups): http://www.nytimes.com/2009/02/27/business/media/27adco.html?adxnnl=1&adxnnlx=1269796090-dAy7Jkx4 XGUQxoRpQwit0g (accessed 3/28/10). For an amusing comparison of the Snuggie and the Slanket, and two other similar products (the Freedom Blanket and the Blankoat), see http://gizmodo.com/5190557/ultimate-battle-the-snuggie-vs-slanket-vs-freedom-blanket-vs-blankoat (accessed 3/28/10).

41 *$412 billion.* http://www.intenseinfluence.com/blog/how-much-money-is-spent-on-advertising-per-year (accessed 4/26/10).

42 *every year from diarrhea.* http://www.who.int/water_sanitation_health/publications/factsfigures04/en/ (accessed 3/28/10).

43 *ashamed to eat [them].*" http://people.ischool.berkeley.edu/~hal/people/hal/NYTimes/2006-06-01.html (accessed 3/3/10).

44 *Sendhil uses in many of his talks.* One of the talks where Sendhil explains the Last-Mile Problem is available to the public thanks to TED. You can find it at http://www.ted.com/talks/sendhil_mullainathan.html (accessed 3/28/10).

45 *designed an RCT.* Marianne Bertrand, Dean Karlan, Sendhil Mullainathan, Eldar Shafir, and Jonathan Zinman. "What's Advertising Content Worth? A Field Experiment in the Consumer Credit Market." *Quarterly Journal of Economics*, 125(1), February 2010.

49 *did a choice experiment.* S. S. Iyengar and Mark Lepper. 2000. "When Choice Is Demotivating: Can One Desire Too Much of a Good Thing?" *Journal of Personality and Social Psychology* 79:995–1006.

50 *designed an RCT to find out.* Shawn Cole, Xavier Giné, Jeremy Tobacman, Petia Topalova, Robert Townsend, and James Vickery. 2008. "Barriers to Household Risk Management: Evidence from India." Mimeo, World

Bank. The working paper is at http://www.hbs.edu/research/pdf/09-116
.pdf (accessed 4/26/10).

Chapter 4

58 *go beyond the tangible.* The story of Mrs. Potosí comes from FINCA's Web
site. http://www.villagebanking.org/site/apps/nlnet/content2.aspx?c=er
KPI2PCIoE&b=5004173&ct=7159949 (accessed 1/5/10).

59 *to change lives.* The newsletter featuring Marta's story is available at:
http://www.opportunity.org/wp-content/uploads/2010/06/Impact-2008-
Spring.pdf (accessed 1/5/10). It appeared originally in *Impact* (spring 2008
edition), published by Opportunity International, 2122 York Road, Suite
150, Oak Brook, IL 60523. Janna Crosby, editor.

60 *banking services to the poor.* For the full story, told in his own words, see:
Muhammad Yunus and Alan Jolis. 2003. *Banker to the Poor: Micro-lending
and the Battle Against World Poverty.* New York: Public Affairs, hardcover
pp. 20–29. ISBN 978-1-89162-011-9.

61 *approaching $650 million.* These figures are taken from Mix Market, a
great source of industry data on microfinance: http://www.mixmarket
.org/mfi/grameen-bank (accessed 3/7/10).

61 *some 155 million borrowers. State of the Microcredit Summit Campaign
Report 2009.* Washington, DC: Microcredit Summit Campaign.

62 *will eat for a lifetime.* http://www.nytimes.com/2005/09/21/readersopinions/
bono-questions.html (accessed 4/9/10).

65 *82 percent APR yield.* APR (for "annual percentage rate") is the most
common way to quote interest rates. It's the way we usually talk about
costs and returns for borrowing, saving, and investments. Credit card
agreements, certificate of deposit accounts, car financing, and mortgages are just a few places where you'll find APR being discussed. These
microcredit interest rate figures are portfolio yield numbers, from publicly available accounting data. See, for example, http://www.themix
.org for how these data are calculated.

67 *that would serve everybody.* Dean Karlan and Jonathan Zinman. January
2010. "Expanding Credit Access: Using Randomized Supply Decisions to
Estimate the Impacts. "*Review of Financial Studies,* 23(1).

70 *the poor really had.* Suresh de Mel, David McKenzie, and Christopher
Woodruff. 2008. "Returns to Capital: Results from a Randomized Experiment." *Quarterly Journal of Economics* 123(4):1329–72. The same researchers are also replicating and expanding the study in Ghana and Sri Lanka
with the help of IPA in the field.

72 *less than $2.50 per day.* http://www.globalissues.org/article/26/poverty-
facts-and-stats (accessed 4/4/10).

73 *returns were actually negative.* For a more complete analysis of the gender results, see Suresh de Mel, David McKenzie, and Christopher Woodruff. 2009. "Are Women More Credit Constrained? Experimental Evidence on Gender and Microenterprise Returns." *American Economic Journal: Applied Economics,* 1(3):1–32. This is the companion paper to the *Quarterly Journal of Economics* article cited above.

75 *made entrepreneurial loans.* Dean Karlan and Jonathan Zinman. 2010. "Expanding Microenterprise Credit Access: Using Randomized Supply Decisions to Estimate the Impacts in Manila." Working Paper.

78 *to conduct an RCT.* Abhijit Bannerjee, Esther Duflo, Rachel Glennerster, and Cythia Kinnan. May 2009. "The Miracle of Microfinance? Evidence from a Randomized Evaluation." Poverty Action Lab Working Paper 101.

Chapter 5

89 *work on a given day.* Colin Camerer, Linda Babcock, George Loewenstein, and Richard H. Thaler. 1997. "Labor Supply of New York City Cab Drivers: One Day at a Time." *Quarterly Journal of Economics* 112(2):407–441.

92 *self-employed or casual workers.* http://www.wiego.org/stat_picture (accessed 3/30/10). Microcredit clients are doubly unlikely to be formally employed because so much of microcredit is directed toward individuals who own their own businesses.

93 *skills they already know. . . .* Muhammad Yunus and Alan Jolis. 2003. *Banker to the Poor: Micro-Lending and the Battle Against World Poverty.* New York: Public Affairs, p. 140.

94 *Peruvian microlender FINCA Peru.* FINCA Peru is not affiliated with FINCA International, the organization I worked with in El Salvador. It shares the name because it was originally founded as an arm of FINCA.

95 *their weekly meetings.* Dean Karlan and Martín Valdivia. "Teaching Entrepreneurship: Impact of Business Training on Microfinance Clients and Institutions." *Review of Economics and Statistics,* forthcoming.

96 *business training for its clients.* http://personal.lse.ac.uk/fischerg/Assets/Drexler%20Fischer%20Schoar%20-%20 keep%20it%20Simple.pdf.

97 *enterprises in this study.* Miriam Bruhn, Dean Karlan, and Antoinette Schoar. May 2010. "What Capital Is Missing from Developing Countries?" *American Economic Review Papers & Proceedings.*

104 *same technique in a project.* Dean Karlan and Jonathan Zinman. 2010. "A Methodological Note on Using Loan Application and Survey Data to Measure Poverty and Loan Uses of Microcredit Clients." Working paper.

105 *proceeds for consumption.* October 2008. "The Unbanked: Evidence from Indonesia." *World Bank Economic Review* 22(3):517–537.

Chapter 6

111 *Ghana's per capita annual income.* The UN statistics division, reported here by UNICEF, states Ghana's 2008 gross national income (GNI) per capita as $670: http://www.unicef.org/infobycountry/ghana_statistics .html#69 (accessed 5/7/10).

114 *Who Is the Borrower?* The economic jargon for this phenomenon is "adverse selection." It was first explicitly written out in economics by Nobel laureate Joseph Stiglitz and Andrew Weiss. The paper is: Joseph Stiglitz and Andrew Weiss. June 1981. "Credit Rationing in Markets with Imperfect Information." *American Economic Review* 71(3):393–410.

115 *How Do We Know the Borrower Can Pay?* The economic jargon for this phenomenon, where a lack of incentives to repay (e.g., not holding collateral) causes borrowers to try less hard to repay their loans or take bigger risks with borrowed funds, is "moral hazard in effort" or "ex-ante moral hazard."

116 *most employment in Ghana is informal.* http://unstats.un.org/unsd/ demographic/products/indwm/ww2005/tab5e.htm (accessed 3/30/10).

120 *to children's education.* http://www.grameen-info.org/index.php?option= com_content&task=view&id=22&Itemid=109 (accessed 3/30/10).

124 *3.7 million by 2004.* Again, this is thanks to the Mix Market. The client figures for Grameen are found at http://mixmarket.org/node/3110/ data/100636/products_and_clients.total_borrowers/usd/2000-2004 (accessed 4/26/10).

125 *group-liability loans head-to-head.* Xavier Giné and Dean Karlan. May 2010. "Group versus Individual Liability: Long Term Evidence from Philippine Microcredit Lending Groups." Working Paper.

129 *FINCA Peru's loan clients.* Dean Karlan. December 2005. "Using Experimental Economics to Measure Social Capital and Predict Financial Decisions." *American Economic Review* 95(5):1688–1699.

134 *better performance as clients.* Dean Karlan. February 2007. "Social Connections and Group Banking." *Economic Journal* 117:F52–F84.

136 *frequency, group dynamics, and client default.* Benjamin Feigenberg, Erica Field, and Rohini Pande. June 2010. "Building Social Capital through Microfinance." Harvard Kennedy School Working Paper No. RWP10-019.

139 *Kiva.org, the $2 million.* From the Whole Planet Foundation's 2009 annual report, available at http://www.wholeplanetfoundation.org/files/ uploaded/WPF_2009_Audited_Financials.pdf (accessed 3/25/10).

141 *most of the time—it's savings.* Stuart Rutherford's *The Poor and Their Money* is a wonderful quick read that talks a lot about this basic idea, and also makes the point that what the poor need more than anything is a

way of making small deposits and large withdrawals. The order isn't quite so important to them, in many cases.

Chapter 7

149 *for either saving or borrowing.* The Financial Access Initiative offers a wealth of information about banking and other financial services in the developing world and beyond. This particular figure is the subject of one of their informative focus notes, available at http://financialaccess.org/sites/default/files/110109%20HalfUnbanked_0.pdf (accessed 4/26/10).

149 *western Kenya in 2006.* Pascaline Dupas and Jonathan Robinson. September 2010. "Savings Constraints and Microenterprise Development: Evidence from a Field Experiment in Kenya." Working Paper.

155 *SEED, the savings account.* Nava Ashraf, Dean Karlan, and Wesley Yin. May 2006. "Tying Odysseus to the Mast: Evidence from a Commitment Savings Product in the Philippines." *Quarterly Journal of Economics* 121(2):635–672.

158 *a little nudge.* A "nudge" is a tweak that changes our decisions without changing the underlying alternatives we have to choose from. An example of a nudge is changing the order of food in a buffet line: If you put the fruit before the brownies, people will probably choose more fruit. Thaler and Sunstein coined the term *nudge* and wrote a fascinating book about using nudges to help us make the choices we want to make. Richard Thaler and Cass Sunstein. 2008. *Nudge: Improving Decisions About Health, Wealth, and Happiness.* New Haven: Yale University Press.

159 *employees' saving progress.* Shlomo Benartzi and Richard Thaler. February 2004. "Save More Tomorrow: Using Behavioral Economics to Increase Employee Savings." *Journal of Political Economy* 112.1, Part 2: S164–S187. This study, in contrast with most of the other studies discussed in this book, was not implemented with a randomized control trial. The paper discusses the selection biases that would have to be present to pose serious concerns, and they are fairly stark and odd, thus leaving the reader (at least me) quite convinced of their findings. An important question does remain: Does the increase in retirement savings come at the cost of lower current consumption, or higher debt? If the latter, then this could be a smudge to the nudge.

163 *Bolivia, Peru, and the Philippines.* Dean Karlan, Maggie McConnell, Sendhil Mullainathan, and Jonathan Zinman. April 2010. "Getting to the Top of Mind: How Reminders Increase Saving." Working Paper.

164 *people were also 6 percent.* This figure of 6 percent is calculated from Table 4, Panel A, Column 3 of the paper cited above, as follows. The effect of receiving a reminder on the likelihood of reaching one's savings goal was

estimated at 3.1 percent. Across the entire sample, 54.9 percent of people reached their goals. So the reminders constitute a (3.1/54.9=)5.6 percent improvement.

164 *Peter Orszag, and Emmanuel Saez.* Esther Duflo, William Gale, Jeffrey Liebman, Peter Orszag, and Emmanuel Saez. November 2006. "Savings Incentives for Low- and Middle-Income Families: Evidence from a Field Experiment with H & R Block." *Quarterly Journal of Economics* 121(4):1311–1346.

165 *an RCT on retirement savings.* Emmanuel Saez. 2009. "Details Matter: The Impact and Presentation of Information on the Take-up of Financial Incentives for Retirement Saving." *American Economic Journal: Economic Policy* 1(1):204–228.

Chapter 8

167 *over a billion of the world's poor are farmers.* WB World Development Report 2008, p.1. http://siteresources.worldbank.org/INTWDR2008/Resources/WDR_00_book.pdf

170 *evaluate DrumNet with an RCT.* Nava Ashraf, Xavier Giné, and Dean Karlan. November 2009. "Finding Missing Markets (and a Disturbing Epilogue): Evidence from an Export Crop Adoption and Marketing Intervention in Kenya." *American Journal of Agricultural Economics* 91(4).

172 *a simple RCT to find out.* Esther Duflo, Esther, Michael Kremer, and Jonathan Robinson. 2008. "How High Are Rates of Return to Fertilizer? Evidence from Field Experiments in Kenya." *American Economic Review* 98(2):482–488.

176 *price/service combination highest.* Richard Thaler. 1991. *The Winner's Curse: Paradoxes and Anomalies of Economic Life.* New York: Free Press, p. 69.

176 *pull on them as well.* Shlomo Benartzi and Richard Thaler. 2001. "Naïve Diversification Strategies in Defined Contribution Saving Plans." *American Economic Review* 91(1):79–98.

177 *following a major earthquake.* M. H. Bazerman. 1986. *Judgment in Managerial Decision Making.* Hoboken, NJ: John Wiley & Sons, Inc., p. 19.

178 *likelihood of an event happening.* Amos Tversky and Daniel Kahneman. 1973. "Availability: A Heuristic for Judging Frequency and Probability." *Cognitive Psychology* 5:207–232.

179 *Africa on this and other projects.* Esther Duflo, Michael Kremer, and Jonathan Robinson. July 2009. "Nudging Farmers to Use Fertilizer: Theory and Experimental Evidence from Kenya." NBER Working Paper No. 15131.

181 *adopt new tools and techniques.* Timothy Conley and Christopher Udry. March 2010. "Learning About a New Technology: Pineapple in Ghana." *American Economic Review* 100(1):35–69.

184 *For promised joy!* The lines come from Robert Burns's poem "To a Mouse." The actual (older) Scots text is: "The best laid schemes o' Mice an' Men,/ Gang aft agley,/An' lea'e us nought but grief an' pain,/For promis'd joy!"

185 *grandparents had for ages.* DrumNet does continue to operate, but not in that area, and not working on those crops.

186 *track the sales of fish over time.* Robert Jensen. August 2007. "The Digital Provide: Information (Technology), Market Performance, and Welfare in the South Indian Fisheries Sector." *The Quarterly Journal of Economics* 122(3):879–924.

188 *the story of the challenger.* Michael Kremer. August 1993. "The O-Ring Theory of Development." *The Quarterly Journal of Economics* 108(3):551–575.

Chapter 9

192 *and greater gender equality.* Educated people have better jobs, better health, and greater gender equality. "Education and the Developing World." Center for Global Development, 2006.

198 *children around the world aren't in school.* "Education and the Developing World." Center for Global Development, 2006.

199 *a simple solution with an RCT.* David Evans, Michael Kremer, and Muthoni Ngatia. 2008. "The Impact of Distributing School Uniforms on Children's Education in Kenya." Mimeo.

202 *Progresa's impact on schools enrollment.* T. Paul Schultz. 2004. "School Subsidies for the Poor: Evaluating the Mexican Progresa Poverty Program." *Journal of Development Economics* 74(1):199–250.

203 *to design an evaluation.* Felipe Barrera-Osoria (World Bank), Marianne Bertrand (University of Chicago), and Francisco Pérez (GI Exponential). 2010. "Improving the Design of Conditional Transfer Programs: Evidence from a Randomized Education Experiment in Colombia." *American Economic Journal: Applied Economics,* forthcoming.

204 *counterparts in the control group.* These figures come from the paper cited in the previous endnote, Table 3, Column 7 as follows. The control group's average attendance rate of .786 implies an absence rate of .214. Treatment effects of attendance increases of .025, .028, and .055 for the basic program, first variation, and second variation represent decreases in absence of (.025/.214=)11.6 percent, (.028/.214=)13.1 percent, and (.055/.214=)25.7 percent, respectively.

205 *the second more than tripled it!* Evaluating the impact of school-based deworming on student health and attendance in Kenya. These figures come from the same paper, Table 7, Column 6, as follows. For the first variation, a treatment effect of .094 on the control group mean of .205

represents a 46 percent increase in tertiary enrollment. For the second variation, a treatment effect of .487 on the control group mean of .205 represents a 237 percent increase in tertiary enrollment.

206 *is about twenty cents per pill.* http://Web.worldbank.org/WBSITE/ EXTERNAL/TOPICS/EXTHEALTHNUTRITIONANDPOPULATION/ EXTPHAAG/0,contentMDK:20785786~menuPK:1314819~pagePK:6422 9817~piPK:64229743~theSitePK:672263,00.html (accessed 3/31/10).

207 *in western Kenya in 1998.* Edward Miguel and Michael Kremer. 2004. "Worms: Identifying Impacts on Education and Health the Presence of Treatment Externalities." *Econometrica* 72(1):159–217.

208 *preschool students in Delhi, India.* Gustavo Bobonis, Edward Miguel, and Charu Puri-Sharma. 2006. "Iron Deficiency Anemia and School Participation." *Journal of Human Resources* 41(4):692–721.

209 *higher incomes in the long run.* Hoyt Bleakley. 2007. "Disease and Development: Evidence from Hookworm Eradication in the American South." *Quarterly Journal of Economics* 122:73–117.

209 *rolling in from Kenya.* Sarah Baird, Joan Hamory Hicks, Michael Kremer, and Edward Miguel. "Worms at Work: Long-run Impacts of Child Health Gains." Working Paper.

212 *school-age children.* http://data.un.org/Data.aspx?q=India+population+ age+5-14&d=PopDiv&f=variableID:20;crID:356 (accessed 3/31/10). This figure comes from a query of the UNdata online database, a useful resource for country-level statistics on economics, demographics, health, education, and more. The quarter-billion figure is the 2005 estimate for India population ages five to fourteen (returned 246,293,000).

212 *couldn't do basic arithmetic.* Pratham Organization. 2006. *Annual Status of Education Report 2005.* Mumbai: Pratham Resource Center.

215 *affected students' learning.* Abhijit Banerjee, Shawn Cole, Esther Duflo, and Leigh Linden. 2007. "Remedying Education: Evidence from Two Randomized Experiments in India." *Quarterly Journal of Economics* 122(3):1235–1264.

217 *designed another RCT.* Esther Duflo, Pascaline Dupas, and Michael Kremer. November 2008. "Peer Effects and the Impact of Tracking: Evidence from a Randomized Evaluation in Kenya." *American Economic Review,* forthcoming.

218 *A 2005 survey.* Pratham Organization. 2006. *Annual Status of Education Report 2005.* Mumbai: Pratham Resource Center.

220 *village education into gear.* Abhijit Banerjee, Rukmini Banerji, Esther Duflo, Rachel Glennerster, and Stuti Khemani. February 2010. "Pitfalls

of Participatory Programs: Evidence from a Randomized Evaluation in Education in India." *American Economic Journal: Economic Policy* 2(1):1–30.

Chapter 10

227 *scheduled operating hours.* Abhijit Banerjee, Angus Deaton, and Esther Duflo. 2004a. "Wealth, Health, and Health Services in Rural Rajasthan." *AER Papers and Proceedings* 94(2):326–330.

228 *evaluate it with an RCT.* Abhijit Banerjee, Esther Duflo, and Rachel Glennerster. 2007. "Putting a Band-Aid on a Corpse: Incentives for Nurses in the Indian Public Health Care System." *Journal of the European Economics Association* 6(2–3):487–500.

229 *looked as if they had been hurled into a wall.* From the footnote on p. 11 of "Putting a Band-Aid on a Corpse," cited previously.

232 *use of the public clinics.* Paul Gertler. 2004. "Do Conditional Cash Transfers Improve Child Health? Evidence from Progresa's Control Randomized Experiment." *American Economic Review* 94(2):336–341.

233 *Paul's study of it.* Paul Gertler and Simone Boyce. 2001. "*An Experiment in Incentive-Based Welfare: The Impact of Progresa on Health in Mexico.*" Working Paper.

234 *A separate study.* John Hoddinott, and Emmanuel Skoufias. October 2004. "The Impact of Progresa on Food Consumption." *Economic Development and Cultural Change* 53(1):37–61.

235 *are being rigorously evaluated.* Laura Rawlings. 2005. "Evaluating the Impact of Conditional Cash Transfer Programs." *The World Bank Research Observer* 20(1):29–55.

236 *and test it with an RCT.* Xavier Giné, Dean Karlan, and Jonathan Zinman. 2010. "Put Your Money Where Your Butt Is: A Commitment Savings Account for Smoking Cessation." *American Economic Journal: Applied Economics* 2(4):1–26.

244 *malaria worldwide in 2007 alone.* This figure is from a press release about the president and CEO of PSI, Karl Hofmann. http://mim.globalhealth strategies.com/blog/wp-content/uploads/2009/10/Karl-Bio.pdf (accessed 4/26/10).

245 *who worked together on an RCT.* Jessica Cohen and Pascaline Dupas. 2010. "Free Distribution or Cost-Sharing? Evidence from a Randomized Malaria Prevention Experiment." *Quarterly Journal of Economics* 125(1):1–45.

246 *each year worldwide.* From the World Health Organization Web site's fact sheet on water, sanitation, and hygiene: http://www.who.int/water_sanita tion_health/publications/factsfigures04/en (accessed 3/28/10).

248 *stacked up against one another.* Michael Kremer, Edward Miguel, Send-hil Mullainathan, Claire Null, and Alix Peterson Zwane. 2009. "Making Water Safe: Price, Persuasion, Peers, Promoters, or Product Design?"

Chapter 11
254 *went to Mexico City.* Paul Gertler, Manisha Shah, and Stefano Bertozzi. 2005. "Sex Sells, but Risky Sex Sells for More." *Journal of Political Economy*, 113:518–550.
256 *that's the truth."* This and many other disheartening quotes from "Dr. Beetroot" can be found at http://www.southafrica.to/people/Quotes/Manto/MantoTshabalalaMsimang.htm (accessed 3/15/10).
259 *near Busia in 2004.* Pascaline Dupas. 2007. "Relative Risks and the Market for Sex: Teenage Pregnancy, HIV, and Partner Selection in Kenya." Mimeo, Dartmouth.
263 *"Use Condoms."* Available on YouTube: http://www.youtube.com/watch?v=0ed1m16L1so.
264 *to buy condoms.* Rebecca L. Thornton. 2008. "The Demand for, and Impact of, Learning HIV Status." *American Economic Review* 98(5):1829–1863.
264 *0.6 percent in the United States).* The UNICEF Web site has a wealth of economic, demographic, epidemiological, and other statistics for hundreds of countries. These were found at http://www.unicef.org/infobycountry/malawi_statistics.html#66 (accessed 6/22/10) and http://www.unicef.org/infobycountry/usa_statistics.html#66 (accessed 6/22/10), respectively.
265 *worth ten times as much.* In Thornton's paper, see the discussion on p. 14 and Table 4 on p. 51.

ACKNOWLEDGMENTS

Dean's Acknowledgements

I found writing the acknowledgments very challenging. How do you really express how grateful you are, without sounding soppy or saccharine? I am grateful to many, to those who have worked with me, advised me, worked for me, and those who had nothing to do with me but produced great work that we can write about here.

Professionally, I thank my advisers for life, Esther Duflo and Abhijit Banerjee. Their leadership on the founding board of Innovations for Poverty Action and in creating the Jameel Poverty Action Lab has changed the world for the better, and I'm forever proud to be their advisee. Sendhil Mullainathan was both my adviser and now coauthor, and one of the most fun and creative people around. His influence on this book, and me, is throughout. I thank Richard Thaler, for introducing me to behavioral economics when getting my MBA, taking me on as an advisee from afar when I continued on for my Ph.D., and last but not least, providing so much of the motivation behind the work here. I thank Michael Kremer for advising me in my early days of graduate school, including one particularly memorable (for me) coffee when I was first thinking about running experiments to tackle empirical challenges, and for his leadership in starting up randomized trials in the pre-IPA and pre-JPAL days. I thank Jonathan Morduch, for guiding me and teaching me so much about the economics and politics of microfinance. And lastly, only chronologically, I thank Chris Udry. Esther told me one day in graduate school to get on a train and go visit Chris for a few hours in New Haven, and Chris was gracious enough to meet me even though I wasn't a student at Yale. Hard to say of course (I have no control group "me" who didn't get on the train!), but I think that train ride made a huge impact on my life. A great example of Esther's stellar life-changing advice. Thank you, Esther (and Chris).

Jonathan Zinman is a unique force in my life, both as a brother and my most common collaborator. It is trite but true to say that the research here that I have done with him would not have been done, or would not have been done as well, were it not for him. Although less frequent in my collaboration, I am grateful to my other collaborators in development projects talked about in this book: Nava Ashraf, Marianne Bertrand, Miriam Bruhn, Xavier Giné, Maggie McConnell, Jonathan Morduch, Antoinette Schoar, Eldar Shafir, Martín Valdivia, and Wesley Yin.

I cannot thank enough the team at Innovations for Poverty Action and the Jameel Poverty Action Lab. The current leadership team at IPA—Annie Duflo, Kathleen Viery, and Delia Welsh—helps me sleep a few hours each night, and helps IPA grow two-fold year-in and year-out. Our staff on the ground are some of the hardest working, most dedicated, and smartest individuals. They come at this with different motivations and paths, and it is always an absolute pleasure and thrill to work with each of them. Without them none of this would be possible. Wendy Lewis has provided me and IPA the support these past few years to keep it all straight and orderly—thank you.

This leads me to the next group: the academics. I am just one of many on this quest. I thank the field researchers whose work

I discuss in this book for generating the knowledge I'm able to discuss here: Abhijit Banerjee, Stefano Bertozzi, Suresh de Mel, Esther Duflo, Pascaline Dupas, Paul Gertler, Xavier Giné, Rachel Glennerster, Robert Jensen, Cynthia Kinnan, Michael Kremer, David McKenzie, Edward Miguel, Clair Null, Jonathan Robinson, Emmanuel Saez, Manisha Shah, Rebecca Thornton, Chris Woodruff, Dean Yang, Alix Zwane.

I thank the people who have been on the board of Innovations for Poverty Action: my advisers Esther, Abhijit, and Sendhil, and Ray Fisman, for agreeing to be on the board when their crazy fresh-out-of-graduate school advisee thought creating such an organization would be a good idea (rather than the more sensible focus-on-your-research-only strategy of an untenured professor). And I thank the current board—Greg Fischer, Jerry McConnell, Paras Mehta, Jodi Nelson, J. J. Prescott, Steve Toben, and Kentaro Toyama for carrying the torch and providing the leadership and guidance IPA needs to take us to the next level—as well as three former board members, Wendy Abt, Ruth Levine, and Alix Zwane, for being on the board during our critical growth over the past few years.

The organizations we have worked with deserve particular recognition. Although some of the research here is not testing the core mission of an organization, some of it is. There is nothing more impressive than someone so dedicated to poverty that they are willing to put their beliefs and hopes aside and ask for the evidence, even if it goes against what they have been saying they think should be done. More donors should reward failure. The organizations behind the work reported in this book are all exemplary groups willing to put it all out there in their strive for improvement. For my research projects discussed in this book, I've had the pleasure of working with Omar Andaya, Gerald Andaya, Jonathan Campaigne, Chris

Dunford, Bobbi Gray, Mandred Kuhn, Iris Lanao, Reggie Ocampo, and John Owens. I thank them for their dedication to learning what works.

My favorite times in the field are when my family joins me. It is a true blessing to not have to choose between work and family. Although I like to think my family has gotten a lot out of the experience (they say they have!), I know I'm clearly the one who benefits the most. I get to do my work without having to sacrifice one tiny bit. But this wouldn't be possible if Cindy weren't so flexible and supportive, and our kids weren't such great travelers: able to have fun anywhere, ride on long rickety drives through Ghana, sleep in bedbug-ridden cots in rural Mali, and learn to eat just about anything (enjoying the good food and merely laughing about the bad).

I recently read the acknowledgments in my dissertation and was struck by my closing thanks, and how something so true then could be even more true now. So I repeat them word for word (except now with Gabi added, as she was not born until after graduate school): "Most of all, I thank my family: my wife, Cindy, my son, Maxwell, my daughter Maya and one daughter to be named soon [Gabi]. Having Cindy and Max and Maya [and Gabi] with me on my research travels made all the difference for getting these projects done. I would not be a development economist if it were not for Cindy's support, flexibility, and enthusiasm. . . . This [book] is dedicated to my wife, best friend and love of my life, Cindy, and to Maxwell and Maya [and Gabi]."

Jake's Acknowledgements

Traveling to the field to visit project sites throughout 2009 was a thrill and an adventure and an absolute hoot, and would have been impossible were it not for the help, hospitality, enthusiasm, and heroics of dozens of people.

First and foremost there are the men and women who shared their time and their experiences with me—including, but not limited to, the people whose stories were featured throughout the book. Almost without exception, these were folks who, unsolicited and with no promise of compensation, dropped whatever they were doing to welcome a complete stranger and make him feel at home. I am grateful for their kindness and was humbled by their generosity more times than I can count. Thank you.

I would never have met those extraordinary people, though, had it not been for the efforts of researchers and partner organization staff, who hosted, guided, translated, planned, recommended, coordinated, and generally went above and beyond in service of this project. In India, thanks to Justin Oliver and Joy Miller, the entire CMF team, Selvan Kumar, Nilesh Fernando, Abhay Agarwal, Sree Mathy, Jyothi, and Srikumar Ramakrishnan. In Peru, thanks to Tania Alfonso, David Bullon-Patton, Wilbert Alex Yanqui Arizabal, Silvia Robles, and Kartik Akileswaran. In Bolivia, thanks to Doug Parkerson, Martin Rotemberg, Maria Esther, and Chris from Minuteman Pizza in Uyuni. In Uganda, thanks to Pia Raffler, Sarah Kabay, Becca Furst-Nichols, and William Bamusute. In Kenya, thanks to Karen Levy, Andrew Fischer Lees, Jeff Berens, Owen Ozier, Jinu Koola, Blastus Bwire, Leonard Bukeke, Grace Makana, Moses Baraza, and Adina Rom. In Malawi, thanks to Niall Keheler, Jessica Goldberg, Lutamyo Mwamlina, Cuthbert Mambo, and Mr. Phiri of MRFC. In the Philippines, thanks to Rebecca Hughes, Megan McGuire, Nancy Hite, Yaying Yu, Ann Mayuga, Mario Portugal, Primo Obsequio, Alex Bartik, and Adam Zucker. In Colombia, thanks to Angela Garcia Vargas.

Thanks to the indomitable Wendy Lewis and everyone at IPA, both in New Haven and abroad, for invaluable support throughout.

Thanks to everybody who read and commented on drafts, who brainstormed, and who helped talk through ideas. Thanks especially to Laura Fillmore for valuable discussions at every stage of the process. Thanks to Helen Markinson for all the encouragement. Thanks to Chelsea DuBois for supplying the opening story and much, much more besides.

Finally, infinite thanks to Mom, Dad, Naomi, and Julie, who are without a doubt the best people I know.

Dean and Jake's Collective Acknowledgements

We thank our agent, Jim Levine, who swore when we signed with him that he wasn't a sign-and-leave kind of agent. Trust him we did, and he came through, working with us on the manuscript (and title—that was hard!) all the way to the end. We thank Jim's team at Levine Greenberg for all of their work along the way, including Elizabeth Fisher, Sasha Raskin, and Kerry Sparks. We thank our editor, Stephen Morrow at Dutton, Penguin Books, for his valuable insights and edits and guidance throughout, and patience as we rejected title after title after title. We thank Andrew Wright for valuable input, both substantive and stylistic.

We are grateful to many for reading draft (and often draft after draft) of the manuscript, including David Appel, Julie Appel, Naomi Appel, Scott Bernstein, Kelly Bidwell, Laura Fellman, Erica Field, Laura Fillmore, Sally Fillmore, Alissa Fishbane, Nathanael Goldberg, Cindy Karlan, Karen Levy, David McKenzie, Ted Miguel, Cleo O'Brien-Udry, Tim Ogden Rohini Pande, Jonathan Robinson, Richard Thaler, Rebecca Thornton, and Chris Udry.

INDEX